RUSSIAN
FEDERATION

MONGOLIA

NORTH
KOREA

Beijing

*BO
HAI*

SOUTH
KOREA

*YELLOW
SEA*

*EAST
CHINA SEA*

Shanghai

VIETNAM

*SOUTH
CHINA SEA*

LAOS

SHANGHAI
*See pp120–67
Street Finder maps
pp168–73*

EYEWITNESS TRAVEL

BEIJING &
SHANGHAI

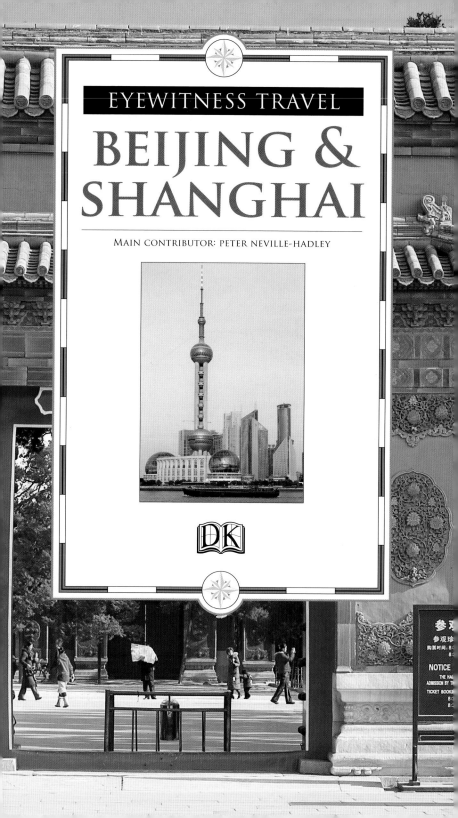

EYEWITNESS TRAVEL

BEIJING & SHANGHAI

MAIN CONTRIBUTOR: PETER NEVILLE-HADLEY

DK

LONDON, NEW YORK,
MELBOURNE, MUNICH AND DELHI
www.dk.com

PRODUCED BY BRAZIL STREET
PROJECT EDITOR Andrew Humphreys
ART EDITOR Gadi Farfour

DORLING KINDERSLEY
SENIOR EDITOR Hugh Thompson
DTP DESIGNER Natasha Lu
PICTURE RESEARCHERS Ellen Root
PRODUCTION Linda Dare

CONTRIBUTORS
Peter Neville-Hadley, Donald Bedford, Christopher Knowles

PHOTOGRAPHERS
Chen Chao, Colin Sinclair, Linda Whitwam

ILLUSTRATORS
Gary Cross, Richard Draper, Paul Guest,
Chapel Design & Marketing, John Mullany

Reproduced in Singapore by Colourscan
Printed in Singapore by KHL Printing Co. Pte. Ltd.

First American Edition 2007
07 08 10 9 8 7 6 5 4 3 2 1

Published in the United States by Dorling Kindersley Publishing,
Inc., 375 Hudson Street, New York 10014

Copyright © 2007 Dorling Kindersley Limited, London
A Penguin Company

Published in Great Britain by Dorling Kindersley Limited.

A CATALOGING IN PUBLICATION RECORD IS
AVAILABLE FROM THE LIBRARY OF CONGRESS.

ISSN 1542-1554
ISBN: 978-0-75662-500-9

FLOORS ARE REFERRED TO THROUGHOUT IN ACCORDANCE WITH
US USAGE; IE THE "FIRST FLOOR" IS AT GROUND LEVEL.

Front cover main image: Huxinting Teahouse, Shanghai

**The information in this
DK Eyewitness Travel Guide is checked regularly.**

Every effort has been made to ensure that this book is as up-to-date
as possible at the time of going to press. Some details, however,
such as telephone numbers, opening hours, prices, gallery hanging
arrangements and travel information are liable to change. The
publishers cannot accept responsibility for any consequences arising
from the use of this book, nor for any material on third party
websites, and cannot guarantee that any website address in this
book will be a suitable source of travel information. We value the
views and suggestions of our readers very highly. Please write to:
Publisher, DK Eyewitness Travel Guides, Dorling Kindersley,
80 Strand, London, WC2R 0RL.

CONTENTS

Gateway, Lama Temple, Beijing

INTRODUCING BEIJING AND SHANGHAI

**A colonial-era lion guarding a
doorway on the Bund, Shanghai**

BEIJING

The Huangpu River and Pudong skyline, Shanghai

TRAVELERS' NEEDS

SURVIVAL GUIDE

Players and spectators at a game of
mah jong, Hou Hai, Beijing

SHANGHAI

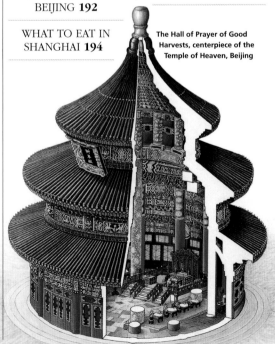

The Hall of Prayer of Good
Harvests, centerpiece of the
Temple of Heaven, Beijing

INTRODUCING
BEIJING & SHANGHAI

FOUR GREAT DAYS IN BEIJING

Rapidly redeveloping Beijing changes on an almost weekly basis, so here are four days largely dedicated to giving a flavor of an older China before it vanishes. Famous sights like the Temple of Heaven and the Forbidden City, are safe from the bulldozers, but traditional *hutong* life is certainly under threat, as are the old open-air markets visited here, such as Guanyuan and

Panjiayuan. There's also a day spent away from the city at the Great Wall, a must for all visitors to Beijing. Energetic sightseers should manage everything on these itineraries, but this selection can also be dipped into for ideas. All walks are reachable by public transport. Price guides are for two adults or for a family of two adults and two children, excluding meals.

Practicing tai ji quan

EMPIRE TO REPUBLIC

- **The imperial splendor of the Forbidden City**
- **Stand on the spot where modern China began**
- **Pay your respects to the embalmed Chairman Mao**

TWO ADULTS allow ¥300

Morning
Start early at **Jing Shan Park** *(see p68)* at the east side where the last Ming emperor hanged himself on a tree known as the Guilty Sophora. Climb to the top of the hill for a spectacular view south across the roofscape of the **Forbidden City** *(see pp62–7)*. Just below is the northern entrance to the palace. It would be easy to spend a day here, but for a first taste rent an audio guide and travel south along the main axis, through the emperors' private quarters, and past the great halls of audience and administration. Just a simple walk through such as this will still take up much of the morning. There are snack restaurants dotted around the interior, marked on maps.

Heroic Socialist sculptures in front of Mao's Mausoleum

Afternoon
Leaving the palace by the main entrance you pass through the **Tian'an Men** *(see p59)*; buy a ticket that allows you to mount the Ming-era gate and stand where Mao stood to announce the formation of the People's Republic on October 1, 1949. The Chairman's embalmed body lies in his **mausoleum** *(see p58)*, which is straight ahead (not open every day), but first deposit bags to the south of the **China National Museum** *(see p59)*. The museum can be visited afterwards. It presents a

manipulated history of China through some the most famous treasures of the imperial era. Finish the day by walking to the southern end of Tian'an Men Square and ascending the **Qian Men** *(see p58)*, another great city gate and one of the last relics of the Ming city walls. The views back across the square to the Forbidden City are the stuff of memories.

FAMILY BEIJING – INSECTS TO ACROBATS

- **To market, for flowers, birds, fish, and insects**
- **Let the children run wild in the park**
- **Partake in a tea ceremony**
- **See an acrobatic show**

FAMILY OF FOUR allow ¥800

Morning
Recent years have seen a revival of Beijing's traditional pastimes: *hua, niao, yu, chong* – flowers, birds, fish, and insects. Take a taxi to the **Guanyuan Market** *(see p103)* to see the revived popularity of all four, especially the insect vendors in the alley at the rear. Jump on the subway at nearby Fucheng Men and ride four stops north to Jishuitan. This is the beginning of the Hou Hai walk *(see pp100–101)*, which you can follow as far as the restored **Mei Lanfang Memorial Hall**. At this point taxi south for lunch at **Lao Beijing Zhajiang Mian Da Wang** *(see p198)*.

Tian'an Men, the imposing gate from which the square takes its name

Afternoon

From the restaurant it is a short walk to the magnificent **Temple of Heaven** *(see pp74–7)*, where you can see locals enjoying the green spaces, playing board games, and exercising. Plus of course there are the many and varied historical buildings. Then back north to the **Purple Vine Teahouse** *(see p108)*, just outside the Forbidden City's west gate, for tea in a traditional setting. In the evening, you have the option of **Beijing Opera** or **traditional acrobatic performances** in historic surroundings at either the Huguang Guildhall or Zhengyici Theater *(see p107)*. Children will definitely prefer the latter.

Practicing *tai ji quan* at the Temple of Heaven

ANCIENT ARCHITECTURE AND MODERN ART

- Walk the Great Wall
- Visit the resting place of Ming emperors
- View cutting-edge art in a former factory compound

TWO ADULTS allow ¥600

Morning

Arrange an early start with your taxi – hired in advance – for a trip to the **Great Wall at Badaling** *(see p92)*. Once there, head off along the right hand section of wall for a longer hike – once you clear the crowds you can better enjoy the expansive views and fresh air without being

The Great Wall – the great unmissable daytrip from Beijing

jostled for space. If you haven't brought your own packed lunch you can eat at one of the restaurants at the site, but they are touristy and fairly expensive.

Afternoon

Most organized tours head off to the **Ming Tombs** *(see pp88–9)* but these are not especially compelling unless you're really interested in Ming funerary architecture or are enjoying your break from the city. Keep the visit short then, and have the driver head back to central Beijing via the **798 Art District** *(see p85)* for a former industrial compound now busy with artists' studios, galleries, and a handful of suitably cool cafés in which to observe Beijing's boho scene.

DISCOUNT SHOPPING

- **Explore Beijing's biggest flea market**
- **Hunt clothing bargains**
- **Lunch on Chinese dumplings**

TWO ADULTS ¥200 plus shopping

Morning

Make an early morning start – the earlier the better – for a trip to **Panjiayuan Market** *(see p103)*, best at weekends but still busy on other days, too. Here you'll find just about any and every kind of souvenir imaginable at prices far lower than tourist shops. From the market take a short taxi ride to nearby **Hong Qiao Market** *(see p103)* to browse the shoes and

clothes in the main market, pearls upstairs (beware the low quality, though), or everything from PlayStations to jigsaws and radio-controlled models in Toy City, which is in an annexe to the rear. If you can haul yourself away, aim to grab lunch on **Qian Men Dajie**, which is just a short ride west and is lined with restaurants, some specializing in *jiaozi* (dumplings).

Afternoon

After dining, stroll to the **Beijing Silk Store** *(see p104)*, which is just off Qian Men. From here, take a taxi on to **Bai Nao Hui** *(see p104)* for computer accessories and other electronics, then further east to **Yaxiu Market** for cheap clothing *(see p104)*. This is a good place to finish up as you are now in the heart of Sanlitun, with its vast array of bars and restaurants in which to help you recover.

A seller of bead, coral and stone necklaces at Hong Qiao Market

FOUR GREAT DAYS IN SHANGHAI

One of the greatest pleasures of a visit to Shanghai lies in observing the contrast between the solid civic worthiness of the foreign buildings on one side of the Huangpu, and the newly erected glitzy towers that face them across the water. The first day out samples both, while the second focuses on the city's excellent

Fan dancer on the Bund

art collections. The third returns to the contrast of old and new, but tells the story through retail, after which, a break from the bustle with an expedition out of town to the so-called "Venice of the East," the canal town of Suzhou. Price guides are for two adults or for a family of two adults and two children, excluding meals.

The gleaming skyscrapers of Pudong, seen from the Bund promenade

OLD AND NEW SHANGHAI

- Colonial architecture on the Bund
- Lunch on the waterfront
- The skyscrapers of Pudong
- Tunnel rides, express elevators, and ferry trips

FAMILY OF FOUR allow ¥1,000 plus meals

Morning
Start at the south of the **Bund** *(see pp122–3)* around the Fangbang Zhong Lu junction. If you get there early enough you can watch locals perform their morning exercises of *tai ji quan* or sword play on the promenade. Spend a few hours wandering the grand riverfront sweep enjoying the early 20th-century foreign architecture and the striking views across to Pudong. Some of the buildings can be entered to view original murals and period fittings. Reaching Suzhou Creek, double back via **Huangpu Park** for a cheap lunch at one of numerous waterside snack restaurants or dine

more luxuriously with views from the terrace at **M on the Bund** *(see p206)*.

Afternoon
The well-signposted **Bund Sightseeing Tunnel** *(see p136)* offers a ride beneath the river in electric gondolas. You emerge near the base of the **Oriental Pearl TV Tower** *(see p136)*. Here, you can either buy a ticket for the **Shanghai History Museum** or visit the **Shanghai Ocean Aquarium** *(see p136)* next door, which is one of the best of its kind. Afterwards, it's a short walk to the **Jinmao Tower** *(see p137)* and a stomach-churning elevator ride to the 88th floor for some of the most spectacular views in Shanghai. Once you have recovered, there's a food court in the basement, and a Starbucks nearby on the embankment, or stay for dinner at one of the Grand Hyatt's restaurants, all with staggering views. Walk back to the riverside and the ferry terminal and pay ¥2 for a brief ride across the river back to where you started the walk in the morning.

ALL ABOUT ART

- Fabulous artifacts at the Shanghai Museum
- Lunch on a rooftop terrace
- Visits to working artists' studios and shops

TWO ADULTS allow ¥200 plus meals and show tickets

Morning
The former race course, now **People's Park** (subway: Renmin Park) has become the center of Shanghai's cultural life. Start with the **Shanghai Museum** *(see pp126–9)*, which is one of the best in China. How you divide your visit depends on your preferences for ancient artifacts or modern art, but either way it would be easy to spend a whole morning here. Afterwards cross the park to the **Shanghai Art Museum** *(see p125)*, housed in a building that was once the race course clubhouse. Lunch upstairs on the terrace of restaurant **Kathleen's 5**.

Modern sculpture displayed at the Shanghai Art Museum

Afternoon

For a further dose of modern Chinese art there's the nearby **MOCA (Museum of Contemporary Art)** *(see p124)*, which is worth visiting for the architecture alone. Pass the strikingly modern **Shanghai Grand Theater** *(see p125)* and check what's on during your stay; your hotel can help make a booking if necessary. For a terrific view of the places you have just visited, cross the road to the Tomorrow Square building and take the elevator up to the reception of the **J.W. Marriott** *(see p186)* on the 38th floor. Finally, take a short taxi ride south to the **Taikang Lu Art Street** *(see p162)* for unique creations from contemporary galleries, or buy straight from the artists themselves.

Taikang Lu Art Street, the place to pick up paintings and applied art

ALLEYWAYS AND AVENUES

- **Shop on Nanjing Lu**
- **Compare the old Chinese and foreigner quarters**
- **Drink at a colonial villa**

TWO ADULTS allow ¥500.

Morning

The pedestrianized part of **Nanjing Lu** (Henan Lu to Xizang Lu) was once known as the best shopping street in China. It may no longer be cutting-edge, but the goods are better value than some of Shanghai's more fashionable places. From here

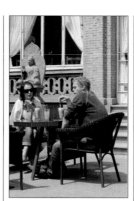

The garden terrace of Face, part of the Ruijin Guesthouse complex

you can walk or take a taxi to the Old City and the busy **Yu Gardens Bazaar** *(see p130)*. Most of the flying-eaved buildings here are of fairly recent construction but there is the working City Temple, the Yu Gardens and the very picturesque Huxinting Teahouse as well as lots of shops. Enjoy lunch in one of the dumpling restaurants around the teahouse but aim to be there early as these places get very busy.

Afternoon

Walk west from the bazaar among the winding alleyways of the Old City to get a taste of the past – old people sitting outside their homes playing *mah jong* while the washing billows overhead and bicycles cut through the narrow paths. Pass old temples, mosques, and markets, before cutting north to **Huaihai Zhonglu**, once the grand Avenue Joffre and now where the chic department stores and malls reside. This isn't the place for bargains but it is fun window-shopping alongside the Chinese.

Finish the day by taking a taxi farther west for an early evening stroll around the leafy estate of the **Ruijin Guesthouse** *(see p132)*, perhaps dropping in for a drink at **Face** *(see p165)*. This is the heart of the French Concession and, after drinks, there are a great many fine restaurants nearby.

GARDENS OF SUZHOU

- **Enjoy a canal boat ride**
- **Dine on Suzhou specialties**
- **Stroll around gardens designed over generations**

TWO ADULTS allow ¥350.

Morning

Suzhou *(see pp144–9)* is close to Shanghai but an early start by train or bus is still recommended (you can also join an organized tour). This is one of many canal towns around Shanghai nicknamed the "Venice of the East." That may be something of an exaggeration, but most visits do begin with a ride in the local equivalent of a gondola, taken from across the road from the railway station, to alight at the **Pan Men Scenic Area** *(see p149)*. This is where you find the famous double gate and climb the Ruiguang Pagoda.

Afternoon

Taxi north to Guanqian Jie to try Suzhou specialities for lunch at **Deyue Lou** *(see p207)* before tackling your choice of the gardens for which Suzhou is famed, such as the sprawling **Humble Administrator's Garden** *(see pp146–7)*, the quieter and more intimate **Ou Yuan** *(see p144)*, or the **Master of the Nets Garden**, which Chinese often consider the most satisfying for its balanced *feng shui*.

Tour boats awaiting passengers for a canal cruise

Putting Beijing & Shanghai on the Map

Beijing sits on a plain 25 miles (40 kilometers) east of the mountains that once offered protection from the war-like tribes of the provinces beyond. It is one of very few capitals not sited on a major river system. By contrast, Shanghai sits on the banks of the Huangpu River, on silt carried down in the muddy waters of the Yangzi and washed up the Huangpu with the tide. Since rapid development began in the 19th century, constant dredging has been necessary.

Datong

Baoding

307

Taiyuan

Shijiazhuang

HEBEI

Xingtai

SHANXI

Handan

Yan'an

309

Changzhi

Hebi

210

Tongchuan

Kaifeng

Xianyang

Luoyang

Zhengzhou

Xi'an

Xuchang

Zhouk

Pingdingshan

SHAANXI

312

HENAN

209

Nanyang

CENTRAL AND EASTERN ASIA

RUSSIAN FEDERATION

KAZAKHSTAN

UZBEKISTAN

TURKMENISTAN

KYRGYZSTAN

MONGOLIA

Harbin

Xilinhot

Ürümqi

NORTH KOREA

JAPAN

Xinyang

AFGHANISTAN

TAJIKISTAN

Beijing

SOUTH KOREA

Suizhou

PAKISTAN

Golmud

CHINA

Xi'an

Ji'nan

Lhasa

Chengdu

Shanghai

East China Sea

NEPAL

Guiyang

Nanchang

BHUTAN

Nanning

TAIWAN

PACIFIC OCEAN

INDIA

BANGLADESH

MYANMAR

Hong Kong

Bay of Bengal

LAOS

South China Sea

PHILIPPINES

Wuhan

THAILAND

VIETNAM

SRI LANKA

CAMBODIA

Han Shui

LIAONING

LIAONING

201

HEBEI

Qinhuangdao

BEIJING

Tangshan

TIANJIN

Tianjin

Dalian

Bo Hai

0 km   100

0 miles   100

Cangzhou

Botou

Yantai

Dezhou

Binzhou

206

YELLOW SEA

Zibo

309

Ji'nan

Weifang

Yellow River

Qingdao

KEY

SHANDONG

204

☐ Greater Beijing

☐ Greater Shanghai

✈ International airport

Jining

☒ Domestic airport

Zaozhuang

National highway

Lianyungang

Major road

Shangqiu

Railroad

Xuzhou

JIANGSU

Provincial border

Great Wall

Suzhou

Huaiyin

Yancheng

Dongtai

Bengbu

Fuyang

Huainan

Yangzhou

Taizhou

ANHUI

Nanjing

SHANGHAI

Lu'an

Hefei

Suzhou

☒

✈

Wuhu

Tai Hu

Yangzi

Tongling

Hangzhou

Ningbo

206

Anqing

Shaoxing

ZHEJIANG

A PORTRAIT OF BEIJING & SHANGHAI

he two cities of Beijing and Shanghai have long loomed large in the Western imagination, one as the capital of an ancient and cultured civilization, all temples and ceremony, and the other as a legendarily louche colonial-era collision of Western and Eastern cultures, famed as the "Paris of the East."

The modern-day realities are rather different. Standing in the shadow of forests of cranes and partly obscured by clouds of construction dust and traffic pollution, the two cities seem to be rapidly converging towards a culturally unspecific modernity that already sees Shanghai appearing as an anonymous urban landscape of the future in Western science fiction films. In both cities, boulevards have been driven through narrow alleys, ancient courtyard housing is disappearing beneath shopping malls and tower blocks, and largely foreigner-designed complexes of epic proportions are springing up in readiness for the forthcoming 2008

Tile relief from the Forbidden City

Beijing Olympics and 2010 Shanghai World Expo. Change and growth are common to all developing cities, but in these two great Chinese metropolises they are happening much faster and on a much larger scale than anywhere else.

Beyond the similarities are some profound regional differences and petty rivalries – the citizens of Beijing and Shanghai are particularly well-known for needling each other, each with a sense of pride based on their home cities' fundamentally different histories.

Despite the long periods spent under foreign rule, Beijingers see themselves as the truly Chinese inheritors of a rich imperial culture,

Shanghai's high-rise skyline, a symbol of the city's booming prosperity

◁ Red flags flying next to Qian Men on Tian'an Men Square

Early morning exercises along the waterfront promenade of The Bund, Shanghai

while Shanghainese hark back to their city's foreign-run heyday in the 1920s and 1930s, and see themselves as the open-minded absorbers and interpreters of foreign culture to the rest of China. The Shanghainese inevitably look east from the Bund across the river to the gleaming towers of Pudong, a brand new mini-Manhattan, where the soaring 88-story Jin Mao tower is soon to be surpassed by a 101-story structure going up just a few yards away. Pudong is a three-dimensional advertisement for Shanghai's booming economy, designed to increase the confidence of foreign investors.

Shanghai has the highest average income per household in China, and leads the emergence of a middle class, tiny as a percentage of the overall population of China, but still larger than the populations of many a European nation.

THE POLITICAL CAPITAL

Beijing's response to Pudong has been to embark on a concerted building program of its own, with a roster of spectacular architecture. There is the newly christened Central

Business District to either side of the East Third Ring Road, which features the flamboyant creations of internationally famous architects such as Holland's Rem Koolhaas. Elsewhere, Frenchman Paul Andreu's startling egg-shaped Grand National Theater rises immediately west of Tian'an Men Square, Briton Norman Foster's dragon-shaped terminal increases capacity at the international airport, and a Swiss-designed Olympic Stadium in the shape of a giant bird's nest is auspiciously located on the city's historic main axis, north of the Forbidden City.

And while Shanghai may be the country's commercial center, political shifts register on Beijing's seismometer first. Word-of-mouth from within the government's high-security Zhong Nan Hai compound, the modern equivalent of the Forbidden City, typically fuels whispered debate amongst the city's inhabitants, who see themselves as the closest to power.

On a more personal level, Beijingers consider themselves cultured but lazy, and both admire and resent the notorious business acumen of their big-city rivals to the south. The former consider the latter *jinjinjijiaode* or calculating. In return, the Shanghainese consider Beijingers to be no less calculating – it's just that they hide it behind a smoothly political exterior. The Shanghainese are proud of their familiarity with foreign things, and foreigners on the street attract less attention there than they do in Beijing. Quentin Tarantino's visit to Beijing for *Kill Bill* caused considerable buzz amongst the class tuned in to foreign culture. In contrast, Tom Cruise's visit to Shanghai for *Mission: Impossible III* produced only a studied yawn. Shanghainese often consider Beijingers, and especially any still speaking the outmoded language of politics, as country bumpkins.

Praying at the Lama Temple, Beijing

CITY TALK

Beijingers often regard Mandarin, the official national language of China, of administration, and of a classical education, as their own dialect. But the local habit of adding a retroflex "r" suffix to many words gives their pronunciation a non-standard growl, and makes it sound as if they are rolling the language around their mouths like wine-tasters, before spitting it out.

Shanghainese, a language incomprehensible to all other Chinese except some from neighboring Zhejiang and Jiangsu Provinces (the original homes of most Shanghai people or their forebears), often sounds like a series of ill-suppressed sneezes.

In anticipation of a larger than usual influx of visitors for internationally high-profile events, the government is calling for increased levels of culture and civilization, sometimes despairing of the citizens of both cities. Some Beijing men have a habit of taking off their shirts and rolling up their trousers above the knee in hot weather, while Shanghainese of both sexes wear Western-style pajamas in the street. Campaigns against such behavior have joined those against spitting and swearing.

But, however much the government strives to dress up both populations and skylines into a uniform readiness to receive visitors, no one should regard either city as representing any more than itself, each with a distinctly

Window shopping on Shanghai's Nanjing Xi Lu different spirit.

Language and Script

The Chinese script can be traced back to the oracle bones of the Shang dynasty (16th–11th centuries BC) that were inscribed with symbols representing words and used for divination. Despite changes brought about by different writing materials, Chinese characters have remained remarkably consistent. It is said that to read a newspaper takes knowledge of at least 3,000 characters but an educated person would be expected to know over 5,000. Since 1913 the official spoken language has been *Putonghua* (Mandarin) but there are many regional dialects. Although people from different parts of China may not be able to understand each other, they can use a shared written script.

Cang Jie, *minister of the legendary Yellow Emperor, was supposedly inspired to invent the Chinese script one morning after seeing bird and animal tracks in the snow.*

A BEAUTIFUL SCRIPT

Writing was elevated to an art form considered on a par with painting as a visual aesthetic *(see pp26–7)*. As the process changed from inscribing bone, brass or stone to using a brush on silk and paper, a more fluid writing style became possible.

Seal, in red cinnabar – this may be a name seal, or inscribed with other characters.

Oracle bones *display China's first examples of seal script. Questions were inscribed on the bones which were then burnt – the way cracks divided the inscriptions was deemed significant.*

Bamboo slats *were used from around the 5th century BC. These were tied together to make the earliest type of books. Used for administrative and philosophical texts, the script runs from top to bottom.*

Writing materials were silk, stone, or paper, which was first invented around the 2nd century BC.

Cursive script *(cao shu)* has strokes that run into each other. Fluid and dynamic, it allows for great expressiveness.

The Diamond Sutra (AD 868) *is the world's first block-printed book to bear a date. Printing was probably invented about a century earlier. Movable block printing was developed in the 11th century but had less social impact than in Europe because of the thousands of symbols required.*

CHINESE CHARACTERS

May be composed of pictographic, ideographic and phonetic elements. The radical (or root), an element that appears on the left or at the top of a character, usually gives a clue as to sense. Here, in the character for "good," pronounced *"bao,"* the radical combines with another meaning element "child." The concept, therefore, is that "woman" plus "child" equals "good."

"Woman"

The Chinese character for "Good"

"Child"

Combining element for "child," is here an ideographic (meaning) element. The combining element may alternatively be phonetic, giving a clue for pronunciation of the character.

The radical for "woman" appears in characters with "female" associations, such as "milk," "wife," and "sister."

Pinyin is a **Romanization** *system that was introduced in 1956. While Pinyin will never replace the character forms, it is an easier method for children to start learning the language and useful for input to computers.*

STYLES OF CALLIGRAPHY

Zhuanshu, or seal script, was developed during the Zhou era and used for engraved inscriptions.

Lishu, or clerical script, probably evolved during the Han era and was used for stone inscriptions.

Kaishu, or regular script, developed from Lishu after the Han era, is the basis of modern type.

Cao shu, or cursive script, literally grass script, has strokes that are reduced to abstract curves or dots.

Xingshu, or running script, has strokes that run together, and is a semicursive script.

Simplified script was introduced in 1956 to make it easier for peasants to learn to read.

Chinese typewriters were very difficult to use. The typist had to find each character in a tray of thousands. Computers have made typing Simplified script much easier – the user types in the Pinyin and gets a sub-menu of several possible characters.

Chinese Literature

Dating back to the sixth century BC, the earliest Chinese texts were primarily philosophic, such as the Confucian *Analects* and Daoist *Daode Jing*. History as a literary genre was not established until the Han period (206 BC–AD 220) with Sima Qian's *Historical Records*: thereafter each dynasty wrote a history of the preceding one. As for the novel, a fully fledged Chinese example did not appear until the Ming period (1368–1644) and was developed during the Qing dynasty until it was eventually stifled by Communism. Since the 1980s Chinese authors have been allowed greater freedom of expression, although, in 2000, news of exiled writer Gao Xingjian's Nobel Prize for Literature was suppressed.

Confucius, author of the *Analects*, and his disciples

CLASSICS

Post-Qin dynasty, once Confucianism had become the state orthodoxy, five early works were canonized as the Five Classics: *the Book of Changes, Book of Documents, Book of Songs, Spring and Autumn Annals* and *Book of Ritual*. These books were established as the basis for Chinese education.

The scholar class or literati *achieved the status of government official through success in the civil service examinations, based on detailed knowledge of the Classics and accomplishment in writing.*

TANG POETS

With early beginnings in the *Book of Songs* and *Elegies of Chu*, Chinese poetry reached its height more than twelve hundred years later in the Tang period (618–907). The two greatest Tang poets are considered to be Du Fu and Li Bai. Others include the Buddhist Wang Wei, also 8th-century, and slightly later Bai Juyi (772–846).

Baoyu prefers to flirt with the women rather than obey his father and study hard to advance his career.

Du Fu *(AD c.712–770) wrote of suffering in war, as well as of family life. His keynote is compassion, considered a Confucian virtue. His poems display enormous erudition.*

Li Bai *(AD c.701–761) was a more ebullient figure. A prolific poet, his favorite subjects were moon gazing and carousing. The theme of freedom from constraint is a Daoist one.*

EPIC NOVELS

In the Ming era, the novel developed from folk tales and myths into classics such as *Journey to the West, Romance of the Three Kingdoms* and *The Water Margin* – a tale of the heroic fight against corruption. Later, the Qing novels used a more elevated language and subtle characterization, culminating in the romantic novel, *Dream of the Red Chamber*. These novels contain many characters that reoccur in other cultural contexts from Beijing Opera to popular television serials and films.

Guandi, God of War, *derives from Guan Yu, a general of the state of Shu, portrayed in* Romance of the Three Kingdoms. *This novel was based on historical figures from the Three Kingdoms Era (AD 220–80). A symbol for justice, honesty, and integrity, his figurines are found in temples throughout China.*

Journey to the West *is a comic fantasy based on the pilgrimage to India of the Buddhist monk Xuanzang. The late Ming novel centers on Monkey, one of the monk's companions who represents carefree genius, bravery, and loyalty.*

DREAM OF THE RED CHAMBER

Perhaps the greatest Chinese novel, this portrays the decline of an aristocratic Qing household. Infused with a Daoist sense of transcendence, it focuses on the life and loves of the idle Baoyu and twelve perceptively drawn female characters.

20TH CENTURY

In the early 20th century, fiction writers and playwrights addressed social issues in a new realist style. However Communism demanded revolutionary themes. After the persecution of writers during the Cultural Revolution *(see pp50–51)*, experimental forms and styles gradually emerged. However, the books of Chinese authors may still be banned if they are openly critical of the government or are "spiritual pollutants"; nevertheless pirated versions are often widely available.

Mo Yan *is a post-Cultural Revolution fiction writer. Best known for his novel* Red Sorghum *(1986), made into a major film, he writes in a rich style, often graphic, fantastic, and violent.*

Lu Xun, *early 20th-century writer of short stories and novellas, is known as the father of modern Chinese literature. His realist, satirical style is indebted to such writers as Dickens. He is renowned for his humorous depiction of Ah Q, an illiterate but enthusiastic peasant, done down by the forces of convention.*

Religion and Philosophy

Traditionally, the three strands in Chinese religion and philosophy are Confucianism, Daoism, and Buddhism. An eclectic approach to religion allows the three to coexist, often within a single temple. Confucianism, the first to gain real influence, can be seen as a manifestation of the public, socially responsible self. Daoism represents a personal and wilder side; its emphasis on the relativity of things contrasts with Confucian concern for approved roles. Buddhism, a foreign import, is spiritual and otherworldly, offering an alternative to Chinese pragmatism. During the Cultural Revolution, religion was outlawed as contrary to Communist ideas. Today, people are largely able to express their beliefs.

Laozi, Buddha, and Confucius

CONFUCIANISM

Originated by Confucius (551–479 BC) and developed by later thinkers, Confucianism advocates a structured society in which people are bound to each other by the moral ties of the five familial relationships: parent-child, ruler-subject, brother-brother, husband-wife, and friend-friend. In Imperial China, Confucianism was the philosophy of the elite scholar-gentleman class. For much of the Communist era, it was reviled as a reactionary philosophy linked to the former ruling aristocracy.

Confucius *was a thinker and teacher whose philosophy of family obligations and good government is based on the principles of* ren *(benevolence) and* yi *(righteousness). He died unknown, his disciples spreading his teachings.*

Filial piety, *or* xiao, *another Confucian precept, consists of obedience to and reverence for one's parents, and by extension respect for other family members and one's ruler.*

The birth of Confucius *is celebrated in the philosopher's home town of Qufu in late September. Many thousands of his descendants, all surnamed Kong, still live in the city.*

The paying of respects *to one's ancestors is based on filial piety and runs throughout Chinese culture. During the Qing Ming festival in April, Chinese traditionally clean and upkeep their ancestors' tombs.*

Scholars *collated the Confucian Classics including the* Lunyu *(Analects), a series of Confucius's sayings, well after his death. The Classics were the basis of education until 1912.*

DAOISM

Strongly linked with early folk beliefs, Daoism incorporates the traditional concepts of an ordered universe, *yin* and *yang*, and directed energy, *qi*. Over time, Daoism developed into a complex religion with an extensive pantheon. Daoist philosophy encourages following one's intuition and following the grain of the universe by living in accordance with the Dao.

Laozi, *the founder of Daoism, is a shadowy figure, who may have lived in the 6th century BC. The Daode Jing, which introduces the idea of Dao or the Way that permeates reality, is attributed to him.*

Han Xiangzi, *one of the Eight Immortals, a popular group of Daoist adepts, is believed to have fallen from a sacred peach tree, which bestowed eternal life. He is usually shown playing a flute.*

Daoist alchemists *aimed to find an elixir for eternal life, winning influence with emperors. Daoism influenced scientific development, and contributed to the discovery of gunpowder in the 9th century.*

In "Peach Blossom Spring" *by Daoist poet Tao Qian, a fisherman chances upon a lost idyllic world and encounters Immortals. Daoist reverence for nature led to the creation of numerous paradises.*

BUDDHISM

In China the Mahayana school of Buddhism, which promises salvation to anyone who seeks it, is followed. Enlightened ones, *bodhisattvas*, remain in this world to help enlighten others. Through deeds and devotion believers gain merit and maintain their connections with the *bodhisattvas*, bringing them closer to nirvana.

The Laughing Buddha, *or Milefo, is an adaptation of the Maitreya, the Future Buddha. His large belly and laughing face are signs of abundance and he is worshiped in the hopes of a happy, affluent life.*

The Guardian King *of the South (left) is coiled by a snake; the King of the North holds a parasol. Kings of the four directions guard the entrance to many temples protecting the main deity from evil influences.*

Luohans *or* arhats *are the Buddha's disciples and often appear in temples in groups of 18. Their holiness is thought to enable them to achieve extinction (nirvana) on death.*

A Buddhist supplicant *burns sticks of incense in aid of prayer. Buddhist temples throb with spiritual energy, as worshipers pray and make offerings to gain merit.*

Architecture

Tiled imperial dragon

For over two thousand years, the Chinese have used the same architectural model for both imperial and religious buildings. This has three elements: a platform, post-and-beam timber frames, and non-loadbearing walls. Standard features of building complexes include a front gate, four-sided enclosures or courtyards, and a series of halls in a linear formation running north. Most Chinese buildings were built of wood, but because wooden buildings tend to catch fire, only a few structures remain; the earliest date from the Tang period.

Aerial view of the Forbidden City, showing the traditional linear layout

HALL

In every context, the Chinese hall or *tang* follows the same pattern: a platform of rammed earth or stone, and timber columns arranged in a grid. The front of the hall always has an odd number of bays. Between the columns and beams are brackets (*dougong*), cantilevers that support the structure, allowing the eaves to overhang. The timber is brightly painted, the roof aesthetically curved, and tiled or thatched.

Gate of Heavenly Purity (see p64)
An archetypal Chinese hall, the central doorway and uneven number of bays emphasize the processional element.

Base gives monumentality

Bay, or space between columns

Standard Hall
Buildings in China conformed to a set of rules about proportions. This uniform architecture created a sense of identity – useful in a large and disparate country.

STORIED BUILDING (LOU) AND STORIED PAVILION (GE)

Multi-story buildings in China predate pagodas and varied from two-storied private homes to huge seven- or more story towers built to enjoy the scenery. Storied pavilions were used for storage and had doors and windows only at the front. Both types of building kept the standard elements of base, columns, and hanging walls.

Storied Pavilion
These were used for storing important items, such as libraries of Buddhist sutras or colossal statues.

Characteristic "flying eave"

Symmetrical façade

Storied Building
The construction of tall buildings relied heavily on the dougong *bracket.*

PAGODA

Based on the Indian stupa, the Chinese pagoda, or *ta*, was developed in the first century AD along with the arrival of Buddhism. Multi-storied pagodas appeared in Buddhist temple complexes (although later they often stood on their own) and were originally intended to house a religious relic. They were built of brick, stone, or wood.

Top resembles Indian stupa

Base, usually with an underground chamber

ORNAMENTAL ARCHWAY

The *pailou*, or *paifang*, is a memorial or decorative archway. Made of wood, brick, or stone, and sometimes with glazed tiles, it often bears an edifying inscription. *Pailou* were erected at crossroads, temples, bridges, government offices, parks, and tombs.

Ornamental, multi-sectioned roof

Inscription typically four characters

CITY WALLS

Early defensive walls, like other early architectural forms, were made of earth – either pounded hard by pestles or moistened to make a clay and pressed around reed frames. Later walls were often built using brick. City walls were traditionally square, with the main gate to the south. The Chinese for "city" *(cheng)* also means "wall."

Easy to defend with a bow

Gate tower, often a two-story *lou*

City wall and gate
The towers on top of walls can vary from small buildings to palatial multi-story structures.

City Walls
Typically made of rammed earth and brick, ramparts and watchtowers were an effective defense. Both Beijing and Shanghai were originally surrounded by such walls.

ARCHITECTURAL DETAILS

It is interesting to interpret the architectural detail on Chinese buildings. The use of yellow tiles, for example, was reserved for the emperor. The Nine-Dragon Screen, which occurs in the Forbidden City and elsewhere, is also imperial since the dragon symbolizes the *yang*, or male principle, and by extension the emperor.

Chiwen
Able to douse flames with water, the Chiwen often appears at the end of a roof ridge (see p63) as a protection against fire.

Dougong
A bracket (dougong), transmits the load from roof to column. It's a traditionally complex, nail-free, and ornamental construction method.

Traditional Arts

Funerary bronze bell

The earliest Chinese artifacts were found in royal tombs. These include bronzes, ceramics, and jades from the Shang and Zhou period, as well as terracotta warriors from the Qin period. Of the many rich art forms that subsequently developed in China, painting and pottery are perhaps the most important, and have reached the highest aesthetic level. Other significant art forms include sculpture, notably the Buddhist sculpture of Western China. There are also many distinctive and popular forms of Chinese decorative art.

Buddhist sculpture in the Gandharan style

Ritual bronze tripod *from an early royal tomb, decorated with a mythical animal design known as a* taotie.

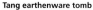

Wet and dry ink used to give the detail of the trees.

POTTERY

Since inventing porcelain, China developed a huge range of potting, decorating, and glazing techniques that were imitated from Europe to Japan. Chinese ceramics led the world in aesthetic taste and technique up until the demise of the Qing dynasty.

Tang earthenware tomb figure *representing a fierce warrior, with typical rough* sancai *(three-color) drip glaze. This was a lead-based glaze, fired at a low temperature.*

Textured strokes give the rocks depth.

Song celadon bowl, *with incised floral design. Celadon was the European name given to the refined gray-green glaze of this type of stoneware and porcelain.*

Ming vase *in the blue-and-white style known and imitated internationally. The technique involves underglaze painting in cobalt blue before the pot is fired.*

Qing famille-rose vase, *a delicate porcelain in a distinctive palette. The name comes from the use of bright pink enamel.*

Bird-and-flower painting *(including the depiction of fruit and insects) reveals the Chinese Daoist interest in observing the natural world. Despite the lightness of subject, the paintings have an intense, quasi-scientific depth.*

CHINESE PAINTING

Considered the highest traditional art form, Chinese painting is executed on silk or paper using a brush and inks or watercolors. **Landscape painting**, associated with the scholar class, reached a highpoint in the Northern Song and Yuan periods. Huang Gongwang *(see below)*, a master of the Yuan, was admired for his simple calligraphic style.

Religious painting *first appeared along the Silk Road with the arrival of Buddhism from India. The Chinese soon developed an individual style.*

Ink wash is used for the hills in the distance.

Bamboo painting *was a genre of the scholar class. Bamboo symbolized the scholar-gentleman who would bend but not break in the face of adversity.*

TRADITIONAL CRAFTS

As well as the traditional high art forms of painting and pottery, China has a wealth of beautiful decorative arts. Delicate carvings in lacquer, ivory and jade are popular, as are colorful cloisonné items, decorated inksticks (or cakes), snuff bottles, and fans.

Snuff bottles *were produced in large numbers during the Qing period. Made of glass, jade, mother-of-pearl, or semi-precious stones, they were delicately carved or painted on the inside in exquisite detail.*

Lacquer carving *is distinctive for its deep red color and floral designs, and is often used on boxes.*

Cloisonné *is a style of enameling. Individual metal cloisons, usually made of copper, are soldered together and inlaid with different colored enamels. The object is then fired and polished.*

Traditional Chinese Gardens

Lotus, a favorite symbolic flower

The Chinese garden developed as a synthesis of two concepts linked in Daoist philosophy *(see p23)* – scenery and serenity: the contemplation of nature in isolated meditation led to enlightenment. Therefore, the educated and wealthy built natural-looking retreats for themselves within an urban environment. The garden creates poetic and painterly concepts, and aims to improve on nature by creating a picture that looks natural but is in fact entirely artificial. For this the Chinese garden designer used four main elements: rocks, water, plants, and architecture.

Classical Chinese garden design *was considered a type of three-dimensional landscape painting or solid poetry.*

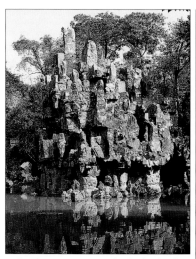

Rocks: *There were two main kinds of rock – the eroded limestones from lakes, often used as sculptures, or the yellow rock piled up to recall mountains and caves to the mind of the viewer. The beauty and realism of the rockery usually determined the success or failure of the garden.*

Water: *An essential element of life, water also could be used in the garden as a mirror and so appear to increase the size of the garden. Water also serves as a contrasting partner and therefore a balance to the hard stone. Finally it is a home for goldfish, symbols of good fortune.*

Corridors, paths, and bridges *link the different areas and give the artist control over how the views are presented to the visitor.*

Interiors *of pavilions were important as the venues for creativity. A lot of care was taken to select an appropriate and poetic name for each building.*

Patterns and mosaics *brighten up the garden and are also symbolic. Cranes represent longevity, while the* yin *and* yang *symbol often appears where a path forks in two.*

GARDEN VIEWS

Using these four elements the garden is like a series of tableaux painted onto a roll of silk. One by one they come before your eyes just as the artist intended them to. As you follow the paths, you see just what he wanted you to see. These may be borrowed views, where the scenery from somewhere else is made to look part of the picture; hidden views, where you round a corner to come upon an unexpected scene; or contrasting views where leafy bamboo softens the view of rock, or opposite views as the *yin* element water balances the *yang* element rock.

A moon gate *is a round door that neatly frames a view as though it were a picture. Gates can be square-, jar-, or even book-shaped.*

Patterned screens *allow in a certain amount of light and may be used to cast patterned shadows on white walls. They are also sometimes used to give tempting partial views through to other areas of the garden.*

Plants: *Plants were used sparingly and usually for their symbolic qualities. Thus the lotus is purity, as it flowers from the mud; bamboo is resolve, it is difficult to break; plum is vigor, as it blooms in winter; the pine is longevity, for it is an evergreen; the imperial peony, is wealth.*

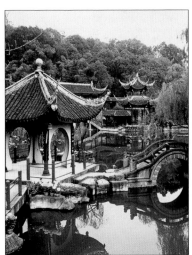

Buildings: *An intrinsic part of the garden, these pavilions and waterside halls provide a place for contemplation and more importantly a specific viewpoint, as well as shelter from the sun and rain. They could range from open kiosks to multi-story halls and meeting rooms.*

PENJING

Dating as far back as the Tang dynasty (618–907), *penjing* is the art of creating a miniature landscape in a container. Not limited to small trees, the artist may use rocks and specially cultivated plants to portray a scene of natural beauty, as though it were a landscape painting. As well as being beautiful, the harmony in these creations is seen as the spiritual expression of man's relationship with nature, the meeting of the temporal with the omnipresent. Often part of a Chinese garden will be devoted to the display or cultivation of this delicate art.

The Chinese art of *penjing*, the forerunner to Japanese bonsai

Beijing Opera

Souvenir mask

One among many hundreds of local operas across China, Beijing Opera began in the Qing dynasty. It is said that Emperor Qianlong (r.1736–96), on a tour of the south, was rather taken by the operas of Anhui and Hebei and brought these troupes back to Beijing, where a new form of opera was established. The Guangxu emperor and Dowager Empress Cixi were also keen devotees and helped develop the art form. Beijing Opera has proved remarkably resilient, surviving the persecution of actors and the banning of most of the plays during the Cultural Revolution.

Emperor Qianlong, credited with starting Beijing Opera

BEIJING OPERA

Visually stunning and with a distinct musical style, the plays are based on Chinese history and literature. Beijing Opera is a form of "total theater" with singing, speech, mime, acrobatics, and symbolic visual effects.

Monkey *is one of the favorite characters – clever, resourceful, and brave. He appears in Chinese classic literature (see p21).*

The colors of the painted faces *symbolize the individual character's qualities. Red, for example, represents loyalty and courage; purple, solemnity and a sense of justice; green, bravery and irascibility.*

The acrobatics *of Beijing Opera combine graceful gymnastics and movements from the martial arts. Training is notoriously hard. The costumes are designed to make the jumps seem more spectacular by billowing out as they spin.*

Riding a horse *is represented by raising a tasseled horsewhip. Other actions and movement on the stage are similarly stylized rather than realistic.*

MUSICAL INSTRUMENTS

Despite the dramatic visual elements of Beijing Opera, the Chinese say that they go to "listen" to opera, not to see it. The importance of the musical elements should not therefore be underestimated. Typically six or seven instrumentalists accompany the opera. The stringed instruments usually include the *erhu* or Chinese two-stringed violin, *sanxian* or three-stringed lute, and moon guitar, or possibly *pipa* (traditional lute). The main function of the instruments is to accompany the singing. Percussion instruments include clappers, gongs, and drums. These are used largely to punctuate the action; movement and sound are intimately linked. Wind instruments also sometimes feature, such as the Chinese horn, flute, and *suona*.

Gong

Suona   **Pipa**   **Erhu**

Mei Lanfang *was the foremost interpreter of the female role type or* dan *during the opera's heyday in the 1920s and 1930s. Traditionally all female roles were played by male actors, although that has now changed.*

THE FOUR MAIN ROLES

There are four main role types in Beijing Opera: the *sheng* (male) and *dan* (female) roles have naturalistic make-up. The *jing* or "painted faces," in contrast, have stylized patterned, colored faces, while the *chou* are comic characters.

Chou: with a white patch on his face, the *chou* is usually dim but amusing.

Sheng: these may be young or old, with beard or without.

Dan: there are six parts within this role from virtuous girl to old woman.

Jing: the most striking looking, they also have the most forceful personality.

Modern Arts

The birth of modern art in China at the start of the 20th century coincided with greater contact with the West. Experiments with new materials and styles in the visual arts, Western-style music, "spoken drama" (*huaju*), cinema, and modern literary forms such as free verse all took root at this time. However, after 1949, this creativity was stifled by Soviet-influenced Socialist Realism. During the Cultural Revolution many artists were even persecuted on the grounds that their works were "reactionary." Since the 1980s and 1990s, however, there has been some liberalization in the arts and new, exciting forms have developed.

The Oriental Pearl TV Tower, *Pudong, Shanghai is the epitome of China's high-rise architecture boom since the early 1990s.*

This example of performance art *is by Cang Xin, a Beijing-based conceptual artist, active since the mid-1990s. The title of this piece,* Unification of Heaven and Man, *alludes to classical Chinese philosophical concepts.*

Shaven-headed man

MODERN ART
This painting, *Series 2 No. 2,* is by Fang Lijun, leader of the Cynical Realism school, which came about as a reaction to the demise of the pro-democracy movement in 1989. Rejecting idealism, these artists make fun of the problems of life in China.

Sculpture *entitled* Torso, *by Zhan Wang, a Shanghai-based conceptual artist. Zhan uses reflective steel sheets to give the illusion of solidity.*

Orchestral and chamber music *has been popular in China since the early 20th century. Today, there are many schools specializing in Western-style music, and several high-quality ensembles and artists on the world scene.*

CHINESE CINEMA

From early classics such as *Street Angel* (1937), made in the (then) foreign enclave of Shanghai, Chinese cinema has scaled new heights of international success, with the work of such acclaimed directors as Zhang Yimou.

Farewell My Concubine *(1993), directed by Chen Kaige, a post-Cultural Revolution filmmaker, who gave expression to new moral uncertainties, is set in the world of traditional Beijing Opera.*

The Hong Kong film industry *followed its own path and became primarily famous for its action movies. Renowned martial arts star Jackie Chan, seen above in an early acting and directorial debut,* Fearless Hyena, *made many films and successfully crossed over from Hong Kong to Hollywood.*

Background is a hazy blue, making it appear dream-like

Wei Wei *is one of the bestselling pop stars in China today. Rock music only took off in the 1980s: Cui Jian, the "grandad" of Chinese rock is seen as a rebel by the authorities. Hong Kong's less controversial Canto-pop singers, in contrast, have had more freedom.*

Anonymous figures seem threatening

Main figure is yelling or yawning – is he angry or just bored?

Ballet *in contemporary China mixes traditional Chinese and Western influences. Here, the ballet version of Zhang Yimou's film* Raise the Red Lantern *is performed by members of the National Ballet.*

Modern theater *provides an expression of Chinese life in the 21st century. Here, a scene from* Toilet (2004), *a black comedy, is performed by the National Theater company in Beijing. The play broke taboos with its frank portrayal of urban life and treatment of homosexuality.*

THROUGH THE YEAR

The dates of traditional Chinese festivals are tied to a lunar calendar, which has 29.5 days a month. This means that festival dates move around in the same manner as the Christian Easter does. Public holidays associated with Communism – National Day and International Labor Day, for example – are fixed on the familiar Gregorian (Western) calendar. Some

Chinese New Year banner

celebrations of Western origin, such as Christmas, are also observed. Very few Chinese have any sort of discretionary holiday from work, so on the longer public holidays a large proportion of the population takes to the road all at the same time. At such times it is unwise to attempt much travel, and many tourist attractions may be shut for a day or two *(see p37)*.

SPRING

The four seasons are far more clearly marked in Beijing than in Shanghai, which tends to be either cool and humid, or hot and humid, year round. Spring in Beijing sees seeds from the many scholar trees blown into drifts by winds that clear away the pollution. However, those same winds also sometimes bring scouring clouds of sand from the arid northwest, turning the skies dark and yellow.

A red lantern – lucky symbol

Festival, which is also known as Chinese New Year, is a time when wage packets contain bonuses, debts must be settled, and everyone who can heads for their family home. Many temple fairs take place at this time, especially in Beijing, and these often feature stilt-walkers, acrobats, opera singers, and other traditional entertainments. Museums and most offices are shut for at least three days, many for longer, although a great deal of shopping goes on, commonly encouraged by department store sales.

JANUARY–FEBRUARY

Spring Festival (Chun Jie)
Beijing, Shanghai. This occurs with the first new moon after January 21, which will be February 18 in 2007, February 7 in 2008, January 26 in 2009, and February 14 in 2010. Spring

FEBRUARY–MARCH

Lantern Festival Beijing, Shanghai. Coinciding with a full moon, this festival marks the end of the 15-day Spring Festival period. Lanterns bearing auspicious characters or in animal shapes are hung

Lion dancing, performed as part of Spring Festival celebrations

everywhere. It is also a time for eating the sticky rice balls known as *yuanxiao*.

MARCH

International Women's Day *(March 8)*, Beijing, Shanghai. A holiday, or half-day holiday, for the female part of the population; men go to work as usual.

MARCH–APRIL

Peach Blossom Festival Shanghai. This festival takes place among more than 6,175 acres (2,500 hectares) of peach orchards in the Nanhui District outside Shanghai over a two-week period in late March and early April, depending on the progress of the blossom. Visitors come to admire the trees and to eat at local

Red lanterns form a tunnel in a Beijing park during the Lantern Festival

AVERAGE DAILY HOURS OF SUNSHINE

BEIJING
SHANGHAI

Sunshine Chart
Although Beijing appears to receive a generous number of hours of sunshine throughout the whole year, the reality is that air pollution often creates a haze over the city that prevents the sun getting through. Shanghai has similar problems with smog.

homes that have temporarily become cafés, restaurants, and guesthouses, in a tradition called *nongjia le*.

APRIL

Clear Brightness Festival (Qing Ming Jie) *(April 5)*, Beijing, Shanghai. Also known as the Tomb-Sweeping Festival, this takes place two weeks after the vernal equinox, usually April 5, but April 4 in leap years. Those who still live close enough to their ancestors' graves pay a visit to tidy them up and make offerings of snacks and alcohol, an event which often turns into a picnic. Around this time, the Shanghainese like to eat *qingtuan*, which are sticky rice balls that have been dyed green.

SUMMER

Shanghai steams and drips as the heat steadily rises, and the increased usage of air-conditioning units causes electricity shortages and black-outs. On a more northerly latitude, Beijing is washed clean by intermittent showers, but it is otherwise similarly hot and sticky.

MAY

International Labor Day *(May 1)*, Beijing, Shanghai. This has now expanded into a week-long holiday, which marks the start of the domestic travel season. Shops, offices,

A dragon boat, with the drummer setting the rhythm for the rowers

and other businesses close for at least three days, and often for the whole week.
Meet in Beijing Beijing. This is a cultural festival running throughout all of May with an unpredictable mix of Chinese and foreign elements at a variety of venues around the city.

JUNE

Dragon Boat Festival (Duanwu Jie) Beijing, Shanghai. Held on the fifth day of the fifth lunar month (usually June), this popular festival features races between colorful dragon-headed boats. On-board drummers set the tempo and keep the twin rows of paddlers in unison. The festival honors the honest official, Qu Yuan, who drowned himself after banishment from the court of the Duke of Chu nearly 2,500 years

ago. Shocked citizens threw rice cakes into the water to distract the fish from his body. Rice cakes are eaten today in the form of *zongzi*, pyramids of glutinous rice wrapped in river reeds and tied up with string. Races and pageantry can be seen at Qinglong Hu near the Ming Tombs outside Beijing, and on various lakes and rivers around Shanghai.
Shanghai International Film Festival Shanghai. Held over one week in mid-June, this celebration of celluloid showcases plenty of Chinese cinema unlikely to be seen much in the West – but don't expect anything beyond officially approved projects – along with a selection of unchallenging foreign fare. However, the festival is still important enough for international stars to put in an appearance.

Shanghai International Film Festival poster

AVERAGE MONTHLY RAINFALL

Rainfall Chart
Typically for a coastal city, Shanghai is wet throughout the year. Beijing receives its greatest rainfall during the height of summer, when the prolonged and heavy downpours provide a welcome release from the seasonal heat.

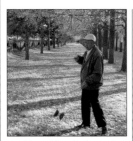

Exercising with a spinning top in a Beijing park in fall

FALL

The months of September and October are easily the best time to visit Beijing. The summer heat has gone and in its place are warm, dry days, with frequent cool breezes that clear the smog-laden skies. Farther south, the baking temperatures and

humidity associated with summers in Shanghai have also dropped to more comfortable levels.

JULY–AUGUST

Qi Xi Beijing, Shanghai. Taking place on the seventh day of the seventh lunar month, which is usually August, Qi Xi celebrates the story of the earthly cowherd and celestial weaving girl who were separated by the gods but who are annually reunited in the heavens by a bridge of magpies. It is the Chinese equivalent of Valentine's Day, and it's going through something of a modern revival, especially in Shanghai, where it involves much shopping for gifts and fully-booked restaurants.

Mooncake

AUGUST–SEPTEMBER

Mid-Autumn Festival (Zhong Qiu Jie) Beijing, Shanghai. On the 15th day of the eighth lunar month (usually in September), this festival, also known as the Harvest or Moon Festival is traditionally a time for family reunions and reading poetry under the full moon. Shops fill with boxes of mooncakes (*yuebing*), the extremely fattening pies filled with bean paste that are exchanged as gifts at this time.

OCTOBER

National Day (*October 1*), Beijing, Shanghai. Marking the anniversary of Mao's speech in which he declared

National Day's massed military parades – a throwback to the days of Communist-era China

AVERAGE MONTHLY TEMPERATURE

BEIJING
SHANGHAI

Temperature Chart
*Beijing annually
endures extremes of
temperature, with the
thermometer often
dropping below zero
in winter and then
threatening to blow in
the heat of summer.
Shanghai ranges from
sultry to sweaty, with
the heat exacerbated
by humidity.*

the foundation of the People's Republic. Crowds turn out to watch massive parades, particularly at Beijing's Tian'an Men Square. This is another three-day holiday that for most people and businesses expands into a full week. Every city sight and scenic rural tourist destination is crowded to its limits and beyond.

Shanghai Formula One Grand Prix Shanghai. This is an entirely foreign event with, for the time being at least, no Chinese competitors, but in its way it is entirely in keeping with Shanghai's tradition of foreign entertainments. The event fills the city's hotels, so if you are visiting at this time check the exact dates well ahead. The 56-lap race around a brand new 3.3-mile (5.5-km) circuit annually raises the city's international profile. Taxi drivers love to talk about *F-yi* year-round, and many drive as if they dream of participating.

WINTER

Beijing winters are not only bitterly cold but the briefest exposure to the arid atmosphere desiccates the face instantly. The dry air and cool temperatures also accentuate the creation of static electricity so be wary reaching for taxi and hotel door handles. By contrast, Shanghai is traditionally deemed to be warm enough year-round for private homes

**Typical Beijing winter weather –
heavy snow and icy roads**

not to be heated, but although temperatures do not drop as low of those of Beijing, the humidity makes the cold more penetrating. Occasional strong winds make viewing Shanghai panoramas from a cosy room in your hotel seem far more attractive than actually venturing out.

DECEMBER

Christmas Day *(December 25)*, Beijing, Shanghai. Although not a traditional holiday in China, this day has been adopted via Hong Kong, which means, of course, that there is a stress on the commercial aspect. Shopping malls and foreign-run hotels have conspired to press this idea upon the Chinese in major cities to the point that it is now rare for a high-street store not to acknowledge the holiday with images of *Shengdan Laoren*, the Chinese version of Father Christmas.

JAN

New Year's Day *(January 1)*, Beijing, Shanghai. Although overshadowed by the Spring Festival (Chinese New Year) celebrations that take place soon after *(see p34)*, Western New Year is still a public holiday, celebrated with gusto by the large number of expatriate foreigners living in Beijing and Shanghai.

PUBLIC HOLIDAYS

New Year's Day (Jan 1)
Spring Festival or Chinese New Year (Feb 18, 2007; Feb 7, 2008; Jan 26, 2009; Feb 14, 2010)
International Labor Day (May 1–3)
National Day (Oct 1–3)

Avoid traveling during Spring Festival and the first weeks of May and October. At these times all Chinese get five days off work and everyone who can afford to takes to the road, either on holiday or to visit relatives. Prices for hotels and transportation rise accordingly, and it is impossible to get a bus or train ticket, or an internal flight. However, since Shanghainese and Beijingers are among those with the highest disposable incomes, and thus most likely to travel, traffic in the two cities thins and it can be a pleasant time to spend in either place.

THE HISTORY OF CHINA

*C*hina boasts one of the longest single unified civilizations in the world. Its history is characterized by dramatic shifts in power between rival factions, periods of peace and prosperity when foreign ideas were assimilated and absorbed, the disintegration of empire through corruption and political subterfuge, and the cyclical rise of ambitious leaders to found each new empire.

FIRST SETTLERS

From around 8000 BC, settlements of populations based on a primitive agricultural economy began to emerge in the eastern coastal regions and along the rich river deltas of the Huang He (Yellow River), the Yangzi, and the Wei. These civilizations focused on hunting, gathering, and fishing, and the cultivation of millet in the north and rice in the south. Each civilization is notable for its own distinct style of pottery, such as the bold earthenware of the Yangshao (5000–3000 BC) and the black ceramics of the Longshan (3000–1700 BC).

Yangshao pottery amphora

BRONZE AGE CHINA AND THE FIRST KINGDOMS

The first dynasty in China was founded by the Shang around 1600 BC. The Shang lived in large, complex societies and were the first to mass-produce cast bronze. Power centered on the ruling elite who acted as shamans of a sort, communicating with their ancestors and gods through diviners. Elaborate bronze food and wine vessels were used both for banqueting and for making ancestral offerings. Inscriptions on oracle bones provide the first evidence of writing, dating from around 1300 BC.

In 1066 BC, the Zhou seized power, establishing their western capital at present-day Xi'an. The Western Zhou initially sustained many of the traditions of the Shang, but later reorganized the political system, and replaced the use of oracle bones with inscriptions on bronze and, later, writing on silk and strips of bamboo.

The Eastern Zhou (770–221 BC) is divided into the Spring and Autumn period (770–476 BC) and the Warring States period (475–221 BC). The Eastern Zhou period was dominated by political conflict and social unrest, as rival factions jockeyed for power. It also saw economic expansion and development as the use of iron revolutionized agriculture. It was in this climate of unrest that the philosophical ideologies of Confucianism, Daoism, and Legalism emerged.

TIMELINE

		5000–3000 BC Yangshao culture based around the Wei river		2200–1600 BC Existence of semimythical first dynasty, the Xia	1300 BC First writing on oracle bones		
8000– 6500 BC Neolithic period						c. 551–479 BC Life of Confucius	475–221 BC Eastern Zhou: Warring States

8000 BC	6000 BC	4000 BC	2000 BC	1000 BC	500 BC

	6500–5000 BC Earliest settlements in northern China		1600–1050 BC Shang dynasty		770–476 BC Eastern Zhou: Spring and Autumn period	513 BC First mention of iron casting
	Bronze food vessel, Shang		1066–771 BC Power seized by Zhou			

◁ **Detail from "The first Emperor of the Han Dynasty Entering Guandong" by Song painter Chao Pochu**

Dynasty Timeline

China was ruled by a succession of dynasties, broken by periods of fragmentation and civil war. The emperor's authority was divinely granted through a mandate of heaven and was thus unlimited. Leaders of succeeding dynasties claimed that the previous leadership had displeased the gods and had therefore had its heavenly mandate withdrawn.

SHANG DYNASTY

1600–1050 BC

The Shang dynasty marked the emergence of Bronze Age China and palace culture. A semi-divine king acted as a shaman and communicated with the gods.

Bronze tripod food vessel, Shang

WESTERN HAN

206 BC–AD 9

Gaozu	206–195 BC
Huidi	195–188 BC
Shaodi	188–180 BC
Wendi	180–157 BC
Jingdi	157–141 BC
Wudi	141–87 BC
Zhaodi	87–74 BC
Xuandi	74–49 BC
Yuandi	49–33 BC
Chengdi	33–7 BC
Aidi	7–1 BC
Pingdi	1 BC–AD 6
Ruzi	AD 7–9

Broken terracotta heads found at Jingdi's tomb

EASTERN HAN

AD 25–220

Guang Wudi	25–57	Chongdi	144–145
Mingdi	57–75	Zhidi	145–146
Zhangdi	75–88	Huandi	146–168
Hedi	88–105	Lingdi	168–189
Shangdi	106	Xiandi	189–220
Andi	106–125		
Shundi	125–144		

TANG

618–907

Gaozu	618–626	Jingzong	824–827
Taizong	626–649	Wenzong	827–840
Gaozong	649–683	Wuzong	840–846
Zhongzong	684 & 705–710	Xuanzong	846–859
Ruizong	684–690	Yizong	859–873
	& 710–712	Xizong	873–888
Wu Zetian	690–705	Zhaozong	888–904
Xuanzong	712–756	Aidi	904–907
Suzong	756–762		
Daizong	762–779		
Dezong	779–805		
Shunzong	805		
Xianzong	805–820		
Muzong	820–824		

Sancai-glazed dancing tomb figures

FIVE DYNASTIES & TEN KINGDOMS

907–960

Based north of the Yangzi, five successive dynasties swiftly usurped one another, with no dynasty lasting for more than three reigns. The Ten Kingdoms to the south went through a similarly turbulent period.

Throughout this period and most of the Song dynasty, the northern frontiers were dominated by the semi-nomadic Liao dynasty (907–1125) in the east, and by the Western Xia (990–1227) in the west. In 1115, the Liao were overthrown by the Jin (1115–1234), who forced the Song southwards in 1127.

YUAN

1279–1368

Genghis Khan (1162–1227) united numerous Mongol speaking tribes and captured Beijing in 1215. His grandson, Kublai, completed the conquest of China by finally defeating the Southern Song in 1279.

Kublai Khan	1279–1294
Temur Oljeitu	1294–1307
Khaishan	1308–1311

Ayurbarwada	1311–1320
Shidebala	1321–1323
Yesun Temur	1323–1328
Tugh Temur	1328–1329,
	1329–1333
Khoshila	1329
Toghon Temur	1333–1368

MING

1368–1644

Hongwu	1368–1398	Longqing	1567–1572
Jianwen	1399–1402	Wanli	1573–1620
Yongle	1403–1424	Taichang	1620
Hongxi	1425	Tianqi	1621–1627
Xuande	1426–1435	Chongzhen	1628–1644
Zhengtong	1436–1449		
Jingtai	1450–1457		
Tianshun	1457–1464		
(Zhengtong restored)			
Chenghua	1465–1487		
Hongzhi	1488–1505		
Zhengde	1506–1521		
Jiajing	1522–1567		

WESTERN ZHOU DYNASTY

1066–771 BC

The Zhou founded their capital at Chang'an (Xi'an). They continued some Shang traditions, but reorganized the political system, dividing the nobility into grades. The feudal system of the Western Zhou broke down after the capital was sacked and the king slain.

EASTERN ZHOU DYNASTY

770–221 BC

Spring and Autumn
770–475 BC

Warring States
475–221 BC

The Zhou dynasty ruled at its eastern capital of Luoyang alongside numerous rival states. This long period of almost constant warfare was brought to an end when the Qin emerged victorious.

QIN DYNASTY

221–206 BC

Qin Shi Huangdi   221–210 BC
Er Shi   210–207 BC

Statue of attendant from the tomb of Qin Shi Huangdi

PERIOD OF DISUNITY

220–589

China was divided into the warring Wei, Wu, and Shu kingdoms. The Wei briefly re-united China under the Western Jin (280–316), the first of the six Southern Dynasties (280–589), with their capital at Jiankang (Nanjing). The north was ruled by a succession of ruling houses – the 16 Kingdoms (304–439). The nomadic Toba Wei set up the Northern Wei dynasty, the first of five Northern Dynasties (386–581) with a capital first at Datong, then at Luoyang.

SUI

581–618

China was once more united by the short and decisive rule of the Sui.

Wendi   581–604
Yangdi   604–617
Gongdi   617–618

Emperor Wendi's flotilla on the Grand Canal

NORTHERN SONG

960–1126

Taizu	960–976	Shenzong	1068–1085
Taizong	976–997	Zhezong	1086–1101
Zhenzong	998–1022	Huizong	1101–1125
Renzong	1022–1063	Qinzong	1126–1127
Yingzong	1064–1067		

Painting by Emperor Huizong

SOUTHERN SONG

1127–1279

Gaozong	1127–1162
Xiaozong	1163–1190
Guangzong	1190–1194
Ningzong	1195–1224
Lizong	1225–1264
Duzong	1265–1274
Gongdi	1275
Duanzong	1276–1278
Di Bing	1279

QING

1644–1911

Shunzhi	1644–1661
Kangxi	1661–1722
Yongzheng	1723–1735
Qianlong	1736–1795
Jiaqing	1796–1820
Daoguang	1821–1850
Xianfeng	1851–1861
Tongzhi	1862–1874
Guangxu	1875–1908
Pu Yi	1909–1912

Emperor Zhengde's love of leisure led to a relaxation of imperial control

Imperial dragon detail on the back of a eunuch's official court robe

FOUNDATION OF IMPERIAL CHINA

The Warring States Period was finally brought to an end as the Qin emerged victorious. In 221 BC, Qin Shi Huangdi pronounced himself the first emperor of China and ruled over a short yet decisive period of history. The Qin state was based on the political theories of Legalism, which established the role of the ruler as paramount and espoused a system of collective responsibility. Following unification, Qin Shi Huangdi conscripted thousands of workers to join together the defensive walls to the north, creating the Great Wall. He standardized the system of money, and weights and measures, and laid the foundations for a legal system. A ruthless ruler, Qin Shi Huangdi died in the belief that his famous terracotta army would protect him in the afterlife from his numerous enemies.

Archer from Qin terracotta army

The founding of the Han dynasty (206 BC–AD 220) heralded a "golden age" in Chinese history. Emperor Gaodi (r. 206–195 BC) established the capital of the Western Han (206 BC–AD 9) at Chang'an (Xi'an), and retained much of the centralized administration established by the Qin. Subsequent emperors developed the civil service examination to select able men for state office. Han society was founded on the principles propounded by Confucius, and the Confucian classics formed the basis of the civil service examination. Daoism and *yin-yang* theory coexisted with ancestor worship and

would form the basis of indigenous Chinese belief *(see pp22–3)*.

The Han empire expanded with regions of Central Asia, Vietnam, and Korea being brought under Chinese control. In 138 BC, General Zhang Qian was sent to establish diplomatic links with Central Asia and returned with tales of rich pastures and "heavenly horses." The fine thoroughbreds of Ferghana (in modern Uzbekistan) were traded in exchange for Chinese silk, starting the flow of goods along the fabled Silk Road.

Han rule was briefly interrupted as Wang Mang seized power in AD 9, only to be restored by Guang Wudi (r. AD 25–57), who established the Eastern Han capital in Luoyang. Once more, the Han expanded Chinese territory. Paper was by now in use for much official documentation and the first Chinese dictionary was produced. Buddhism began its spread to China with the first Buddhist communities being established in Jiangsu province.

Chariot and footmen, impressed into a tomb's brick, Han

TIMELINE

213 BC Burning of the books as part of process of "unification"

206 BC–AD 9 Western Han capital established at Chang'an (Xi'an)

c. 139–126 BC Official envoy Zhang Qian establishes first diplomatic and trading links of Silk Road

AD 2 First known census: 57,671,400 individuals

Bronze horse and rider, Han

c. 100 First dictionar *Shuo Wen* produced with more than 9,00 characters

200 BC   **100 BC**   **1**   **AD 100**

221–206 BC Qin dynasty under first emperor, Qin Shi Huangdi

Tomb figure, Qin

165 BC First official examinations for the selection of civil servants

25–220 Eastern Han dynasty capital at Luoyang

65 First mention of Buddhist community established at court of Prince Ying of Chu

Sui emperors Yangdi and Wendi in a detail from "Portraits of the 13 Emperors" by Tang painter Yen Li Pen

PERIOD OF DIVISION

From the rule of Hedi (r. AD 88–105), the Eastern Han declined. Civil war finally split the country in 220. The next 350 years were characterized by almost constant warfare as China was ruled by over 14 short-lived dynasties and 16 "kingdoms."

China was divided into the Northern and Southern dynasties (265–581), each region taking on its own distinct character. Foreign peoples took control of the North, such as the Toba branch of the Xianbei, who founded the Northern Wei in 386. These rulers were receptive to foreign ideas and religions, creating some of the finest Buddhist cave complexes first at Yungang, near their capital in Datong, and from 494, at Longmen, when they moved their capital to Luoyang.

Apsara from Buddhist cave, Northern Wei

As foreign invaders took control of the North, the Han Chinese retreated south to establish their new capital at Jiankang (Nanjing). In a climate of relative stability, the south became the economic and cultural center as the population shifted to the Yangzi delta. Philosophy and the arts flourished alongside a renewed interest in Daoism and a growing interest in Buddhism.

UNIFICATION AND STABILITY

Following military successes against the Liang and the Chen, the Northern Zhou general Yang Jian (541–604) pronounced himself emperor, taking the name Wendi, and founded the Sui dynasty in 581. This brief but significant dynastic rule established political and social stability. He undertook an extensive program of works including extending the Great Wall and the beginnings of the Grand Canal. The second emperor, Yangdi (569–617), restored diplomatic relations with Japan and Taiwan and extended trade to Central Asia.

190 Communications with central Asia are cut		**310** Massive exodus of Chinese upper classes to South	*Colossal Buddha at Yungang Caves, Northern Wei*	**581–618** Sui dynasty, initiated by Wendi's reunification of China	
AD 2 First known census: 57,671,400 individuals					
200	**300**		**400**	**500**	**600**
220 Civil war breaks out between the ngdoms of Wei, Shu, and Wu	**265–581** China divided into Northern and Southern dynasties		**386–535** Northern Wei, first of the ruling houses to adopt Buddhism	**c. 6th C** First true porcelain produced	**c. 7th C** Woodblock printing first used in China

GLORY OF THE TANG

The Tang dynasty (AD 618–907) marks a high point in Chinese history. During this golden age, China enjoyed an extended period of peace and prosperity. The arts flourished and were enriched by foreign styles, motifs, and techniques such as silverworking. Foreign religions, such as Nestorian Christianity, were tolerated and co-existed alongside native Daoism and Confucianism. Woodblock printing was invented by the Chinese some time during the 7th century and hastened the spread of Buddhism.

Following the An Lushan rebellion of 755, the Tang became increasingly inward looking. The great Buddhist persecution of 841–46 was symptomatic of a dynasty in decline, which finally fell in 907.

THE LIAO DYNASTY (907–1125)

The Liao dynasty, which at its largest covered much of Mongolia, Manchuria, and northern China, was ruled by semi-nomadic and pastoral people, the Qidan. The Liao maintained a dual administration, Qidan and Chinese, and even a prime-ministership, to ensure the survival of their own customs and traditions whilst utilizing the efficiency of Tang structures of government. In 1115, the Qidan were overthrown by another semi-nomadic people, the Ruzhen (Jurchen).

Sancai glazed horse, Tang

With the support of the Northern Song, the Ruzhen took control of the north and founded the Jin dynasty. The Liao were forced westwards to the region of the Tian mountain range in present-day Xinjiang, where they established the Western Liao (1125–1211). The rest of northwest China was dominated by the Western Xia, a Tibetan related people who recognized the Liao as their overlords.

FIVE DYNASTIES AND TEN KINGDOMS (907–960)

While the north of China was dominated by the insurgence of semi-nomadic peoples from the steppe regions, the south was ruled by a series of short military dictatorships. The Song dynasty was founded in 960 by Zhao Kuangyin, a military commander of the later Zhou (951–960), whose imperial name became Shizong. In the Yangzi delta and regions to the south, the Ten Kingdoms existed in relative peace and stability and were reunited by the Song in 979.

Painting of an official celebrating, Five Dynasties (923–938)

TIMELINE

618–907 Tang heralds new golden age	**690–705** Empress Wu Zetian rules as first empress of China	**755–763** An Lushan rebellion drives emperor and court from Chang'an to Sichuan	**806** Earliest dated printed manuscript, the Diamond Sutra	**907–60** Period of division known as Five Dynasties and Ten Kingdoms	**10th c.** Gunpowder and fire arms first used	

700	**750**	**800**	**850**	**900**

661 Chinese administration in Kashmir, Bokhara, and the borders of eastern Iran	**705** Famous poet Li Bai born	**806–820** First bankers' bill	**907–1125** Qidan people rule northeastern China as the Liao dynasty, making Beijing their southern capital	
	Tang silver	**770** Death of great poet Du Fu		

THE SONG DYNASTY (960–1279)

The Song presided over a period of cultural brilliance and unprecedented growth in urban life during which the social makeup of China fundamentally changed. Less territorially ambitious than the Tang, the Song stimulated economic development through improved communications and transport. New industries based on mass production began to emerge, notably the porcelain industry based in Jiangxi province. During the Southern Song, China underwent an industrial revolution producing quantities of raw materials such as salt and iron on a scale that would not be seen in Europe until the 18th century.

In this buoyant economic climate a new middle-class emerged, stimulating demand for the new range of consumer goods. Power shifted from the aristocratic elite to government bureaucrats, who spent their spare time practising the arts of poetry, calligraphy, and painting. Collecting and connoisseurship led to an artistic renaissance and the founding of the first Imperial collections. Emperor Huizong was a great patron of the arts who used ancient precedents and values to buttress his own position.

Illustration of Song Emperor Huizong, r. 1101–1125

Neo-Confucianism and a renewed interest in Daoism marked a return to indigenous beliefs and traditional structures of power.

The Northern Song repeatedly came under attack from the Western Xia in the northwest and the Jin in the northeast. Only 12 years after joining forces with the Song against the Liao, the Jin invaded the Northern Song capital at Bianliang (Kaifeng), capturing emperor Qinzong and forcing the court to flee southwards. The capital of the Southern Song (1127–1279) was established at Lin'an (Hangzhou) south of the Yangzi.

Early movable type, Song

JIN DYNASTY (1115–1234)

The Jin were a semi-nomadic Tungusic people originating from Manchuria. War with the Song and persistent attacks from the Mongols resulted in a weakening of the Jin state which by the early 13th century formed a buffer state between the Song in the south and the Mongols in the north. In 1227, Mongol and Chinese allied forces defeated the Jin and in 1234 the Jin emperor committed suicide. The Jin state was integrated into the rapidly expanding Mongol empire.

	1127–1279 Southern		
960–1126 Northern Song reunites China and bases capital at Bianliang (Kaifeng)	*Detail of painting by Emperor Huizong*	Song dynasty with capital at Hangzhou, after being forced south by the Jin	**1154** First issue of paper money (Jin)	**1206–1208** Song and Jin at war

950	1000	1050	1100	1150	1200

990–1227 Western Xia people establish kingdom dominating northwest China	**1041–8** First attempts at printing with movable type	**1115–1234** Jin dynasty founded in northeast China forcing Liao westwards	**1214** Jin move capital from Beijing to Kaifeng in Henan province
	1090 First attested use of compass on Chinese ships		

MONGOL RULE (1279–1368)

The Mongol leader Genghis Khan united the various Mongol-speaking tribes of the steppes and in 1215 conquered northern China. He divided his empire into four kingdoms, each ruled by one of his sons. His grandson Kublai Khan (r. 1260–94), ruler of the eastern Great Khanate, finally defeated the Southern Song in 1279 and proclaimed himself emperor of the Yuan dynasty. China now became part of a vast empire which stretched from the East China Sea across Asia as far as Russia, the Ukraine, and Baghdad.

Buddhist deity, Yuan

Two capitals were maintained at Dadu or Khanbalik (present-day Beijing) and Yuanshangdu (Xanadu). The Silk Routes opened once more, connecting China to the Middle East and Medieval Europe. Direct contact was now made for the first time between the Mongol court and European diplomats, Franciscan missionaries, and merchants. According to the writings of Marco Polo, the Italian merchant spent 21 years in the service of Kublai and his court.

The Mongols ruled through a form of military government, in contrast to the bureaucratic civil service established by the Chinese. Although Chinese and Mongol languages were both used for official business, the Chinese were not encouraged to take up official posts. Muslims from Central and Western Asia took their place, and the Chinese increasingly retreated from official life.

As there were no clear rules for succession, civil war broke out in 1328 between Mongol nobles. The secret societies of the Red Turbans and the White Lotus led peasant rebellions and in 1368 General Zhu Yuanzhang forced the Mongols out of China, becoming the first emperor of the Ming dynasty.

MING DYNASTY (1368–1644)

The Ming (literally "brilliant") dynasty was one of the longest and most stable periods in China's history. The founder of the Ming, Zhu Yuanzhang, rose from humble beginnings to become a general, ruling as emperor Hongwu ("vast military accomplishment"). During his reign, Hongwu introduced radical changes to both central and local government, which he made binding on his successors. The emperor's role became more autocratic as Hongwu dispensed with the position of Prime Minister, taking direct responsibility for overseeing all six ministries himself.

Hongwu appointed his grandson to be his successor. Upon his death, his son the Prince of Yan, who controlled the region around Beijing, led an army

Genghis Khan (c.1162–1227), Persian miniature

TIMELINE

1215 Mongols capture Beijing	**1234** Jin emperor commits suicide and Jin integrated into Mongol empire		**1368–1644** Ming dynasty, founded by rebel leader General Zhu Yuanzhang	**1403** Construction of Great Walls in North China

Mongol on horseback

1250	**1300**	**1350**	**1400**

| **1227** Genghis Khan dies, having united various Mongol speaking tribes of the steppe | **1279–1368** Kublai Khan defeats Southern Song and rules China as emperor of the Yuan dynasty | **1328** Civil war breaks out between Mongol nobles | |

Jade elephant, Ming

The existing battlements of the Great Wall, reinforced and joined together during the Ming dynasty

against his nephew, taking Nanjing and proclaiming himself emperor Yongle ("Eternal Joy"). Yongle (r. 1403–24) moved the capital to his power base in Beijing, where he created a new city based on traditional principles of Chinese city planning. At its core lay the Forbidden City *(see pp62–7)*, the imperial palace and offices of government, surrounded by a grid system of streets, with four imperial altars at the cardinal points. The entire city was walled to provide both protection and enclosure. In 1421, Beijing became the official capital and, bar a short interlude during the Nationalist era in the early 20th century, would remain so until the present day.

By the 15th century, China had become a significant maritime power, its ships dwarfing those of contemporary Europe. Blue and white porcelain, silk, and other luxury items were in high demand in the foreign markets of Japan, Southeast Asia, and the Middle East. Yongle sent six maritime expeditions under the Muslim eunuch admiral Zheng He, which reached as far as the east coast of Africa. In 1514 Portuguese traders first landed in China, purchasing tea which then became a fashionable drink in European society. Porcelain provided ballast for the ships, and other luxury items were brought back along with the cargo. Trade was dominated by the Dutch in the 17th century, only to be surpassed by the British a hundred years later. Jesuit missionaries, who arrived in the 16th century, claimed few converts but gained access to the emperor and the inner court.

The arts thrived under emperor Xuande (r. 1426–35), an artist and poet, who patronized the arts, notably the porcelain industry at Jingdezhen. In literature, the late Ming is noted for its great dramas and classical novels, such as *Journey to the West (see p21)*. Philosophy of the time reinforced the Neo-Confucianism of the Song.

The late Ming was dominated by peasant uprisings, incursions by Japanese pirates and Mongolian tribes, and excessive eunuch power. Rebellions within China eventually joined with external forces to end Ming rule.

Wedding jewelry, Ming

Gilt bronze bowl, Ming

1426–35 Xuande emperor becomes first Ming emperor to patronize the arts extensively	**1514** Portuguese land in China, becoming the first Europeans to trade in tea and porcelain			**1573–1620** Wanli reign begins well but dynasty declines as emperor takes little interest in duties	**1620** Emperor Taichang poisoned by eunuchs

1450	**1500**	**1550**	**1600**

420 Construction of the Forbidden City in Beijing completed	**Early 16th century** Later Ming monarchs neglect duties of government and eunuch power increases	**1538** Jesuit Father Matteo Ricci enters southern China and begins missionary duties	**1570** Popular novel *Xi Yu Ji* (Journey to the West) published	**1600s** Dutch dominate European trade with China	**1601** Jesuit missionary Matteo Ricci allowed to enter Beijing

QING RULE (1644–1911)

The Manchu leader Nurhachi established the Later Jin in 1616, organizing the scattered tribes of the north into eight banner units. In 1636, the Manchu ruler Abahai changed the name to Qing, literally "pure," and prepared the way for the capture of Beijing in 1644. Under Manchu control, China was once more ruled by a foreign people. The Manchus were keen to adopt the Chinese method of rule, encouraging Chinese scholars into the service of the new empire. Dual administration at national and provincial levels meant Manchu and Chinese bureaucrats worked side by side using first Manchu and later Chinese as the official languages of government. However, despite the close interaction of Manchu and Chinese, the ruling Manchus were careful to maintain a distinct separation in order to protect their own privileges and cultural traditions.

Emperor Kangxi, r. 1661–1722

The first emperors of the Qing were enlightened rulers who presided over one of largest and most populous countries in the world. The territorial aspirations of Emperor Kangxi brought the regions of Central Asia and southern Siberia once more under Chinese control. Kangxi was succeeded by Emperor Yongzheng. It was his fourth son, Emperor Qianlong, "Lasting Eminence," (r. 1736–96) who heralded another golden age. An ambitious ruler, Qianlong was determined to extend China's borders beyond those of the Tang, personally leading campaigns to Burma, Vietnam, and Central Asia.

During the 18th century, contact with the west increased through Jesuit missionaries and trade. By the mid-18th century, the Chinese sought to control trade by refusing all official contact with Westerners and opening only Canton to foreign merchants. Pressure from European embassies increased as the British sent Lord Macartney in 1792–94 to establish diplomatic relations and open China to trade. China refused to grant a single concession to the British.

THE DECLINE OF THE EMPIRE

The 19th century is one of the most turbulent periods of Chinese history, as internal uprisings, natural disasters, and the relentless encroachment of the West culminated in the end of the empire. A succession of weak rulers were manipulated and controlled by

Lord Macartney's massive entourage arriving at Qianlong's tent

TIMELINE

	1644–1800 Military expansion into Central Asia and Siberia; colonization of new territories Yunnan and Xinjiang	1723–1735 Kangxi's son Yin Zhen seizes power ruling under name of emperor Yongzheng	*Emperor Shunzhi, r. 1644–61*	1747 Qianlong builds Yuanming Yuan *(see p84)* in western style
1650	**1675**	**1700**	**1725**	**1750**
1644–1911 Manchus establish Qing dynasty	**1650** First Catholic church in Beijing	**1661–1722** Rule of Kangxi emperor. Appoints Jesuits to run Board of Astronomy	**1736–1795** Qianlong, a great patron of the arts, rules over another golden age	**1757** Chinese restrict all foreign trade to Canton

A merchant testing tea quality in a Cantonese warehouse

the Dowager Empress Cixi, who ruled for much of the late Qing from "behind the curtain." The Taiping Rebellion of 1850–64 devastated south and central China.

Western powers, frustrated by the reluctance of the Chinese to open to foreign trade, brought the Chinese under increasing pressure. Keen to protect the trade of opium from their colonies in India, the British engaged in the First Opium War (1840–42), which culminated in the Treaty of Nanjing, resulting in the opening of four new ports to trade, the payment of huge indemnities, and the ceding of Hong Kong to Britain. Following the Arrow War (Second Opium War) with Britain and France (1856), the European forces divided China into "spheres of influence" – the British strongest along the Yangzi and in Shanghai, the Germans controlling Shandong province, and the French controlling the borders with Vietnam.

In 1900 the Boxers allied with imperial troops and attacked the foreign legations in Beijing. An eight-nation army defeated the onslaught, and Cixi fled to Xi'an, blaming everything on the emperor. The Chinese government paid once more for the loss of life and Cixi returned to Beijing until her death in 1908. The child emperor Pu Yi lived in the Forbidden City as the last emperor until his abdication. On 1 January 1912 the Republican leader Sun Yat Sen inaugurated the Chinese Republic.

FROM EMPIRE TO REPUBLIC

In the final years of the empire, many Chinese intellectuals recognized the need to modernize. Supporters of the Reform Movement of 1898 propounded the adoption of western technology and education, and, following the Boxer Rebellion, a number of reforms were adopted. Elected regional assemblies were set up, further undermining the power of the Qing. In 1911 the empire collapsed completely. Sun Yat Sen was elected provisional President of China, but was soon forced to resign in favor of general Yuan Shikai, who sought to become emperor. Yuan was forced to back down when governors revolted and he died soon after in 1916. China then came under the control of a series of regional warlords until it was united once more with the founding of the People's Republic of China in 1949.

Sun Yat Sen, 1866–1925

The Cultural Revolution

In 1965, Mao Zedong set in motion a chain of events that were to unleash the turmoil now known as the Cultural Revolution. Having socialized industry and agriculture, Mao called on the masses to transform society itself – all distinctions between manual and intellectual work were to be abolished and class distinction disappear. The revolution reached its violent peak in 1967, with the Red Guards spreading social unrest. The People's Liberation Army (PLA) finally restored order, but the subsequent years were characterized by fear, violence, and mistrust.

Actor in opera

Children were encouraged *to take part in the Revolution. Their enthusiasm led to the destruction of family photographs and posses- sions. In some cases, children denounced their own parents.*

THE RED GUARD

Mao appealed to students to form the Red Guard, in whom he entrusted the fate of the revolution. The movement rapidly gathered momentum and the Red Guard, who raised Mao to godly status, traveled China spreading Mao Zedong "Thoughts," smashing remnants of the past, vandalizing temples, and wreaking havoc.

Mass public meetings *were held as part of the Socialist Education Movement, a precursor of the Cultural Revolution intended to reverse "capitalist" and "revisionist" tendencies perceived in social and economic life. Everyone was required to attend.*

An injured cadre *is carried away after being denounced. Shamings became the bench mark of public meetings. Many politicians and teachers were paraded and accused, leading to job loss and, in some cases, suicide.*

The *Little Red Book* was essential to the Red Guard and issued to every soldier under Lin Biao's command.

Demonstrating their opposition *to Soviet-style communism and their support for Maoism, Red Guards change a Beijing street sign in front of the Soviet Embassy from East Yangwei to Fanxiu Lu (Anti-revisionism Road).*

Model operas *were the pet project of Mao's third wife, Jiang Qing. She set about creating a politically correct revolutionary culture. Many artists and intellectuals were sent to the countryside for re-education.*

Lin Biao spread the study *of the "Thoughts of Mao" and compiled the* Little Red Book *which became obligatory reading for his army recruits. As head of the PLA, Lin Biao provided essential military backing and was Mao's named successor. He died in a plane crash over Siberia in 1971 amid rumors of an imminent usurpation.*

May 7 Cadre Schools *were set up by the central government in 1968. 100,000 officials plus 30,000 family members were sent to perform manual labor and undergo ideological re-education. An unknown number of lower-ranking cadres were sent to thousands of other cadre schools.*

Liu Shaoqi *(right), president from 1959–66, was one of a number of high officials to be denounced, imprisoned, and paraded in "struggle rallies." He died from his experiences.*

GANG OF FOUR

The Gang of Four, as they became known, orchestrated attacks on intellectuals and writers, high officials, the party, and the state and were responsible for some of the worst excesses of the Cultural Revolution. Zhang Chunqiao, critic and propagandist, Yao Wenyuan, editor-in-chief of *Shanghai Liberation Army Daily*, Wang Hongwen, a young worker, and Mao's third wife Jiang Qing, an ex-film star, dominated the political center unchallenged until Mao's death in 1976. Millions of Chinese citizens watched their televized trial in 1980–81. Jiang Qing, who was singled out by propagandists and became one of the most hated figures in China, was defiant until the end, railing against her prosecutors throughout the trial. She took her own life in 1991, while serving her life sentence.

Lynched effigies of members of the Gang of Four hanging from a tree

Chiang Kai Shek (1887–1975), leader of the KMT

COMMUNISTS AND NATIONALISTS

After the fall of the empire, the political landscape changed dramatically and became dominated by two forces, the Nationalist Party or Kuomintang (KMT) and the Communist Party, founded in 1921. The Nationalists were led first by Sun Yat Sen from his power base in Guangzhou, then by General Chiang Kai Shek who seized power in 1926. In 1923 the two Parties formed a "united front" against the warlords, but in 1926 the Communists were expelled from the KMT. Chiang Kai Shek led his army to Nanjing where he tried to establish a Nationalist capital, and betrayed the Communist-led workers of Shanghai who were massacred by underworld gangsters. The Communists were driven underground and Mao Zedong retreated to the countryside.

High in the mountains of Jiangxi province, Mao and Zhu De founded the Jiangxi Soviet in 1930. From this inaccessible base, the communists began to redistribute land to the peasants and institute new marriage laws. In 1934, Chiang Kai Shek drove the communists from the area, forcing Mao to embark on the legendary Long

March. Yan'an, where the march ended, became the new Communist Party headquarters and would remain so until 1945.

JAPANESE ATTACK

Domestic turmoil laid China open to attack, and in 1931 the Japanese occupied Manchuria, founding the puppet state of Manchukuo and placing the last Qing emperor, Pu Yi, at its head. By 1937 the Japanese had occupied much of northern China, Shanghai, and the Yangzi valley ruthlessly taking cities, wreaking death and devastation. The Japanese were finally driven from Chinese soil in 1945, and China was plunged into civil war.

THE EAST IS RED

By 1947, the Communist policy of land reform was reaping rewards and gaining the support of people in the countryside. In 1948–9, the Communists gained decisive victories over the KMT. On 1 October 1949 Chairman Mao pronounced the founding of the People's Republic of China. Chiang Kai Shek fled to Taiwan, establishing a Nationalist government and taking with him many Imperial treasures.

Communist poster depicting Mao surrounded by the masses

TIMELINE

1912 Abdication of emperor Pu Yi marks the end of Imperial China	**1921** Founding of the Chinese Communist Party	**1945** End of World War II; Japan defeated	**1958** Radical reform of the Great Leap Forward	**1965** Mao launches Cultural Revolution
		1937 Japanese take much of northern China	**1947** Civil War breaks out in China	
1910	**1920**	**1930**	**1940**	**1950**	**1960**
	1926 Chiang Kai Shek seizes leadership of National Party	**1934** Mao leads the Red Army on Long March	**1951–2** Rural co-ops established	
Last Emperor Pu Yi	**1931** Japanese invasion of Manchuria	**1949** Mao proclaims founding of People's Republic of China	

In the early years of the People's Republic, the Chinese worked hard to rebuild a country devastated by 100 years of turmoil. New laws sought to redress inequities of the past, redistributing land and outlawing arranged marriages.

Zhou Enlai with President Nixon

The Party promptly branded intellectuals as "rightists" and sent them to the countryside for re-education. Frustrated with the slow rate of change, Mao launched the Great Leap Forward in 1958. Large communes providing food and childcare replaced the family, releasing manual labor and improving productivity. But unrealistic productivity targets and the falsification of statistics concealed the disastrous effect of Mao's experiment. Agricultural failure coupled with natural disasters resulted in the starvation of millions

Having reformed agriculture and industry, Mao sought to transform society and launched the Cultural Revolution in 1965 *(see pp50–51)*. The greatest excesses of the period were over by 1971, but the country was tightly controlled and directed until Mao's death in 1976. Deng Xiaoping emerged as leader, implementing economic reforms which returned land to the peasants and encouraged greater economic freedom.

The economic liberalization of the 1980s stimulated the economy but was unmatched by political freedom. On 4 June 1989 the democracy movement called for political reform and an end to corruption, but was brutally suppressed in Tian'an Men Square. Whilst many students and intellectuals fled abroad, others remain incarcerated in China's jails. Deng Xiaoping pressed on with economic reform, and the 1990s saw the opening of Special Economic Zones and stock exchanges in most major cities.

By 1992, China's economy had become one of the largest in the world.

The unprecedented rate of economic growth in the 1990s was matched by the transformation of the landscape as traditional buildings made way for modern highrises. The former colonies of Hong Kong and Macau were returned to China and foreign investment flooded in. Entrepreneurs prospered, and the Communist Party has been keen to attract this new class into its ranks. Disbanding the state economy has also spawned inequity, and the gap between rich and poor grows increasingly wider. How the most populous nation on earth resolves the many issues it

Chinese traders on the Stock Exchange

faces is of compelling interest to the rest of a world on whose future a reawakened China is going to have a massive impact. The 2008 Olympics, to be held in Beijing, may provide a glimpse of the shape that future takes.

Little Red Book			
1976 Mao dies	**1993** Jiang Zemin becomes president; construction of Three Gorges Dam begins	**2003** Chinese launch first manned spacecraft; Hu Jintao becomes president	
1978 Deng Xiaoping emerges as leader		**2008** Beijing hosts the 2008 Olympic Games	
1970	**1980**	**1990**	**2000**	**2010**	**2020**
1972 President Nixon is first American president to visit China	**1989** Democracy movement suppressed in Tian'an Men Square	**1997** Hong Kong handed back to China; Macau, two years later	**2001** China admitted as member of World Trade Organization	**2010** Shanghai hosts the 2010 World Expo	

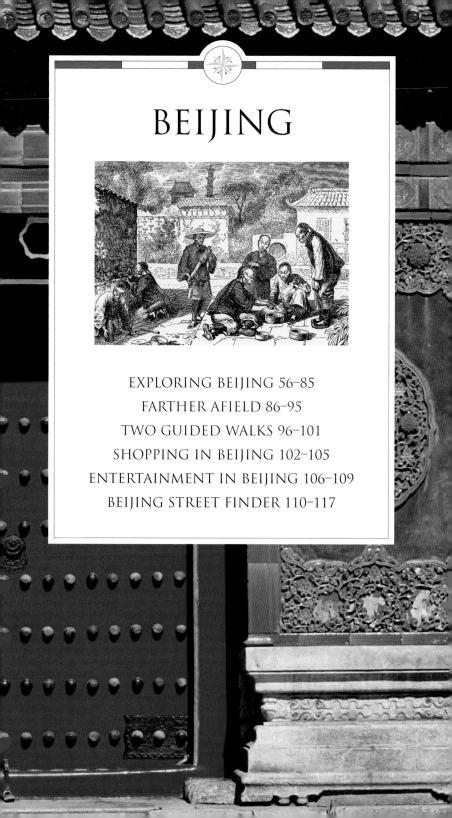

BEIJING

Exploring Beijing

Beijing's most significant sights and districts are marked on this map. At the core is the Forbidden City, with Tian'an Men Square and Qian Men to the south, and the shopping district of Wangfujing to its east. North of the Forbidden City stand the Drum and Bell Towers, and farther northeast is the Buddhist Lama Temple. North of Bei Hai Park, the Mansion of Prince Gong stands in an historic district of *hutongs*, the old alleyways that riddle the city. To the south, Tian Tan, known as the Temple of Heaven, is a majestic example of Ming dynasty design. Beijing's suburbs are also dotted with sites including the magnificent Summer Palace complex.

LOCATOR MAP

KEY

▪	Street-by-Street area: see pp58–9
✈	International airport
▣	Train station
▣	Long-distance bus station
Ⓜ	Subway station
▦	City bus station
▦	Temple
✝	Church
═	National highway
▬	Major road

SIGHTS AT A GLANCE

Historic Buildings, Sites, and Neighborhoods

Ancient Observatory **18**
Dazhalan & Liulichang **4**
Drum & Bell Towers **11**
Forbidden City pp62–7 **6**
Legation Quarter **7**
Mansion of Prince Gong **10**
National Olympic Stadium **33**
Qian Men **2**
Summer Palace pp80–83 **29**
Tian'an Men Square pp58–9 **1**
Underground City **3**
Yuanming Yuan **30**

Shops and Markets

Wangfujing Street **17**

Museums and Galleries

798 Art District **34**
Beijing Natural History Museum **20**
China Railway Museum **35**
Chinese Military History Museum **26**
National Art Museum of China **16**

Temples, Churches, and Mosques

Confucius Temple **13**
Cow Street Mosque **23**
Dong Yue Miao **15**
Fayuan Temple **24**
Great Bell Temple **31**
Lama Temple **12**
Miaoying Temple White Dagoba **27**
South Cathedral **5**
Temple of Heaven pp74–7 **21**
White Clouds Temple **25**
Xiannong Tan **22**

Southeast Corner Watchtower **19**

Parks and Zoos

Bei Hai Park **9**
Beijing Zoo **28**
Di Tan Park **14**
Jing Shan Park **8**
Xiang Shan Park **32**

SEE ALSO

- *Street Finder* pp110–17
- *Where to Stay* pp178–82
- *Where to Eat* pp198–202

GETTING AROUND

A system of ring roads encircles the city center, and the best way to explore this area is by taxi, by subway, or by bicycle (*see pp226–7*). The bus service, though extensive, is generally slow and overcrowded. Organized tours are another option for a quick overview of the sights. Most hotels and agencies operate tour buses for visiting sights outside Beijing, although hiring a taxi for the day allows for greater flexibility.

Street-by-Street: Tian'an Men Square ❶
天安门广场

Chairman Mao

Tian'an Men Guangchang – the Square of the Gate of Heavenly Peace – is a vast open concrete expanse at the heart of modern Beijing. With Mao's Mausoleum at its focal point, and bordered by 1950s Communist-style buildings and ancient gates from Beijing's now leveled city walls, the square is usually filled with visitors strolling about as kites flit overhead. The square has also traditionally served as a stage for popular demonstrations and is most indelibly associated with the student protests of 1989 and their gory climax.

Cyclists along Chang'an Jie

Great Hall of the People
Seat of the Chinese legislature, the vast auditorium and banqueting halls are open for part of the day except when the National People's Congress is in session.

★ Zhengyang Men
Along with the Arrow Tower this tower formed a double gate known as the Qian Men. It now houses a museum on the history of Beijing.

The Arrow Tower or Jian Lou, like Zhengyang Men, was first built in the Ming dynasty.

★ Mao's Mausoleum
Flanked by revolutionary statues, the building contains the embalmed body of Chairman Mao. His casket, raised from its refrigerated chamber, is on view mornings and afternoons.

★ **Tian'an Men**
Mao proclaimed the founding of the People's Republic of China on October 1, 1949 from this Ming dynasty gate, where his huge portrait still remains.

LOCATOR MAP
See p114 Street Finder Map 4 C1

| 0 meters | 20 |
| 0 yards | 20 |

The national flag is raised at dawn and lowered at dusk every day.

China National Museum
Built in 1959, this building was originally home to the Museum of Chinese History and the Museum of the Revolution, now merged. The same exhibits are on display (and the same propagandist lens). The halls also host exhibitions from other world class museums.

Bags, coats, and cameras must be left here before visiting Mao's Mausoleum.

Monument to the People's Heroes
Erected in 1958, the granite monument is decorated with bas-reliefs of episodes from China's revolutionary history and calligraphy from Communist veterans Mao Zedong and Zhou Enlai.

STAR SIGHTS

★ Mao's Mausoleum

★ Zhengyang Men

★ Tian'an Men

Zhengyang Men, Qian Men – part of Beijing's central fortifications

Qian Men **2**
前门

Qian Men Dajie. **Map** 4 C2. **M** *Qian Men.* ◯ *8:30am–3:30pm daily.*

Qian Men or the Front Gate consists of two towers, the **Zhengyang Men**, on the southern edge of Tian'an Men Square, and the **Jian Lou Arrow Tower** just to the south. Zhengyang Men (Facing the Sun Gate) was the most imposing of the nine gates of the inner city that divided Beijing's imperial quarters in the Forbidden City from the "Chinese City," where, during the Manchu Qing dynasty, the Chinese inhabitants lived.

Rising 131 ft (40 m), the gate stands on the north-south axis that runs through the Tian'an Men and the Forbidden City. Its museum has dioramas of the old city walls, and photographs of Beijing's old streets.

The 125-ft (38-m) high Jian Lou (Arrow Tower), originally built in 1439, has 94 windows that were used for shooting arrows. Both the Jian Lou and Zhengyang Men were badly damaged by fire during the Boxer Rebellion. In 1916, the enceinte, a semi-circular wall that connected the two towers, was demolished to make way for a road. Jian Lou is now closed to the public. Across the road to the east, the Old Railway Station was built by the British and now houses a number of shops. The surrounding area comprises the city's old shopping district, with alleys filled with specialty stores. Numerous silk and cloth shops, food stalls and cinemas make it a lively area worth exploring.

⛩ Zhengyang Men
Tel (010) 6522 9386. ◯ *daily.*

Underground City **3**
北京地下城

62 Xi Damo Hutong. **Map** 5 D2.
M *Qian Men.* **Tel** (010) 6702 2657.
◯ *8:30am–6pm daily.*

At the height of the Sino-Soviet rift in the 1960s, Mao Zedong gave orders to carve out a vast network of bombproof tunnels beneath Beijing. Work on this subterranean hideaway was done by hand, and the resulting maze of tunnels was equipped with weapons, hospitals, and large stocks of water and food. Most of the labyrinth's entry points are hard to find, but the one most easily accessible is on Xi Damo Hutong, an alley southeast of Qian Men. Guides show visitors around a circuit of dank tunnels,

战备医院
War Hospital
War Hospital sign, Underground City

where signs illustrate the earlier functions of rooms, and point the way to surface landmarks. Unlit passageways branch off from the main circuit, but many are either damaged or blocked, and it is dangerous to wander off alone. Old ventilation shafts and flood-proof doors can be seen. Rumor has it that a tunnel once connected the Zhongnanhai, the Communist Party Headquarters, to the Western Hills, 12 miles (20 km) west of the city, for the evacuation of China's leaders in the event of an emergency.

BEIJING'S CITY WALLS

The earliest defensive walls around Beijing (then called Yanjing, later Zhongdu) were erected in the Jin dynasty (1115–1234) and modeled on the wall around Kaifeng. The Mongol Kublai Khan rebuilt Zhongdu, naming it Dadu, and encompassed it with a 19-mile (30-km) wall. It was only during the Ming era (1368–1644) that the walls took on their final shape of an Outer Wall with seven gates, and an Inner Wall with nine gates. The magnificent Inner Wall was 38 ft (11.5 m) high and 64 ft (19.5 m) wide. The walls and most of their gates were unfortunately demolished in the 1950s and 60s to make way for roads. Of the inner wall, only Qian Men and Desheng Men survive, while the outer wall retains only Dongbian Men (*see p73*). The old gates live on as place names on the second ring road, and as the names of stations on the Beijing Underground Loop line.

Arrow Tower of Qian Men

Shop selling Communist memorabilia, Dazhalan Jie

Dazhalan &
Liulichang ❹
大栅栏和琉璃厂

Map 4 C2. Ⓜ *Qian Men.*

South of Qian Men are the narrow and lively *hutongs* *(see p69)* of the old Chinese quarter. The inner city wall and its gates separated the "Inner City" containing the imperial quarters of the Manchu emperors from the "Chinese City," where the Chinese lived apart from their Qing overlords. Today, the district buzzes with shops, cinemas, and restaurants. Running west off the northern end of Qian Men Dajie is Dazhalan Jie, whose name "Big Barrier Street" refers to

the now-demolished gates that were closed every night to fence off the residents from Qian Men and the Inner City. The area was damaged during the Boxer Rebellion and later restored. There are *hutong* tours by rickshaw – drivers just wait in the street in Dazhalan.

The area is a great place for browsing, and has several quaint Qing-era specialty shops. Located down the first alley on the left from Dazhalan Jie is the century-old pickle shop **Liubiju**, selling a vast

array of pungent pickles. **Ruifuxiang**, on the right-hand side of Dazhalan, dates from 1893 and is renowned for its silks and traditional Chinese garments. On the south side of Dazhalan Jie is the Chinese medicine shop **Tongrentang Pharmacy**, which has been in business since 1669 and enjoyed imperial patronage. On the same side of the road, the **Zhangyiyuan Chazhuang** or Zhangyiyuan Teashop has been supplying fine teas since the early 20th century. To the west of Dazhalan Jie, Liulichang Jie, with its restored buildings and many stores, is a fascinating place to wander around. It has everything from ceramics, bric-à-brac, paintings, lacquerware, and antique Chinese books to Cultural Revolution-era

Cyclists on restored Liulichang Jie

memorabilia. However, beware of so-called "antiques" which should be judiciously examined before buying.

South Cathedral ❺
南堂

141 Qian Men Xi Dajie. **Map** 4 A2. Ⓜ *Xuanwu Men.*

The first Catholic church to be built in Beijing, South Cathedral (Nan Tang) stands close to the Xuanwu Men

underground station, on the site of Jesuit Matteo Ricci's former residence. Ricci was the first Jesuit missionary to reach Beijing. Arriving in 1601, he sent gifts of European curiosities such as clocks, mathematical instruments, and a world map to the Wanli emperor, thus gaining his goodwill, and was eventually given permission to establish a church.

Like many of China's churches, this restored building has suffered much devastation. Construction first began in 1605, and it subsequently burned down in 1775. It was rebuilt a century later, only to be destroyed once again during the Boxer Rebellion of 1900. The cathedral was rebuilt in 1904. Also known as St. Mary's Church, it is the city's largest functioning Catholic cathedral, and has regular services in a variety of languages including Chinese, English, and Latin. Service timings are posted on the noticeboard. A small gift shop is located near the south gate.

Stained glass at the South Cathedral (Nan Tang)

Forbidden City ❻
故宫

Decorative wall relief

Forming the very heart of Beijing, the Forbidden City, officially known as the Palace Museum (Gugong), is China's most magnificent architectural complex and was completed in 1420. The huge palace is a compendium of imperial architecture and a lasting monument of dynastic China from which 24 emperors ruled for nearly 500 years. The symbolic center of the Chinese universe, the palace was the exclusive domain of the imperial court and dignitaries until the abdication in 1912. It was opened to the public in 1949.

Chinese Lions
Pairs of lions guard the entrances of halls. The male is portrayed with a ball under his paw, while the female has a lion cub.

Storehouses

Offices of the imperial secretariat

★ Golden Water
Five marble bridges, symbolizing the five cardinal virtues of Confucianism, cross the Golden Water, which flows from west to east in a course designed to resemble the jade belt worn by officials.

OUTER COURT
At the center of the Forbidden City, the Outer Court is easily its most impressive part. Most of the other buildings in the complex were there to service this city within a city.

Meridian Gate (Wu Men)
From the balcony the emperor would review his armies and perform ceremonies marking the start of a new calendar.

Gate of Supreme Harmony
Originally used for receiving visitors, the 78-ft (24-m) high, double-eaved hall was later used for banquets during the Qing dynasty (1644–1912).

★ Marble Carriageway
The central ramp carved with dragons chasing pearls among clouds was reserved for the emperor.

Hall of Preserving Harmony

Bronze cauldrons were filled with water in case of fire.

Gate of Heavenly Purity

The Hall of Middle Harmony received the emperor before official ceremonies.

Imperial sundial

VISITORS' CHECKLIST

North of Tian'an Men Square.
Map 2 A4/5. *Tel* (010) 6513
2255. ☐ Apr–Oct: 8:30am–5pm
daily; Nov–Mar: 8:30am–4:30pm
daily. 🖼 🚻 🛒 📷 🏪
www.dpm.org.cn

★ Hall of Supreme Harmony
The largest hall in the palace, this was used for major occasions such as the enthronement of an emperor. Inside the hall, the ornate throne sits beneath a fabulously colored ceiling.

Roof Guardians
An odd number of these figures, all associated with water, are supposed to protect the building from fire.

STAR FEATURES

- ★ Golden Water
- ★ Marble Carriageway
- ★ Hall of Supreme Harmony

DESIGN BY NUMBERS

The harmonious principle of *yin* and *yang* is the key to Chinese design. As odd numbers represent *yang* (the preferred masculine element associated with the emperor), the numbers three, five, seven, and the ultimate odd number – nine, recur in architectural details. It is said that the Forbidden City has 9,999 rooms and, as nine times nine is especially fortunate, the doors for imperial use usually contain 81 brass studs.

Palace door with a lucky number of studs

Exploring the Forbidden City

Magnificent though the Outer Court is, there is still a great deal more to see. A short distance north through the Gate of Heavenly Purity lies the Inner Court with three impressive palaces and the private living quarters of the emperor. Farther on, beyond the Imperial Flower Garden stands the northern Gate of Divine Prowess and exit into Jing Shan Park *(see p68)*. Those wanting to avoid the long queues for tickets at the Meridian Gate can find a more peaceful entrance here, and simply tour the palace in reverse.

officials, and after 1900, even foreign ones, who previously had not been allowed inside the palace. The last emperor's wedding ceremony was also held here. Beyond lies the **Hall of Union**, used as a throne room by the empress, and to house the jade seals of imperial authority. Then comes the **Palace of Earthly Tranquility**, living quarters of the Ming empresses.

The Pavilion of a Thousand Autumns in the Imperial Gardens

🏯 Inner Court

Beyond the Hall of Preserving Harmony *(see pp62–3)* lies a narrow courtyard with gates leading to the open areas east and west of the Outer Court and a main gate, the **Gate of Heavenly Purity**, leading to the Inner Court. Tradition has this gate to be the only building in the whole palace not to have been burned down at least once, and thus the oldest hall of all. The walls to either side that form a boundary between the Outer and Inner Courts only date from the early days of the republic, when the last emperor, Pu Yi *(see p65)* was confined to the rear of the palace until ejected by the Christian warlord Feng Yuxiang in 1924.

To either side of the gate are groups of smaller halls, built on a more human scale, separated by narrow alleys; this area was once the residence of concubines and imperial offspring.

Straight ahead, back on the main axis, stand three splendid palaces, mirroring those of the Outer Court

but on a smaller scale. The double-eaved **Palace of Heavenly Purity** was used as the imperial sleeping quarters. It was here that the last Ming emperor, Chongzhen, wrote his final missive in blood, before getting drunk, killing his 15-year-old daughter and his concubines, and then hanging himself on Jing Shan *(see p68)*, just north of the palace, as peasant rebels swarmed through the capital. In the late Qing era it was used for the reception of

🏯 Imperial Gardens

The **Imperial Flower Garden**, north of the three inner palaces and the Gate of Earthly Tranquility, dates from the reign of the Ming Yongle emperor. It is symmetrically laid out with pavilions, temples, and halls, as well as a rock garden. On the west and east sides of the garden are the charming **Pavilion of a Thousand Autumns** and **Pavilion of Ten Thousand Springs**, each topped with a circular roof. One of these was the site of the school-room used by Sir Reginald Johnston, tutor to the last emperor. Johnston, Pu Yi, and the empress would sometimes have picnics in the gardens.

Positioned centrally in the north of the garden, the **Hall of Imperial Peace** formerly served as a temple, while on top of the lofty rockery in the northeast of the garden the **Imperial View Pavilion** boasts views over the gardens and beyond. During the Qing dynasty, sacrifices were performed in the gardens on Qi Xi, the seventh day of the seventh lunar month, and

The intricately carved and painted ceiling in the Hall of Union

THE FORBIDDEN CITY

① Gate of Heavenly Purity
② Palace of Heavenly Purity
③ Hall of Union
④ Palace of Earthly Tranquility
⑤ Imperial Flower Garden
⑥ Hall of Imperial Peace
⑦ Hall of Mental Cultivation
⑧ Hall of Martial Valor
⑨ Hall for Worshiping Ancestors
⑩ Palace of Abstinence
⑪ Nine Dragon Screen
⑫ Hall of Imperial Zenith
⑬ Palace of Peaceful Longevity
⑭ Flower Garden of the Palace of Peaceful Longevity
⑮ Arrow Tower
⑯ Gate of Divine Prowess

| 0 meters | 300 |
| 0 yards | 300 |

KEY

☐ Area illustrated *(see pp62–3)*

the Chinese equivalent of Valentine's Day *(see p36)*. The sacrifices were made by the emperor and empress, and directed to a pair of stars that represent lovers.

🏵 Western Palaces

Much of the western flank of the Forbidden City remains closed to visitors, but the halls west of the three inner palaces are accessible. South of these, a network of high-walled alleys links a labyrinth of smaller halls that were the residences of imperial concubines. Particularly fine is the **Palace of Eternal Spring**, where *trompe-l'oeil* paintings at the ends of the passageways make them appear to extend to infinity.

The southernmost accessible hall, the **Hall of Mental Cultivation**, was used by the Yongzheng emperor *(see p93)* for his residence, rather than the Hall of Heavenly Purity, where his father, the Kangxi emperor, had lived for 60 years. The East Warm Chamber of the Hall of Mental Cultivation was the site of the formal abdication of Pu Yi, the last emperor. The document was signed by his father, who was regent.

There are also further exhibitions in some of the buildings lining the western side of the Outer Court; these include occasionally changing displays of court insignia, and ancient weapons and musical instruments. Before returning to the main Meridian Gate it is possible to venture farther west to the newly-opened **Hall of Martial Valor** (still

shown as off-limits on palace maps). The hall was the home of the palace's printing workshop and censors. It now contains a model illustrating the layout of the key central halls in miniature. Other exhibits make much of the Manchu emperors' acceptance of Chinese culture, using the Confucian classics to guide their governance.

THE LAST EMPEROR

Aisin Gioro Pu Yi, ascended the Qing throne at the age of three in 1908 after the death of his uncle, the Guangxu emperor. His brief reign as the Xuantong emperor was brought to an end on February 12, 1912, when he abdicated the throne in the Forbidden City to make way for the new Republican government. The powerless Pu Yi continued

to live in the palace until 1924, before being ejected by a warlord and escaping to the Legation Quarter. He was later installed as the Japanese puppet emperor of Manchukuo, residing in his palace in Changchun. At the end of World War II, he was arrested and handed over to the Chinese Communists, who imprisoned him in 1950. In 1959, Mao granted him amnesty. Pu Yi never returned to the Forbidden City, and he died of cancer, childless, and anonymous in 1967, after working for seven years as a gardener at the Beijing Botanical Gardens.

Pu Yi (1905–67), China's "Last Emperor"

✦ Eastern Palaces

On the east side of the Inner Court lies a much closer knit series of smaller palaces and courtyards, formerly used as the residences of imperial concubines. Nowadays, some of these areas serve as museums of jade, paintings, enamels, and other antique collectibles. Among them is the impressive **Clock and Watch Exhibition**, housed in the recently refurbished **Hall for Worshiping Ancestors**, which once held memorial tablets to Qing ancestors. You can walk among the vast pillars, which have recently been replaced, the water-damaged coffer ceiling high above revealing why this was necessary. The sizeable and fascinating display of clocks includes elaborate Chinese, British, and French timepieces collected by Qing emperors, from a clumsy giant multi-bucket clepsydra to fragile bejeweled replicas of balloons and steamships, and delicate automata. One piece is topped by a robotic figure that dips his brush in ink and writes eight Chinese characters, as can be seen on an accompanying video. A limited number of the clocks are gently wound and set off at 11am and 2pm daily.

Decorative gate in the Eastern Palaces quarter

On the east side of the Inner Court is the **Palace of Abstinence**, where the emperor would fast before sacrificial ceremonies. Next to it is the **Palace of Prolonging Happiness**, a bizarre and incomplete structure of rusting steel and carved stone, designed to be surrounded by water, begun only two years before the fall of the Qing dynasty. Wings to either side of the palace, which were once the home of some of the museum's research departments, now house regularly changing exhibitions usually involving calligraphy, painting, and ceramics.

A little further southeast of the exhibition halls stands a beautiful **Nine Dragon Screen**, a 100-ft (31-m) long spirit wall made from richly glazed tiles and similar to the screen in Bei Hai Park (*see p68*). Chinese ghosts only travel in straight lines, and this screen blocked the straight route north through the Gate of Imperial Zenith and the Gate of Peaceful Longevity. Displays of jewelry and other treasures begin in a long passage up the west side of the courtyard, and continue in the **Hall of Imperial Zenith**, the **Palace of Peaceful Longevity**, and farther halls to the north. These halls are where the venerable Qianlong emperor (reigned 1736–95) lived out his retirement.

The infamous Empress Dowager Cixi (*p81*) also retired to these same northern halls a century later during the brief period she allowed the Guangxu emperor to take the throne. Their interiors are in striking contrast to other halls, displaying a taste for dark paneling inset with mother-of-pearl, which is also to be seen at Cixi's complex at the Eastern Qing Tombs (*p93*). Treasures on display here include scroll paintings and calligraphy, as well as everything from magnificent imperial headdresses with golden dragons disporting themselves among clouds of azure enamel, to vast boulders of jade carved into mountain scenes.

Imperial five-clawed dragons on a glazed Nine Dragon Screen

CHINESE DRAGONS

The Chinese dragon is a curious hybrid of sometimes many animal parts – snake's body, deer horns, bull's ears, hawk's claws and fish scales. Endowed with magical characteristics, it can fly, swim, change into other animals, bring rainfall and ward off evil spirits. The five-clawed dragon represented the power of the emperor, and therefore could only adorn his imperial buildings. The Chinese dragon is a beneficent beast offering protection and good luck, hence its depiction on screens and marble carriageways, and its significance, even today, in festivals such as Chinese New Year.

🀫 Pleasure Gardens

Both Qianlong and Cixi kept their keenest pleasures to hand. The retired emperor's was the secluded **Flower Garden of the Palace of Peaceful Longevity** (also known as the Qianlong Garden), which is graced with rockeries, a small theater stage, and, most strikingly, the **Pavilion for Bestowing Wine**. This is where Qianlong and companions would play intellectual drinking games, floating cups of wine along a writhing 88-ft (27-m) long channel in the stone floor, and composing poems.

Cixi's passion was opera, and just to the east of the garden is the three-story **Pavilion of Pleasant Sounds**, a gaudy stage and fly-tower, fully equipped with hoists and trap-doors, its ceiling painted with fluffy clouds. In celebration of her 60th birthday the empress watched some ten consecutive days of performances here. The building opposite, which is where she would sit, contains costumes and scripts used by the imperial troupes.

The less gentle side of Cixi is remembered just to the north at the **Well of the Pearl Concubine**. In 1900, as foreign armies approached to lift the siege of the Legation Quarter (*see p49*), Cixi prepared to flee for Xi'an, intending that the Guangxu emperor should accompany her. His favorite

concubine dared to protest, and was thrown down the well for her temerity.

🀫 Palace Walls and Gates

The fortified wall around the Forbidden City was originally enclosed within a moat. Another wall ran around the grounds of the Imperial City, including what are now Bei Hai Park and Zhong Nan Hai government compound, the "new Forbidden City." The palace's walls are marked at each of its four corners by elaborate **Arrow Towers**, notable for their many eaves. Of the four palace gates, the horseshoe-shaped **Meridian Gate** or **Wu Men** (*see p62*), which is the southern entrance to the Forbidden City, can be climbed to visit the temporary exhibitions displayed in the central pavilion. This was the home of some of the first displays of palace treasures during the Nationalist era. It also affords views down into the bustle surrounding the ticket offices, and along the walls.

The northern gate of the palace is called the **Gate of Divine Prowess** or **Shenwu Men**, and originally served as a combined bell and drum tower. It now hosts an exhibition of old photographs and drawings related to the architecture and construction of the palaces and other buildings. Unfortunately the labeling of all items is in Chinese only.

Glazed tile panel from palace gate

The former City Bank of New York, now Beijing Police Museum

Legation Quarter ❼
东交民巷

Map 5 D1. Ⓜ *Qian Men*. **Beijing Police Museum** *Tel* (010) 8522 5018. ◯ 9am–4pm Tue–Sun.

When the Conventions of Peking ended the Second Opium War in 1860, foreign delegations were permitted to take up residence in a quarter southeast of the Forbidden City. Here, the first modern foreign buildings in Beijing took root.

On the southeast corner of Tian'an Men Square, the distinctive stripey brick building was the first railway station built within the walls of Beijing, constructed by the British in 1901. It is now a shopping mall and theater for Beijing Opera. East of the station, along Dong Jiao Min Xiang, is the former City Bank of New York, now the **Beijing Police Museum**. Displays on the suppression of counter-revolutionaries and drug dealers share space with early tokens of authority from the Jin and Ming eras. There are also live transmissions from a roadside traffic camera.

East again is the Catholic church of **St. Michael's**, built in 1902, and opposite the church, the **former Belgian Legation**, modeled after a villa that belonged to King Leopold II. A rear entrance leads into a square fringed by mock European buildings. Most are now offices, but you can enter the lobby and see traces of the original fittings.

The four corners of the palace walls are guarded by Arrow Towers

Bei Hai with Jing Shan's summit in the background

Jing Shan Park **8**
景山

44 Jingshan Xi Jie, Xicheng. **Map**
2 A3. M *Tian'an Men Xi*. **Tel** *(010)
6403 1102.* 🔲 *6am–9pm daily.* 🈲

Situated on Beijing's north-
south axis, Jing Shan Park has
its origins in the Yuan dynasty
(1279–1368). Its hill was
created from earth that was
excavated while building the
palace moat during the reign
of the Ming Yongle emperor.
In the early years of the
Ming dynasty it was known
as Wansui Shan (Long Life
Hill), but was renamed
Jing Shan (View or
Prospect Hill) in the
Qing era. Foreign
residents also referred
to it as Coal Hill (Mei
Shan), supposedly
because coal was
stored at the foot of
the hill although
other theories exist.

Until the fall of the
Qing, Jing Shan was linked to
the Forbidden City and was
restricted to imperial use. The
hill's purpose was to protect
the imperial palaces within
the Forbidden City from
malign northern influences,
which brought death and
destruction according to
classical *feng shui*. However,
it failed to save the last Ming
emperor Chongzhen, who
hanged himself from a locust
tree *(huaishu)* in the park in
1644, when rebel troops
forced their way into Beijing.
Another tree, planted after the
original tree was cut down,
marks the spot in the park's
southeast. The park is dotted

with several pavilions and
halls, but the highlight of
any visit is the superb view
of the Forbidden City from
the hill's Wanchun Ting
(Wanchun Pavilion).

Bei Hai Park **9**
北海公园

1 Wenjin Jie, Xicheng. **Map** 1 F3.
M *Tian'an Men Xi*. **Tel** *(010) 6403
3225.* 🔲 *6am–8:30pm daily.* 🈲

An imperial garden for more
than 1,000 years, Bei Hai
Park was opened to the
public in 1925. Filled with
artificial hills, pavilions,
and temples, it is
associated with Kublai
Khan, who redesigned
it during the Mongol
Yuan dynasty. The
Tuancheng (Round
City), near the south
entrance, has a huge,
decorated jade urn
belonging to him.
The park is named
after its extensive lake, **Bei
Hai**, whose southern end is
bordered by the inaccessible
Zhong Nan Hai, Communist
Party Headquarters. In the
middle of Bei Hai, Jade Island
was supposedly made from
the earth excavated while
creating the lake. It is topped
by the 118-ft (36-m) high
White Dagoba, a Tibetan-style
stupa built to honor the visit
of the fifth Dalai Lama in
1651. Beneath the huge
dagoba, **Yongan Si** comprises
a series of ascending halls.
The lake's northern shore has
several sights, including the
massive **Nine Dragon Screen**,
an 89-ft (27-m) long spirit

White Dagoba, Bei
Hai Park

wall made of colorful glazed
tiles. Depicting nine
intertwining dragons, it was
designed to obstruct evil
spirits. The Xiaoxitian Temple
lies to the west.

Mansion of Prince Gong **10**
恭王府

17 Qianhai Xi Jie, Xicheng. **Map** 1 F2.
M *Gulou*. **Tel** *(010) 6616 8149.* 🔲
8:30am–4:30pm daily. 🈲

Beijing's most complete
example of a historic mansion
is situated in a charming
hutong district west of Qian
Hai. It was supposedly the
inspiration behind the
residence portrayed by Cao
Xueqin in his classic 18th-
century novel *Dream of the
Red Chamber (see pp20–21).*
Built during the reign of the
Qianlong emperor, the house
is extensive and its charming
garden is a pattern of open
corridors and pavilions, dotted
with pools and gateways.
Originally built for Heshun,
a Manchu official and the
emperor's favorite, the
residence was appropriated
by the imperial household after
he was found guilty of using
regal motifs in his mansion
design. It was later bequeathed
to Prince Gong in the Xianfeng
emperor's reign (r.1851–61).
The house is popular with
tour groups, so early morning
is the best time to visit and
afterwards, the local *hutongs*
can be explored. In summer,
Beijing Opera is performed in
its Grand Opera House.

Elaborate arched gateway, Mansion
of Prince Gong

Beijing's Courtyard Houses

At first glance, Beijing seems a thoroughly modern city, but a stroll through the city's alleyways *(hutongs)* reveals the charm of old Beijing. These *hutongs* – weaving across much of central Beijing – are where many Beijing residents *(Beijingren)* still live. Typically running east to west, *hutongs* are created by the walls of courtyard houses *(siheyuan)*. Formerly the homes of officials and the well-to-do,

Washing the laundry in public

most are now state-owned. The *hutongs* are very easy to find, try the alleyways between the main streets south of Qian Men, or around Hou Hai and Qian Hai. The modernization of Beijing has destroyed many traditional *siheyuan*, but some have been cleaned up and have again become homes. A few have been converted into hotels *(see pp178–82)*, allowing the visitor a closer look at this disappearing world.

Crowded courtyards
As space became an issue in Beijing, additional buildings filled in the large courtyards. Several families may be living together in one siheyuan.

The main hall was the most northerly and usually reserved for the eldest of the family, such as the grandparents.

Wall adds privacy and keeps out spirits as they are unable to turn corners.

The open courtyard lets in both the sunlight and the wind and cold.

The number of halls and courtyards determines the grandeur of the residence.

Entrance is at the southeastern corner as prescribed by *feng shui.*

Walls were important to the Chinese psyche – even in the secure capital, they felt the need to retreat behind them.

Social housing
With several families living together, a strong community spirit is fostered, while the hutong outside becomes an extension of the home.

Typical Beijing *hutong*
You can take organized rickshaw tours of the hutong, sometimes with a visit to the Mansion of Prince Gong (see p68), but it can be more fun to explore them by yourself.

A view of the Bell Tower from Beijing's Drum Tower

Drum & Bell Towers ⓫
鼓楼

Northern end of Di'an Men Wai Dajie, Dongcheng. **Map** 2 A2. Ⓜ *Gulou.* **Tel** *(010) 8402 7869.* ⬡ *daily.* ▨

Located on the north-south meridian that bisects the Forbidden City and Tian'an Men Square, the Drum Tower (Gu Lou) rises up from a historic Beijing *hutong* district *(see p69).* The squat structure seen today was originally built in 1420 during the reign of the Ming Yongle emperor. Visitors can clamber up the steep stairs to look out over the city and inspect the 25 drums there. The one large and 24 smaller drums were beaten to mark the hours of the day. According to the official Chinese accounts, the original drums were destroyed by the foreign soldiers of the international army that relieved Beijing during the Boxer Rebellion.

A short walk north of the Drum Tower, the Bell Tower (Zhong Lou) is an edifice from 1745, which replaced an earlier tower that had burnt down. Suspended within the tower is a 15-ft (4.5-m) high and 42-ton (42,674-kg) bell, that was cast in 1420. During Spring Festival *(see pp34–5)*, visitors can pay to ring the bell for good luck.

Lama Temple ⓬
雍和宫

12 Yonghe Gong Dajie, Dongcheng. **Map** 2 C1. Ⓜ *Yonghe Gong.* **Tel** *(010) 6404 4499.* ⬡ *daily.* ▨

Beijing's most spectacular temple complex, the Lama Temple (Yonghegong) was constructed during the 17th century and converted into a Tibetan lamasery in 1744. Its five main halls are a stylistic blend of Han, Mongol, and Tibetan motifs. The first hall has a traditional display – the plump laughing Buddha, Milefo, is back-to-back with Wei Tuo, the Protector of Buddhist Doctrine, and flanked by the Four Heavenly Kings. **Yonghe Hall** beyond has three manifestations of Buddha, flanked by 18 *luohan* – those freed from the cycle of rebirth. Even farther back, the Tibetan-styled **Falun Hall** or Hall of the Wheel of Law has a statue of Tsongkhapa, the founder of the Yellow Hat sect of Tibetan Buddhism.

The highlight, however, is encapsulated within the towering **Wanfu Pavilion** (Wanfu Ge) – a vast 55-ft (17-m) high statue of Maitreya (the Future Buddha), carved from a single block of

The striking main gateway of the colorful Lama Temple

For hotels and restaurants in Beijing see pp178–82 and pp198–202

Statue of Confucius at the main entrance, Confucius Temple

sandalwood. The splendid exhibition of Tibetan Buddhist objects at the temple's rear includes statues of the deities Padmasambhava (Guru Rinpoche), and the Tibetan equivalent of Guanyin, Chenresig, alongside ritual objects such as the scepter-like *dorje* (thunderbolt) and *dril bu* (bell), symbols of the male and female energies. Few captions are in English.

Confucius Temple ⓭
孔庙

13 Guozijian Jie, Dongcheng. **Map** 2 C1. Ⓜ *Yonghe Gong.* **Tel** (010) 8401 1977. ◯ *daily.* 🗌

Adjacent to the Lama Temple, the Confucius Temple is the largest in China outside Qufu, the philosopher's birthplace in Shandong province. The alley leading to the temple has a fine *pailou* (decorative archway), few of which survive in Beijing. First built in 1302 during the Mongol Yuan dynasty, the temple was expanded in 1906 in the reign of Emperor Guangxu. It is a tranquil place that offers respite from the city's bustle. Around 200 ancient stelae stand in the silent courtyard in front of the main hall (Dacheng Dian), inscribed with the names of those who successfully passed the

imperial civil service exams. Additional stelae are propped up on the backs of *bixi* (mythical cross between a tortoise and a dragon), within pavilions surrounded by cypress trees. On a marble terrace in the main hall are statues of Confucius and some of his disciples.

Di Tan Park ⓮
地坛公园

N of the Lama Temple, Dongcheng. **Map** 2 C1. Ⓜ *Yonghe Gong.* **Tel** (010) 6421 4657. ◯ *daily.* 🗌

An ideal place to stroll amidst trees, Di Tan Park was named after the Temple of Earth (Di Tan), which was the venue for imperial sacrifices. The park's altar (Fangze Tan) dates to the Ming dynasty and its square shape represents the earth. Under the Ming, five main altars were established at the city's cardinal points – Tian Tan (Temple of Heaven) in the south, Di Tan in the north, Ri Tan (Temple of the Sun) in the east, Yue Tan (Temple of the Moon) in the west, and Sheji Tan (Temple of Land and Grain) in the center. Mirroring ancient ceremonies, a lively temple fair *(miaohui)* is held during the Chinese New Year *(see pp34–5)*, to welcome the spring planting season and appease the gods.

Dong Yue Miao ⓯
东岳庙

141 Chaoyang Men Wai Dajie, Chaoyang. **Map** 3 E4. Ⓜ *Chaoyang Men.* **Tel** (010) 6551 0151. ◯ *8:30am–4:30pm Tue–Sun.* 🗌

On Beijing's eastern side near Chaoyang's Workers' Stadium, the mesmerizing Dong Yue Miao takes its name from the Daoist Eastern Peak, Dong Yue, also known as Tai Shan. It is fronted by a fabulous glazed Ming dynasty *paifang* inscribed with the characters "Zhisi Daizong," meaning "offer sacrifices to Mount Tai (Tai Shan) in good order."

This colorful and active temple, dating to the early 14th century, was restored at considerable cost in 1999, and is tended by Daoist monks. The main courtyard leads into the Hall of Tai Shan, where there are statues of the God of Tai Shan and his attendants. The greatest attractions here are over 70 "Departments," filled with vivid Daoist gods and demons, whose functions are explained in English captions. In Daoist lore, the spirits of the dead go to Tai Shan, and many Departments dwell on the afterlife. The Department for Increasing Wealth and Longevity, for example, offers cheerful advice.

Guardian at entrance, Dong Yue Miao

Corn laid out to form Chinese characters, temple festival, Di Tan Park

National Art Museum of China ⑯

中国美术馆

1 Wusi Dajie, Dongcheng. **Map** 2 B4.
Ⓜ *Dong Si.* **Tel** *(010) 8403 3500.*
◯ *daily, last entry 4pm.* 🖼

Hosting a number of exhibitions of Chinese and international art, as well as occasional photographic displays, the National Art Museum of China (Zhongguo Meishuguan) has 14 halls spread over three levels. This quite ordinary building holds an exciting range of Chinese modern art, which suffers less censorship than other media, such as film or literature. Magazines such as *Time Out Beijing* and *that's Beijing* carry details of current and forthcoming exhibitions.

Wangfujing Street ⑰

王府井

Map 2 B5. Ⓜ *Wangfujing.* **Night Market** ◯ *5:30pm–10pm daily.* **St. Joseph's Church** *74 Wangfujing Dajie.* **Tel** *(010) 6524 0634.* ◯ *early morning during services.*

Bustling Wangfujing Street (Wangfujing Dajie), Beijing's main shopping street, is filled with department stores and giant malls such as the Sun Dong'an Plaza *(see p102)*. Everything from curios, *objets d'art*, antiques, clothes, and books are available here. The huge **Foreign Language**

The imposing façade of St. Joseph's Church, Wangfujing Street

Bookstore is a good place to buy a more detailed map of Beijing. The street has a lively mixture of pharmacies, laundry and dyeing shops, as well as stores selling silk, tea, and shoes.

However, the street's highlight is the **Night Market**, with its endless variety of traditional Chinese snacks, including skewers of beef, and more exotic morsels such as scorpions. Other offerings include pancakes, fruit, shrimps, squid, flat bread, and more. The Wangfujing Snack Street, south of the Night Market, also has a range of colorful restaurants.

The impressive triple-domed **St. Joseph's Church**,

known as the East Cathedral, is at 74 Wangfujing Dajie. One of the city's most important churches, it has recently been restored at a cost of US$2 million. It was built on the site of the former residence of Jesuit Adam Schall von Bell (1591–1669) in 1655, and has been rebuilt a number of times after being successively destroyed by earthquake, fire, and then during the Boxer Rebellion. It is fronted by an open courtyard and an arched gateway.

Ancient Observatory ⑱

古观象台

Map 5 F1. Ⓜ *Jianguo Men.* **Tel** *(010) 6524 2202.* ◯ *9am–4pm daily.* 🖼

Beijing's ancient observatory (Gu Guanxiangtai) stands on a platform alongside a flyover off Jianguo Men Nei Dajie. Dating to 1442, it is one of the oldest in the world. A Yuan dynasty (1279–1368) observatory was also located here, but the structure that survives today was built after the Ming emperors relocated their capital from Nanjing to Beijing. In the early 17th century, the Jesuits, led by Matteo Ricci (1552–1610) and followed by Adam Schall von Bell, impressed the emperor and the imperial astronomers with their scientific knowledge, particularly the accuracy of their predictions of eclipses.

The Belgian Jesuit Father Verbiest (1623–88) was appointed to the Imperial Astronomical Bureau, where he designed a set of astronomical instruments in 1674. Several of these were appropriated by German soldiers during the Boxer Rebellion of 1900, and were only returned after World War I. A collection of reproduction astronomical devices lies in

Ecliptic armillary sphere, Ancient Observatory

Delicious street food at the Night Market, just off Wangfujing Street

For hotels and restaurants in Beijing see pp178–82 and pp198–202

The atmospheric Red Gate Gallery, Southeast Corner Watchtower

the courtyard on the ground floor, some decorated with fantastic Chinese designs including dragons. Steps lead to the roof, where there are impressive bronze instruments, including an azimuth theodolite, used to measure the altitude of celestial bodies, and an armillary sphere, for measuring the coordinates of planets and stars.

Southeast Corner Watchtower (Dongbian Men)

Southeast Corner Watchtower ⑲
东边门箭楼

Off Jianguo Men Nan Dajie, Chongwen. **Map** 5 F2. Ⓜ *Beijing Zhan*. **Red Gate Gallery** *Tel (010) 6525 1005.* ◯ *10am–5pm daily.* 🖼 *For exhibition details visit* **www**.redgategallery.com

A short distance south of the Ancient Observatory, an imposing chunk of the Beijing City Walls *(see p60)* survives in the form of the 15th-century Southeast Corner Watchtower (Dongnan Jiao

Lou). After climbing onto the Ming dynasty battlements, visitors can walk along the short but impressive stretch of attached wall to admire the towering bastion, pitted with archers' windows, and look down on the city below. The walls of the tower are engraved with graffiti left by soldiers of the international army that marched into the city to liberate the Foreign Legations during the Boxer Rebellion in 1900.

Within its splendid, cavernous interior, accessed from the battlements, the rooms reveal enormous red wooden columns and pillars, crossed with beams. The **Red Gate Gallery**, one of Beijing's most appealing art galleries, is situated within this superb setting on levels 1 and 4. Originally founded in 1991 by an Australian who came to Beijing to learn Chinese, the gallery exhibits works in a wide variety of media by up-and-coming contemporary Chinese and foreign artists. Forthcoming exhibitions are listed on the gallery's website *(see above)*.

Beijing Natural History Museum ⑳
自然历史博物馆

126 Tianqiao Nan Dajie, Chongwen. **Map** 4 C3. Ⓜ *Qian Men, then taxi.* **Tel** *(010) 6702 4431.* ◯ *9am–5pm Tue–Sat.* 🖼 **www**.bmnh.org.cn

Housed in an enormous 1950s building covered in creepers, this museum is the largest of its type in China, with about 5,000 specimens arranged into three collections: zoology, paleontology, and botany. The most interesting collection is found in the Paleontology Hall which displays a selection of the dinosaurs and prehistoric animals that populated China between 500 million and one million years ago. Exhibits to look out for include the large-handed Lufengosaurus from the early Jurassic period, and a skeleton of the spine-nosed Qingdaosaurus (*Tsintaosaurus spinorbinus*), from the late Cretaceous period, whose skull sported a horn-like crest. The zoology section displays an abundance of marine, bird, and plant life to explain and illustrate the course of evolution from simple aquatic to far more complicated land-based forms. There is a also a display devoted to human evolution, however, many of the braver visitors head for the basement that houses a macabre display of cross-sections of human cadavers, pickled corpses, limbs, and organs. The botany collection is less impressive but also much less disturbing.

Dinosaur skeletons in the Paleontology Hall, Natural History Museum

Temple of Heaven ㉑

天坛

Gate to the Round Altar

Completed during the Ming dynasty, the Temple of Heaven, more correctly known as Tian Tan, is one of the largest temple complexes in China and a paradigm of Chinese architectural balance and symbolism. It was here that the emperor would make sacrifices and pray to heaven and his ancestors at the winter solstice. As the Son of Heaven, the emperor could intercede with the gods, represented by their spirit tablets, on behalf of his people and pray for a good harvest. Off-limits to the common people during the Ming and Qing dynasties, the Temple of Heaven is situated in a large and pleasant park that now attracts thousands of visitors daily.

Qinian Dian, where the emperor prayed for a good harvest

Name plaques are often written in the calligraphy of an emperor.

The circular roof symbolizes the sky.

THE TEMPLE OF HEAVEN COMPLEX

The main parts of the temple complex are all connected on the favored north-south axis by the Red Step Bridge (an elevated pathway) to form the focal point of the park. The Round Altar is made up of concentric rings of stone slabs in multiples of nine, the most auspicious number. The circular Echo Wall is famed for its supposed ability to carry a whisper from one side of the wall to the other.

① Hall of August Heaven
② Qinian Dian (Hall of Prayer for Good Harvests)
③ Red Step Bridge
④ Echo Wall
⑤ Imperial Vault of Heaven
⑥ Round Altar
⑦ Seven Star Rock
⑧ Hall of Abstinence

| 0 meters | 250 |
| 0 yards | 250 |

KEY

☐ Area illustrated

North Heavenly Gate

West Heavenly Gate

TEMPLE OF HEAVEN PARK

East Heavenly Gate

South Heavenly Gate

Red is an imperial color.

Dragon and phoenix motifs inside and out represent the emperor and empress.

STAR FEATURES

★ Caisson ceiling

★ Dragon Well pillars

The golden finial
is 125 ft (38 m) high and prone to lightning strikes.

★ **Caisson ceiling**
The splendid circular caisson ceiling has a gilded dragon and phoenix at its center. The hall is entirely built of wood without using a single nail.

Blue represents the color of heaven.

★**Dragon Well pillars**
The roofs of the hall are supported on 28 highly-decorated pillars. At the center, the four huge columns, known as Dragon Well pillars, represent the seasons, while the other 24 smaller pillars symbolize the months in a year plus the 12 two-hour time periods in a day.

Tablets in memory of his ancestors were worshiped by the emperor.

Symbolic offerings

Marble platform
Three tiers of marble form a circle 300 ft (90 m) in diameter and 20 ft (6 m) high. The balusters on the upper tier are decorated with dragon carvings to signify the imperial nature of the structure.

QINIAN DIAN

Originally built in 1420, the Qinian Dian, or Hall of Prayer for Good Harvests, is often incorrectly called the Temple of Heaven. There is in fact no single temple building as such at Tian Tan, a more literal translation of which is Altar of Heaven – referring to the whole complex.

Exploring the Temple of Heaven

The Temple of Heaven complex (or Tian Tan, which is more correctly translated as Altar of Heaven) is set in one of Beijing's most impressive parks. The temple was the place where earth, signified by square shapes including the bases of the enclosures, communicated with heaven, signified by the rounded top. This motif of square and rounded shapes is repeated in the layout of the park. Today, local retired people, inured both to the magnificence of the buildings and their hordes of visitors, use the site as a public recreational space, practising *tai ji quan (tai chi)*, various martial arts, and other exercises, flying kites, and rehearsing Beijing Opera, all of which add to the charm.

he would have been carried in a yellow palanquin through the shuttered streets of the city in almost complete silence, accompanied by as many as 500 officials and ceremonially dressed eunuchs. The foreign legations, who settled in Beijing after 1860, were sent notice to keep away and not disturb the procession. Services to the British-built railway station at Qian Men had to be halted for the duration of the ceremonies. The Abstinence Hall itself is the Forbidden City in miniature, walled and moated, entered by two great gates accessed by bridges.

Running south from the Qinian Dian, the **Red Step Bridge** is the central axis of the whole complex, an elevated walkway of stone and marble leading to the main altar. Before the altar is the **Imperial Vault of Heaven**, a lower round building used for storing ceremonial equipment. This is surrounded by the perfectly circular **Echo Wall**, with the same sonic effects found in some European cathedrals, where even a whisper travels round to a listener on the other side. A handclap made while standing on different stones at the center produces a different number of echoes. However, since this is one of the most-visited sights in Beijing, it's rarely possible to test either effect amongst the hubbub of everybody else's efforts.

Triple gates for emperor (east), officials (west), and gods (center)

卍 The Tian Tan Complex

Entering through the North Heavenly Gate, the first building encountered is the **Hall of August Heaven**. This once held wooden spirit tablets representing imperial ancestors. It is also where preliminary ceremonies would take place.

But the Hall of August Heaven is dwarfed by the **Qinian Dian**, or **Hall of Prayer for Good Harvests**, which has come to symbolize Beijing almost as much as the Tian'an Men. This circular tower, topped by a conical roof of dark blue tiles and a gold knob, is perhaps the most beautiful building in the entire city, standing on a great triple-layered, circular, marble plinth, and painted in blue, green, and gold, with red latticed doors at ground level. One of its many claims to fame is that it was constructed without the use of a single nail. Visitors should lean inside for a view of the dragon and phoenix, which form the centerpiece of the

caisson ceiling. This central roundel is mirrored by a natural marble slab in the center of the floor, which is where the emperor would make his prayers for good harvest in the autumn.

The emperor would spend the night before the rituals fasting at the **Hall of Abstinence**, southwest of the Qinian Dian. Prior to this

Imperial Vault of Heaven, store for ceremonial equipment

The Round Altar, site of the annual winter solstice sacrifice

Although the Qinian Dian is regarded as the star, in fact the focus of the Tian Tan complex is the vast triple-tiered **Round Altar** that dominates the southern part of the site. The altar is made up of marble slabs laid in nine concentric circles with each circle containing a multiple of nine pieces. The center of the altar represents the center of the world. Supposedly, the extraordinary acoustics of the construction magnify the sound made by anyone speaking at the center. This is where the emperor would perform the annual winter solstice sacrifice of a young bullock.

Various minor buildings around the site were for the use of musicians and other attendants, and for preparation and cremation of the sacrifice.

The park's venerable cypresses were important enough to be the subject of poems, while the seeds of the park's elms were traditionally made into cakes. These cakes, along with a certain "dragon-whisker" vegetable from the grounds, were regarded as delicacies, believed to have added spiritual or medicinal qualities. However, the park's flora has not always been so respected – many of the trees were cut down for firewood during the Nationalist era.

Although the original temple enclosure was off-limits to ordinary people, by the 18th century there were merchants' stalls along both the inside and outside of the north wall, some of which reappeared in the late 1980s, only to be cleared away again in recent times.

Xiannong Tan ㉒
先农坛

West of the Temple of Heaven.
Map 4 C4. Ⓜ *Qian Men, then taxi.*
Tel (010) 6301 7620. 🚐 ◯ 9am–4pm daily.

As late as the 1930s almost half of the land within the southern part of the city walls was still green space, and the Xiannong Tan complex, which was immediately west of Tian Tan, was nearly the same size. Tan is more correctly translated as altar than temple, and as with its better-known neighbor, the emperor came here annually to perform vital ceremonies. On the vernal equinox he would perform various sacrifices then dress as a farmer and, with various officials guiding the oxen, would plough three furrows. This ritual was performed here from 1420, when some of the remaining halls were constructed, until 1906.

The World Monuments Fund has restored several halls, some of which now house an exhibition on the rituals, while the **Hall of Jupiter**, second in size only to the Forbidden City's Hall of Middle Harmony, is now home to the **Museum of Ancient Architecture**. This is an excellent introduction to the construction techniques of so much that has been lost, helpfully illuminated with detailed models. A fascinating three-dimensional plan shows the Beijing of 1949, with the magnificent city walls and gates largely intact.

YUAN SHIKAI

So important were the ceremonies at the Temple of Heaven in demonstrating the right to rule that not long after the founding of the republic in 1912, first president Yuan Shikai insisted that he should use them to reaffirm his unstable authority. His trip to the Temple of Heaven to perform the rites in 1915 was widely viewed as his first step to becoming emperor, although the solemnity of the occasion was some-what ruined by his decision to travel in an armored car, and by the presence of cameras there to record the events. Shortly afterwards he organized a petition demanding that he ascend the throne, and began the process of installing himself as the first emperor of a new dynasty. Protest from overseas and revolt amongst his supporters brought this to a halt in March 1916, and by June an exhausted Yuan was dead, leaving China to decades of civil war and Japanese occupation.

Yuan Shikai, 1859–1916

A decorative ceiling roundel at the Museum of Ancient Architecture

Cow Street Mosque ㉓
牛街清真寺

88 Niu Jie, Xuanwu. **Map** 4 A3.
M *Xuanwu Men, then taxi.* **Tel**
(010) 6353 2564. ○ *8am–4pm
daily. Avoid Fri (holy day).*

Beijing's oldest and largest
mosque dates back to the
10th century. It is located in
the city's Hui district, near
numerous Muslim restaurants
and shops. The Hui, a
Chinese Muslim minority
group mainly from Ningxia
province, are now scattered
throughout China and number
around 200,000 in Beijing.
The men are easily identified
by their beards and
characteristic white hats.

The Cow Street Mosque
is an attractive edifice, with
Islamic motifs and Arabic
verses decorating its halls
and stelae. Its most prized
possession is a 300-year-old,
hand-written copy of the
Koran *(Gulanjing).*

Astronomical observations
and lunar calculations were
made from the tower-like
Wangyue Lou. The graves
of two Yuan dynasty Arab
missionaries engraved with
Arabic inscriptions can be
seen here. The courtyard is
lush with greenery, making it
an idyllic escape from Beijing's
busy streets. Visitors are
advised to dress conservatively.
Non-Muslims are not allowed
to enter the prayer hall.

Buddhist statuary in the main hall, Fayuan Temple

Fayuan Temple ㉔
法源寺

7 Fayuan Si Qian Jie, Xuanwu. **Map**
4 A3. M *Xuanwu Men.* **Tel** *(010)
6353 4171.* ○ *8am–5pm daily.*

A short walk east from Cow
Street Mosque, the Fayuan
Temple dates to AD 696 and
is probably the oldest temple
in Beijing. It was consecrated
by the Tang Taizong emperor
(r.626–49), to commemorate
the soldiers who perished in
an expedition against the
northern tribes. The original
Tang era buildings were
destroyed by a succession
of natural disasters, and the
current structures date from
the Qing era.

The temple's layout is
typical of Buddhist temples.
Near the gate, the incense
burner *(lu)* is flanked by the
Drum and Bell Towers to the
east and west. Beyond, the
Hall of the Heavenly Kings
(Tianwang Dian) is guarded
by a pair of bronze lions, and
has statues of Milefo (the
Laughing Buddha) and his
attendant Heavenly Kings.
Ancient stelae stand in front
of the main hall, where a
gilded statue of Sakyamuni
(the Historical Buddha) is
flanked by bodhisattvas and
luohan – those freed from
the cycle of rebirth.

At the temple's rear, the
Scripture Hall stores *sutras*,
while another hall contains
a 16-ft (5-m) Buddha statue.
The grounds are busy with
monks who attend the
temple's Buddhist College.

White Clouds Temple ㉕
白云寺

6 Baiyuanguan Jie, Xuanwu. M
Nanlishi Lu, then taxi. **Tel** *(010) 6344
3666.* ○ *8am–4pm daily.*

Home to the China Daoist
Association, the White Clouds
Temple (Baiyun Guan) was
founded in AD 739 and is
Beijing's largest Daoist shrine.
Known as the Temple of
Heavenly Eternity, it was one
of the three ancestral halls of
the Quanzhen School of
Daoism, which focused on
right action and the benefits
of good karma. Built largely
of wood, the temple burnt to
the ground in 1166, and since
then has been repeatedly
destroyed and rebuilt. The
structures that survive date
largely from the Ming and
Qing dynasties. A triple-gated
Ming *pailou* (decorative

Resplendent interior of the Cow Street Mosque

archway) stands at the entrance. It is believed that rubbing the carved monkey on the main gate brings good luck. The major halls are arranged along the central axis, with more halls on either side. The Hall of the Tutelary God has images of four marshals who act as temple guardians, while the Hall of Ancient Disciplines is dedicated to the Seven Perfect Ones, disciples of Wang Chongyang, the founder of the Quanzhen School. The Hall of Wealth is popular with pilgrims who seek blessings from the three spirits of wealth, while the infirm patronize the Hall of the King of Medicine.

The temple grounds are full of Daoist monks with their distinctive topknots. It is most lively during the Chinese New Year (*see pp34–5*), when a temple fair (*miaohui*) is held.

Buddhist monks, Miaoying Temple White Dagoba

Chinese Military History Museum 26
军事博物馆

9 Fuxing Lu, Haidian. Ⓜ *Junshi Bowuguan*. **Tel** *(010) 6686 6114.* ◯ *8am–5:30pm daily.*

Topped by a gilded emblem of the People's Liberation Army, the Chinese Military History Museum is devoted to weaponry and revolutionary heroism. It is close to Muxidi, where the People's Liberation Army killed scores of civilians in 1989. Visitors are greeted by paintings of Mao, Marx, Lenin, and Stalin. The ground floor exhibits defunct F-5 and F-7 jet fighter planes, tanks,

and surface-to-air missiles. The top floor gallery chronicles with pride many of China's military campaigns.

Miaoying Temple White Dagoba 27
妙应寺

Fucheng Men Nei Dajie, Xicheng. **Map** 1 D3. Ⓜ *Fucheng Men*. **Tel** *(010) 6616 0211.* ◯ *daily.*

Celebrated for its distinctive Tibetan-styled, 167-ft (51-m) white dagoba (stupa or funerary mound) designed by a Nepalese architect, the

Miaoying Temple (Miaoying Si) dates to 1271, when Beijing was under Mongol rule. In addition to its conventional Drum and Bell Towers, Hall of Heavenly Kings, and Main Halls, this Buddhist temple has a remarkable collection of small Tibetan Buddhist statues in one of its halls. Another hall has a collection of 18 bronze *luohan* (disciples).

Beijing Zoo 28
北京动物园

137 Xizhi Men Wai Dajie, Haidian. Ⓜ *Xizhi Men*, then taxi. **Tel** *(010) 6831 4411.* ◯ *7:30am–6pm.*

West of the Beijing Exhibition Hall, Beijing Zoo is a relic of a bygone era, with outdated concrete and glass cages. The Panda Hall is one of its better enclosures, and the bears are at their liveliest in the mornings. The real reason for visiting is the huge **Aquarium**, with coral reefs, an Amazon rainforest, and an impressive shark pool. An array of aquatic mammals, including whales and dolphins, completes the collection.

F-5 fighter planes, Chinese Military History Museum

Summer Palace ㉙
颐和园

Bronze dragon

The sprawling grounds of the Summer Palace (Yihe Yuan) served the Qing dynasty as an imperial retreat from the stifling summer confines of the Forbidden City. Despite existing as an imperial park in earlier dynasties, it was not until the time of Emperor Qianlong, who reigned from 1736 to 1795, that the Summer Palace assumed its current layout. The palace is most associated, however, with the Empress Dowager Cixi who had it rebuilt twice: once following its destruction by French and English troops in 1860, and again in 1902 after it was plundered during the Boxer Rebellion.

Suzhou Street
A recreation of the shopping street originally built for the Qianlong emperor.

Temple of the Sea of Wisdom

Marble Boat
Cixi paid for this extravagant folly with funds meant for the modernization of the Imperial Navy. The super-structure of the boat is made of wood painted white to look like marble.

Boat pier

The Bronze Pavilion, weighing 207 tons (188 tonnes), is a highly-detailed metal replica of a timber-framed building.

★ Longevity Hill
The Tower of the Fragrance of the Buddha dominates this slope covered with impressive religious buildings.

STAR SIGHTS

★ Longevity Hill

★ Garden of Virtue and Harmony

★ Long Corridor

EMPRESS DOWAGER CIXI

Together with Tang-dynasty Empress Wu Zetian, Cixi is remembered as one of China's most powerful women. Having borne the Xianfeng emperor's son as an imperial concubine, Cixi later seized power as regent to both the Tongzhi and and Guangxu emperors (her son and nephew respectively). Cixi prevented Guangxu from implementing state reforms and, in her alliance with the Boxer Rebellion, paved the way for the fall of the Qing Dynasty in 1911.

Empress Cixi, 1835–1908

VISITORS' CHECKLIST

6 miles (10 km) NW of Beijing.
Tel (010) 6288 1144. 🅼 Xizhi Men then bus No. 32, or 808 from zoo. 🚌 from Yuyuan Tan Park, and Exhibition Center near zoo (not in winter). ⏰ 7am–5pm daily. 📷 🚫 🍴 🛍 ♿ 🔼 🚻

★ **Garden of Virtue and Harmony**
This three-story building served as a theater, where the court's 348-member opera troupe entertained Cixi, who watched from the surrounding gallery.

Back Lake

The Garden of Harmonious Pleasures was Cixi's favorite fishing spot.

Hall of Happiness and Longevity

East Palace Gate (main entrance)

Hall of Jade Ripples

★ **Long Corridor**
The beams along the length of this 2,388-ft (728-m) walkway are decorated with over 14,000 scenic paintings.

Hall of Benevolence and Longevity
The principal ceremonial hall, this single-eaved building houses the throne upon which Cixi sat.

Exploring the Summer Palace

Following the conventions of Chinese gardens *(see pp28–9)* the palace grounds are arranged as a microcosm of nature, its hills *(shan)* and water *(shui)* creating a natural composition further complemented by bridges, temples, walkways, and ceremonial halls. Even after repeated restoration, the Summer Palace tastefully harmonizes the functional and fanciful, with administrative and residential quarters leading to the pastoral vistas of the grounds, as well as numerous peaceful temples and shrines. Despite the Summer Palace's popularity a little walking takes you to peaceful corners among the most idyllic in Beijing.

A pleasure cruise on Kunming Lake aboard a dragon ferry boat

🏯 Palace Complex

The grounds of the Summer Palace are extensive, but the main buildings can all be visited by those with sufficient energy and time.

The main entrance at the **East Palace Gate** (Gong Dong Men) leads to the official and residential halls of the palace complex. Just inside the main gate stands the **Hall of Benevolence and Longevity** (Renshou Dian), where the Empress Dowager Cixi and her nephew the puppet-emperor Guangxu gave audience. The bronze statues in front of this ceremonial hall, include the symbol of Confucian virtue, the mythical *qilin*, a hybrid, cloven-hoofed animal with horns and scales, sometimes incorrectly referred to as China's unicorn.

To the west, by the lakeside, the **Hall of Jade Ripples** (Yulan Tang) is where Cixi incarcerated Guangxu during his extended stays here after he supported the abortive 1898 Reform Movement

betrayed by Yuan Shikai. Cixi's former residence, the **Hall of Happiness and Longevity** (Leshou Tang), is full of Qing-era furniture and supposedly left as it was at the time of her death in 1908. To the south is the jetty from where Cixi would set sail across the lake; to the east is the **Garden of Virtue and Harmony** (Dehe Yuan) with Cixi's private theater. The theater buildings now contain an exhibition of Qing-era artifacts of daily use, from vehicles, to costumes and glassware.

🏯 Longevity Hill

From the Hall of Happiness and Longevity the **Long Corridor** (Chang Lang), decorated with painted landscapes and other scenes, zigzags along the shore of the lake, interrupted along its length by four pavilions.

At the corridor's halfway point, a series of religious and administrative buildings ascends the slopes of **Longevity Hill** (Wanshou Shan), artificially raised to improve the view in Qianlong's time. The start of the sequence is marked at the lakeside by a fabulous decorative gate *(pailou)*, beyond which stands the **Cloud Dispelling Gate**, with two bronze lions sitting alongside it.

The first main hall, the **Cloud Dispelling Hall** (Paiyun Dian), is a double-eaved structure that was the throne room when the court was at the palace. In the center of the hall is the Empress Dowager's nine-dragon throne, where she sat to receive tribute. Above the hall, rising from a great stone platform, stands the prominent, octagonal, four-eaved **Tower of the Fragrance of the Buddha** (Foxiang Ge). The stiff climb is worth the effort for views from the balcony over the yellow roofs of the halls and pavilions to the lake below.

West of the Tower of the Fragrance of the Buddha is the **Bronze Pavilion**, more properly known as the **Precious Clouds Pavilion** (Baoyun Ge), which imitates the construction of other wooden pavilions, but is built entirely in metal. Dating from

Door to the Temple of the Sea of Wisdom with glazed Buddha effigies

Seventeen-arch Bridge linking South Lake Island to the mainland

the 18th century, the building is one of a handful that, although damaged, survived the destruction wrought by English and French troops during the Second Opium War. The same is true of the magnificent **Temple of the Sea of Wisdom** (Huihai Si), which is directly behind the Tower of the Fragrance of the Buddha. It has an exterior decorated with green and yellow tiles and façades embellished with glazed Buddhist effigies, many of which have been vandalized. From here you can look down or descend to the **Back Lake** (Hou Hu) and **Suzhou Street**, a row of recently recreated historical commercial buildings. Here the Qianlong emperor, his concubines and eunuchs, would play at being part of the common herd, acting out the roles of shoppers, shopkeepers, and pickpockets. Today these buildings house snack vendors and souvenir stalls, with staff dressed in Qing-era costume.

South Lake
The buildings at the north end of the lake are more than enough to fill a single day, however the southern end of the grounds can be blissfully free of crowds. Boat trips to **South Lake Island** depart from the jetty near the **Marble Boat**, also known as the Boat of Purity and Ease, which is found at the very westernmost end of the Long Corridor. (North of here are the imperial boathouses.) Alternatively, if time will allow, hire a boat for a leisurely row around Kunming Lake, or in muggy summer heat, a slow but battery-powered alternative. On South Lake Island, the **Dragon King Temple** (Longwang Miao) is dedicated

The eastern shore's bronze ox

to the god of rivers, seas, and rain. Cixi would come here to pray for rain in times of drought. The island is connected to the eastern shore by the elegant **Seventeen-arch Bridge** (Shiqi Kong Qiao). A marble lion crowns each of the 544 balusters along the bridge's length, all supposedly individual. A large **bronze ox**, dating back to 1755 but looking entirely modern, reposes on the eastern shore; it was believed to pacify the waters and prevent floods.

Across on the western side of Kunming Lake, steep-sloped **Jade Belt Bridge** links the mainland to the West Causeway, which slices through the lake to its southern point.

PLAN OF GROUNDS
The grounds of the Summer Palace cover 716 acres (290 hectares), with Kunming Lake lying to the south of Longevity Hill. South Lake Island is just off the east shore and a stroll around the entire shoreline takes about two hours.

① Jade Belt Bridge
② West Causeway
③ South Lake Island
④ Bronze ox

KEY

☐ Area illustrated (see pp80–81)

0 meters 800

0 yards 800

Remnants of the Yuanming Yuan, once said to resemble Versailles

Yuanming Yuan ㉚
圆明园

28 Qinghua Xi Lu, Haidian.
Ⓜ Xizhi Men, then bus 375.
◯ 7am–6:30pm daily. ▨

The Yuanming Yuan (Garden of Perfect Brightness, sometimes called the Old Summer Palace), now sits isolated from the main Summer Palace, but was a collection of princely gardens fused into the main mass by the Qing Qianlong emperor in the mid-18th century. He commissioned Jesuits at his court to design and construct a set of European-style buildings in one corner, which they likened to Versailles. Unfortunately, all the traditional Chinese halls were burned down by British and French troops during the Second Opium War in 1860. Later the European-style buildings were pulled down, and much of the remains were carted away by the locals for building purposes. Chinese narrations of the devastation criticize both the marauding European troops and the ineffectual Qing rulers.

Today, Yuanming Yuan is a jumble of sad, yet graceful fragments of stone and marble strewn in the **Eternal Spring Garden** in the park's northeastern corner. A small museum displays images and models of the palace, depicting its scale and magnificence. The **Palace Maze** has been recreated in concrete to the west of the ruins. The rest of the park is a pleasant expanse of lakes, pavilions, gardens, and walks.

Great Bell Temple ㉛
大钟寺

31a Beisanhuan Xi Lu, Haidian.
🚌 300, 367. **Tel** (010) 6255 0790.
◯ 8am–4pm daily. ▨

Home to a fascinating collection of bells, the 18th-century Dazhong Si follows a typical Buddhist plan, with the Heavenly Kings Hall, Main Hall, and the Guanyin Bodhisattva Hall. Its highlight is the 46.5-ton (47,246-kg) bell – one of the world's largest – that is housed in the rear tower. The bell was cast between 1403 and 1424, and brought here from Wanshou Temple in the reign of the Qianlong emperor. Buddhist *sutras* in Chinese and Sanskrit embellish its surface. During the Ming and Qing dynasties, the bell was struck 108 times to bring in the New Year, and could be heard for 25 miles (40 km). The gallery above has a display on bell casting,

Heng, Biyun Temple deity

and visitors can toss a coin into a gap at the top of the bell for luck. Hundreds of bells from the Song, Yuan, Ming, and Qing eras can be seen in a separate hall on the west side.

Xiang Shan Park ㉜
香山公园

Wofosi Lu, Xiang Shan, Haidian district. 🚌 333 from Summer Palace, 360 from Zoo. ◯ 6am–7pm. ▨
Botanical Gardens ◯ daily. ▨

This wooded parkland area, also known as Fragrant Hills Park, is at its scenic best in the fall, when the maples turn a flaming red. Its main attractions are the fine views from **Incense Burner Peak**, accessible by a chairlift, and the splendid **Biyun Temple**, or Azure Cloud Temple, close to the main gate. The temple is guarded by the menacing deities Heng and Ha in the Mountain Gate Hall. A series of halls leads to the Sun Yat Sen Memorial Hall, where his coffin was stored in 1925, before being taken to Nanjing. At the temple's rear is the distinctive 112-ft (34-m) high Diamond Throne Pagoda. About a mile (2 km) east of Xiang Shan Park are the **Beijing Botanical Gardens**, with pleasant walks and some 3,000 plant species. The gardens' **Sleeping Buddha Temple** is renowned for its magnificent bronze statue of a reclining Buddha. China's last emperor, Pu Yi (see p65), ended his days here as a gardener.

The Great Bell Temple, or Dazhong Si

National Olympic Stadium ㉝
奥林匹克体育中心

Olympic Green. Ⓜ *Olympic Park* ▦ ▤ *Currently under construction.* **www**.beijing2008.com

Beijing's new National Olympic Stadium is designed to be the stunning centerpiece of China's massive building program for the 2008 Olympics. It is part of the city's "Olympic Green" development, which includes a large landscaped park, an Olympic Village, and many other stadia including the National Indoor Stadium and Swimming Center.

Swiss architects Herzog and de Meuron won the competition for the stadium with a bird's nest-like structure of apparently random, intertwined ribbons of steel and concrete that simultaneously form both façade and structure. The gaps in the concrete lattice of the roof are to be filled with translucent inflated bags, making the building waterproof while allowing light to filter down to the spectators. Inflated bags will also be used at various points round the exterior where wind breaks are needed.

Long after the Olympics have gone, the National Stadium will remain one of the most striking buildings anywhere in the world.

798 Art District ㉞
七九八艺术区（大山子）

2-4 Juxian Qiao Lu, Da Shan Zi, Chaoyang. ▦ *915 or 918 from Dong Zhi Men to Da Shan Zi, or 420 from Beijing Station.* ▤ ◷ *10:30am–7:30pm daily.* **www**.798space.com

Although it has spilled out of its original home and into neighboring moribund industrial buildings to form the Da Shan Zi Art District, the lively arts scene here is still mostly known for the abandoned No. 798 Electronics Factory. This was the first to be converted into

Contemporary art meets obsolete industry at 798 Space in Da Shan Zi

a complex of studios, workshops, and galleries called 798 Space. Built in the Bauhaus style in the 1950s by East Germans with Soviet funding, the area was once the center of Chinese hightech, said to have produced parts for China's first nuclear bombs and satellites. Now its industrial chic is put to more peaceful purposes with art in all media for sale both in galleries and directly from the artists themselves. Wandering among the galleries reveals a different and interesting side to the city – there are large Communist-style sculptures making ironic reflections on history and new Mao-kitsch graffiti on the walls next to the original 1950s slogans exhorting workers. Cafés and restaurants have sprung up to add to the allure of the area.

China Railway Museum ㉟
中国铁道博物馆

1 Jiuxiang Qiao Bei Lu, Chaoyang. **Tel** *(010) 6438 1317.* ▤ ◷ *9am– 4pm Tues–Sun.*

The last passenger steam services in China came to an end in 2006, but a short taxi ride northeast of the 798 Art District, the recently opened Railway Ministry Science and Technology Center has a vast modern hall displaying 53 old locomotives. The collection includes some of the vast black engines imported by the Japanese when they controlled Manchuria, as well as huge Chinese beasts from Datong, and tiny Thomas the Tank Engine-scaled machines that once worked narrow-gauge extensions to French-built lines in Yunnan Province. The most ancient model is from Beijing's first railway line, which ran to Tongzhou, east of Beijing, directly connecting the city with the northern terminus of the Grand Canal, and vital food supplies from the south. Some of the cabs can be boarded by those sufficiently agile. An exhibition on the history of China's railways is promised, but in the meantime the engines themselves are a must for small boys of all ages. It is rumored that some machines will occasionally be in steam; call ahead to enquire.

Communist-era locomotives at the China Railway Museum

FARTHER AFIELD

Beijing continues to expand ring road by ring road but – for now – there is still relief from the crowds to be found in the surprisingly lush landscapes beyond the city limits. The Great Wall meanders across hilly territory to the north, always making for the highest point, and frequently doubling back on itself. There are several official access points with coach parks and souvenir shops, and an unlimited number of unofficial ones.

To the west, ancient temples nestle on green hillsides where rural life goes on much as it has for centuries. A trip out here offers a glimpse of the realities of existence for two-thirds of China's population. This is the world of tiny two-stroke tractors and water buffalo; of orderly patchworks of tiny wheat, corn, and sorghum fields; of bee-keeping and pig husbandry. Most temples have simple guest rooms, while at the well-preserved Ming- and Qing-era village of Chuandixia you can stay with the villagers themselves.

The countryside also harbors the vast necropolises of the Ming emperors and, more interestingly, the much less visited but more elaborate resting places of the Qing, to the east and southwest of the city. Also to the southwest is the 300-year-old stone Marco Polo Bridge and neighboring Wanping, a rare surviving example of a walled city. Both are an easy suburban bus ride from the city.

SIGHTS AT A GLANCE

Tombs, Temples, and Historic Buildings
Eastern Qing Tombs ❸
Great Wall of China
 pp90–92 ❷
Jietai Temple ❻
Marco Polo Bridge ❹
Ming Tombs pp88–9 ❶
Tanzhe Temple ❺

Town and Villages
Chuandixia ❽
Shidu ❼

KEY
▢ City limits
✈ International airport

━━ National highway
━━ Major road
═══ Minor road
— Railroad
═╪═ Great Wall of China
- - Beijing Province border

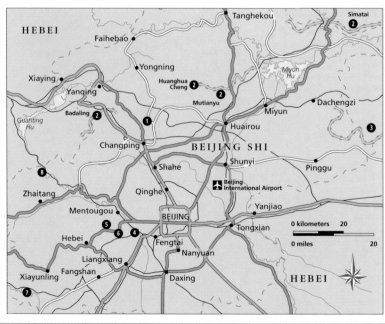

◁ The Great Wall meandering along the ridges of mountainous terrain just north of Beijing

Ming Tombs: Chang Ling ❶
明十三陵

Mythical qilin on Spirit Way

The resting place for 13 of the 16 Ming emperors, the Ming Tombs (Shisan Ling) are China's finest example of imperial tomb architecture. The site was originally selected because of its auspicious *feng shui* alignment; a ridge of mountains to the north cradles the tombs on three sides, opening to the south and protecting the dead from the evil spirits carried on the north wind. The resting place of the Yongle emperor (1360–1424), the Chang Ling is the most impressive tomb and the first to be built. It has been beautifully restored, although the burial chamber, where Yongle, his wife, and 16 concubines are thought to be buried, has never been excavated.

★ Spirit Way
Part of the 4-mile (7-km) approach to the tombs, the Spirit Way is lined with 36 stone statues of officials, soldiers, animals, and mythical beasts.

★ Hall of Eminent Favor
One of China's most impressive surviving Ming buildings, this double-eaved sacrificial hall is erected on a three-tiered terrace.

RECONSTRUCTION OF CHANG LING
This shows the Chang Ling tomb at the time of the burial of the Yongle emperor in the 15th century.

The Stele Pavilion bears inscriptions dating from the Qing dynasty which revered the Ming emperors.

Gate of Eminent Favor

THE MING TOMBS
The 13 tombs are spread over 15 square miles (40 sq km), so are best visited by taxi. Chang Ling, Ding Ling, and Zhao Ling have been restored and are very busy. Unrestored, the rest are open yet quiet.

① Chang Ling (1424)
② Yong Ling (1566)
③ De Ling (1627)
④ Jing Ling (1435)
⑤ Xian Ling (1425)
⑥ Qing Ling (1620)
⑦ Yu Ling (1449)
⑧ Mao Ling (1487)
⑨ Tai Ling (1505)
⑩ Kang Ling (1521)
⑪ Ding Ling (1620)
⑫ Zhao Ling (1572)
⑬ Concubine cemeteries
⑭ Si Ling (1644)

Spirit Way

pailou (archway)

0 kilometers 4
0 miles 4

★ Ding Ling treasures
Artifacts from the Wanli emperor's tomb, such as this threaded-gold crown decorated with two dragons, are on display in the main hall at Chang Ling.

The Spirit Tower marks the entrance to the burial chamber.

VISITORS' CHECKLIST

30 miles (45 km) NW of Beijing.
845 from Xizhi Men (near subway) to Zhengfa Daxue in Changping, then taxi or bus 314 to Da Gong Men. Many tours to the Great Wall (see pp90–92) stop here. **Tel** (010) 6076 1888.
8:30am–5pm daily.
interiors.

An earthen mound, surrounded by a circular rampart, covers the stone burial chamber.

Cedar columns
Supporting the huge weight of the roof, the colossal 43-foot (13-m) nanmu (fragrant cedar) columns are topped with elaborate dougong bracket sets.

Statue of the Yongle Emperor
Yongle, the third Ming emperor, moved the capital from Nanjing to Beijing, where he then oversaw the construction of the Forbidden City.

DING LING BURIAL CHAMBER

Ding Ling, the tomb of the longest reigning Ming emperor, Wanli (r.1573–1620), is the only burial chamber of the 16 tombs to have been excavated and opened to the public. During the 1950s, archeologists were stunned to find the inner doors of the chamber still intact. Inside they found the treasures of an emperor whose profligate rule began the downfall of the Ming dynasty.

Entrance

Side chambers were intended for others of Wanli's courts, but were never used.

The central chamber contains three marble thrones, one for each of the dead.

The coffin chamber held the red lacquer coffins of Wanli and his two wives.

Outer Chamber

Exit (via Spirit Tower)

STAR FEATURES

- ★ Hall of Eminent Favor
- ★ Spirit Way
- ★ Ding Ling treasures

Great Wall of China ❷
长城

A symbol of China's historic detachment and sense of vulnerability, the Great Wall snakes through the countryside over deserts, hills, and plains for several thousand miles. Originally a series of disparate earthen ramparts built by individual states, the Great Wall was created only after the unification of China under Qin Shi Huangdi (221–210 BC). Despite impressive battlements, the wall ultimately proved ineffective; it was breached in the 13th century by the Mongols and then, in the 17th century, by the Manchu. Today, only select sections of its crumbling remains have been fully restored.

Crumbling ruin
Most of the wall is still unrestored and has crumbled away leaving only the core remaining.

★ Panoramic views
Because the wall took advantage of the natural terrain for defensive purposes following the highest points and clinging to ridges, it now offers superb panoramic views.

Ramparts enabled the defending soldiers to fire down on their attackers with impunity.

Surface of stone slabs and bricks

Tamped layer of earth and rubble

Bigger rocks and stones

Kiln-fired bricks, cemented with a mortar of lime and glutinous rice

Large, locally quarried rocks

RECONSTRUCTION OF THE GREAT WALL
This shows a section of the wall as built by the most prolific wall builders, the Ming dynasty (1368–1644). The section at Badaling, built around 1505, is similar to this and was restored in the 1950s and 1980s.

STAR FEATURES

★ Panoramic views

★ Watchtowers

★ Watchtowers
A Ming addition, these served as signal towers, forts, living quarters, and storerooms for provisions.

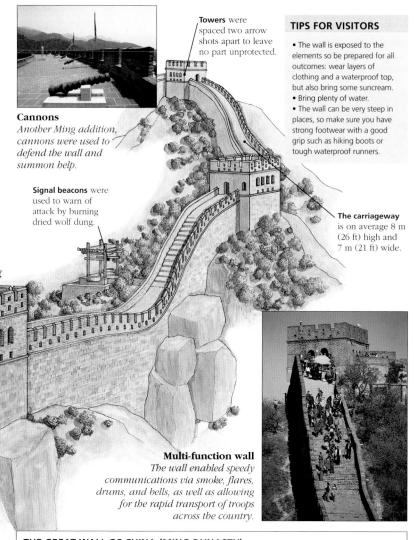

Towers were spaced two arrow shots apart to leave no part unprotected.

Cannons
Another Ming addition, cannons were used to defend the wall and summon help.

Signal beacons were used to warn of attack by burning dried wolf dung.

TIPS FOR VISITORS

• The wall is exposed to the elements so be prepared for all outcomes: wear layers of clothing and a waterproof top, but also bring some suncream.
• Bring plenty of water.
• The wall can be very steep in places, so make sure you have strong footwear with a good grip such as hiking boots or tough waterproof runners.

The carriageway is on average 8 m (26 ft) high and 7 m (21 ft) wide.

Multi-function wall
The wall enabled speedy communications via smoke, flares, drums, and bells, as well as allowing for the rapid transport of troops across the country.

THE GREAT WALL OF CHINA (MING DYNASTY)

0 kilometers 400

0 miles 400

Inner Mongolia

Yellow River

② ③ ④   ⑤
①
Datong   Beijing

Taiyuan   Tianjin

Bo Hai

Qinghai Lake

● Lanzhou

Yellow Sea

Most visitors travel to the wall from Beijing *(see p92)*, but it is worth seeing the wall anywhere along its length. Also impressive are the restored forts at Juyong Guan, Jiayu Guan, and Shanhaiguan.

Places to visit
① Jiayu Guan
② Badaling & Juyong Guan
③ Mutianyu & Huanghua Cheng
④ Simatai
⑤ Shanhaiguan

Exploring the Great Wall of China

A trip to the wall is a must for any visitor to Beijing. Most hotels will be able to organize this for you, usually combined with a visit to the Ming Tombs *(see pp88–9)*. However, be sure to find out whether there are any unwanted diversions planned to cloisonné workshops, jade factories, or Chinese medicine clinics. Small groups can have a more personalized visit, and see the more remote parts of the wall, by hiring a taxi for the day from Beijing and sharing the cost.

Ruins at Huanghua Cheng clinging to the steep hillside

Stall selling tourist paraphernalia at the Great Wall, Badaling

🏯 Badaling

44 miles (70 km) northwest of Beijing. *Tel (010) 6912 1017.* 🚌 *1 from Qian Men.* ⏰ *7:30am–6pm daily.* 🏛️♿🅿️📷

Equipped with guardrails, cable car, pristine watchtowers, and tourist facilities, the restored Ming fortification at Badaling is the most popular section of the Great Wall. The reward for coming to Badaling is the breathtaking view of the wall winding its way over the hills. To fully appreciate this, get away from the crowds by walking as far as you can along the wall either east or west of the entrance. The ticket includes admission to the Great Wall Museum. The pass at **Juyong Guan** is on the way to Badaling and although recently restored, it is often quieter than Badaling. With unscalable mountains on either side it is easy to see why this spot was chosen for defense. There are also some authentic Buddhist carvings on a stone platform, or "cloud terrace," in the middle of the pass that date back to the Yuan dynasty (1279–1368).

🏯 Mutianyu

56 miles (90 km) north of Beijing, Mutianyu Town, Huairou County. 🚌 *6 from Xuanwu Men.* ⏰ *7:30am–6pm daily.* 🏛️♿ *& chair lifts.*

The appeal of Mutianyu lies in its dramatic hilly setting and less intrusive tourist industry. With a series of watchtowers along its restored length, the wall you can see here dates from 1368 and was built upon the foundations of the wall built during the Northern Qi dynasty (AD 550–77).

🏯 Huanghua Cheng

37 miles (60 km) north of Beijing, Huairou County. ⏰ *daily.* 🏛️♿

Situated on the same stretch of wall as Mutianyu, Huanghua is an exhilarating section of Ming wall that is far less developed than other parts of the wall. The great barrier is split into two here by a large reservoir; most travelers take the right hand route on the other side of the reservoir, as the left-hand section is more difficult to reach. Devoid of guardrails, the crumbling masonry at Huanghua Cheng can be uneven and fairly treacherous, so be careful. Due to its crumbling state, access has been limited by the authorities. Because of ongoing reconstruction, it may not always be possible to visit Huanghua Cheng.

🏯 Simatai

68 miles (110 km) northeast of Beijing, Miyun County. 🚌 *6 from Xuanwu Men.* ⏰ *6am–6pm daily.* 🏛️♿ *(Apr–Nov).*

The wall at Simatai has only been partially repaired, affording a more genuine impression of the original wall. The steep and hazardous parts of the wall are also a lot riskier to navigate. Most visitors clamber along the eastern section of wall at Simatai, which leads to much steeper sections of wall, and later, impassable ruins. Despite the tourist trappings, the views are superb here. There is a four-hour trek from Simatai to Jingshanling that provides spectacular vistas, too.

The restored section of the wall at Badaling, northwest of Beijing

Eastern Qing Tombs ❸
清东陵

77 miles (125 km) east of Beijing, Zunhua County, Hebei Province. ☐ May–Oct: 8am–5pm daily; Nov–Apr: 9am–4:30pm daily. 🖼 🎫 📷

The remoteness of the Eastern Qing Tombs east of Beijing and over the border in Hebei province makes them far less popular than the Ming ones *(see pp88–9)*, despite the fact that the setting is even more splendid. In fact, the Eastern Qing tombs make up the largest and most complete imperial cemetery in China, built on as grand a scale as the Forbidden City itself *(see pp62–7)*. Of the many tombs scattered throughout the area,

Spirit Way to Emperor Shunzhi's tomb at the Eastern Qing Tombs

Incense burners in front of a spirit tower at the Eastern Qing Tombs

only five are the burial places of Qing emperors: the tombs of the Shunzhi emperor (r. 1644–61), Kangxi (r. 1661–1722), Qianlong (r. 1736–95), and Xianfeng (r. 1851–61) are open, while that of the Tongzhi emperor (r. 1862–74), at a distance from the main tomb grouping, is not. A 3-mile (5-km) Spirit Way, an approach lined with guardian figures, leads to Shunzhi's tomb, Xiao Ling, at the heart of the main tomb cluster, while several of the other tombs have their own smaller Spirit Ways. Southwest of here lies Yuling, Qianlong's tomb, with its incredible chamber adorned with Buddhist carvings and Tibetan and Sanskrit scriptures (rare features at imperial and principally Confucian tombs). The devious Empress Cixi *(see*

p82) is buried at Ding Dong Ling to the west, in the right-hand tomb of a complex of twin tombs, the other being the resting place of Ci'an, eldest wife of the Xianfeng emperor. Although both tombs were built in 1879, Cixi had her magnificent tomb lavishly restored in 1895. The marble carriageway up to the Hall of Eminent Favor notably locates the carving of the phoenix *(feng)*, symbol of the empress, above the carving of the dragon *(long)*, symbol of the emperor. West of Ding Dong Ling, Ding Ling is partially open and approached via a set of stone animal statues. Look for the smaller tombs of imperial concubines, their roofs tiled in green (not the yellow of emperors and empresses).

EMPEROR YONGZHENG

The son of the Kangxi emperor and a maidservant, Yongzheng (r.1723–35) chose not to be buried at the Eastern Qing Tombs, but perversely started a necropolis as far away as possible in the Western Qing Tombs (Yixian County, Hebei Province). Perhaps, racked with guilt, he could not face burial alongside his father, whose will he had thwarted. For after Kangxi's death, Yongzheng seized the throne from his brother (his father's chosen successor), and declared himself the legitimate heir, ruthlessly eliminating any other brothers and uncles who may have been a threat to his rule. Despite this shaky start, Yongzheng was an able ruler and a devout Buddhist, punishing dishonesty among his officials and seeking to improve the morals and education of his people. Another possible reason for the switch was that he just wasn't satisfied with the Eastern Tombs and chose an area with a better natural setting. Whatever the reason, those keen on Chinese tomb architecture will enjoy the peace of the Western Qing Tombs. Nearby, moved in 1995 to a commercial cemetery, are the remains of Pu Yi, the last emperor of China.

Yongzheng in robes embroidered with symbols of his power

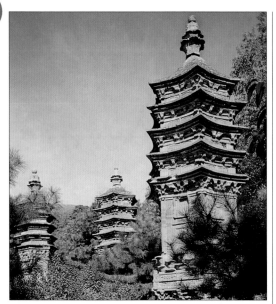

Brick stupas at the Stupa Forest Temple, also known as Talin Si

led to the Japanese occupation of Beijing and a full-scale war. For those with a keen interest in this period of history, the incident is marked by some rather gruesome displays in Wanping's **Memorial Hall**.

Tanzhe Temple ❺
潭柘寺

Mentougou district. 28 miles (45 km) W of Beijing. Ⓜ to Pingguo Yuan (1 hr), then bus 931 or tourist bus 7. **Tel** (010) 6086 1699. ◯ 8am–5:30pm daily. ▨

This enormous temple dates back to the 3rd century AD, when it was known as Jiafu Si. It was later renamed Tanzhe Temple, after the adjacent mountain Tanzhe Shan, which in turn got its name from the nearby Dragon Pool (Long Tan) and the surrounding cudrania *(zhe)* trees. It has a splendid mountainside setting, and its halls rise up the steep incline. The temple is especially famous for its ancient trees, among which is a huge ginkgo known as the Emperor's Tree. A slightly smaller tree close by is called The Emperor's Wife.

The most fascinating sight, however, is the **Stupa Forest Temple** (Talin Si) near the parking lot, with its marvelous collection of brick stupas hidden among the foliage. Each stupa was constructed in memory of a renowned monk. The towering edifices were built in a variety of designs, including the graceful *miyan ta* or dense-eave stupa, characterized by ascending layers of eaves. The earliest among them dates from the Jin dynasty (1115–1234).

Marco Polo Bridge ❹
芦沟桥

Wanping town, Fengtai District. 10 miles (16 km) SW of city center. 🚌 339 from Beijing's Lianhuachi bus station; 309 from WAZI (near Beijing West Railway Station). ◯ 7am–7pm daily. ▨ **Memorial Hall** 101 Wanpingcheng Nei Jie. ◯ 9am–4pm Tue–Sun. ▨

Straddling the Yongding River in Wanping town, the 876-ft (267-m) long marble bridge was first built during the Jin dynasty in 1189 but destroyed by a flood. The current structure dates to 1698. Known as Lugou Qiao in Chinese, the bridge acquired its English name after Marco Polo described it in his famous account of his travels. At the bridge's eastern and western ends are stelae inscribed by the Qing emperors, Kangxi and Qianlong. The poetic observation by Qianlong on a stele at the eastern end reads *"lugou xiaoyue,"* meaning "Moon at daybreak at Lugou." The balustrades along the length of the bridge are decorated by more than 400 carved stone lions, each one slightly different in appearance. Local legend has it that these fierce-looking statues come alive during the night. Despite the widening and extensive restoration work done over the centuries, a surprising amount of the bridge is original. In addition to its antiquity, it is significant as the site of the disastrous Marco Polo Bridge Incident. This is where, on July 7, 1937, the Japanese Imperial Army and Nationalist Chinese soldiers exchanged fire – an event that

Stone lion, Marco Polo Bridge

The 11-arched Marco Polo Bridge, known locally as Lugou Qiao

The gilded Buddha atop its plinth at Jietai Temple

Jietai Temple 6
戒台寺

Mentougou district, 20 miles (32 km) W of Beijing en route to Tanzhe Temple. **M** to Pingguo Yuan (1 hr), then bus 931 or tourist bus 7. **Tel** (010) 6980 6611. ◯ 8am–5:30pm daily. 🖼

The Jietai (Ordination Terrace) Temple has been used for the ceremony of elevating monks to higher levels of the Buddhist hierarchy as far back as the Liao dynasty (907–1125), and it is well worth a visit on the way to or from the nearby Tanzhe Temple. The "terrace" refered to in the temple's name is a finely carved marble plinth used for the ordination ceremonies. Its three layers feature 113 niched statues. Topped with a gilded Buddha and chairs for three masters and seven witnesses, the plinth stands inside a magnificent and unusual square hall, surrounded by lesser courtyards dotted with pines and cypresses. The temple is a half-mile (one-km) walk uphill from the bus stop.

Shidu 7
十渡

Fangshan district. 62 miles (100 km) SW of Beijing. 🚌 bus 917 from Beijing's Tianqiao station to Shidu. **Tel** (010) 6134 9009. 🖼

Shidu offers a fabulous escape from the commotion of urban Beijing and a chance to enjoy some stunning natural scenery. Before the new road and bridges were built, travelers had to cross the Juma River ten times as they journeyed through the gorge between Shidu and nearby Zhangfang village, hence the name Shidu meaning "Ten Ferries" or "Ten Crossings." Pleasant walking trails wind along the riverbank between impressive gorges and jagged limestone formations. Visitors can stop en route to paddle in the shallow river and picnic under the towering peaks. The main sights are around Qingjiang Gou and the lovely Gushan Zhai, marred somewhat by bungee jumping and other entertainment ventures.

Chuandixia 8
川底下

Near Zhaitang town. 56 miles (90 km) NW of Beijing. **M** to Pingguo Yuan (1 hr), then bus 929 to Zhaitang (3 hrs), then taxi. ◯ daily. 🖼

Despite the rather laborious expedition required to get here, a trip to the tiny village of Chuandixia (Under the River) is well worth the effort as the crumbling hamlet survives as a living museum of Ming and Qing dynasty village architecture. Situated on a steep mountainside, it is a picturesque outpost of courtyard houses (siheyuan) and rural Chinese buildings. Because of the close-knit nature of the original village all the courtyards were interconnected by small lanes. The entry ticket allows access to the entire village, all of which can be explored within a few hours. Look out for the Maoist graffiti and slogans that survive on the boundary walls; similar graffiti from the Cultural Revolution has been whitewashed in most other Chinese towns.

Chuandixia's population consists of about 70 people spread over a handful of families. Accommodations can be arranged for those wanting to explore the surrounding hills or simply experience the rural hospitality. Alive to the opportunities brought by tourism, quite a few of the old homesteads provide basic facilities at a reasonable price.

Traditional Ming and Qing dynasty houses, Chuandixia village

TWO GUIDED WALKS

Beijing is famous for its centuries-old alleys known as *hutongs*. The *siheyuan* (courtyard houses) that line them were built with their backs turned on the outside world with the main entrance set in otherwise blank walls. But these alleys and their distinctive homes have been disappearing ever more rapidly since 1949. At first they fell victim to Soviet-style edifices celebrating Communist achievements, then to multi-story apartment towers, and now to road widening and new cross-town highways. These multi-lane highways and burgeoning traffic problems do not always make Beijing the best place to explore on foot but it is worth giving it a go as you can see much more detail at walking pace. Look for the original carved wooden surrounds framing new shop fronts, and the stone "guardians" often found outside the original gates and doors.

Of course, what is charm to some visitors is merely slum living to others. The historic buildings are often almost invisible beneath

Early morning exercise

improvised lean-tos, with windows knocked through external walls to create the tiny and scantily-stocked shops known as *xiaomaibu*.

A walk around Hou Hai *(see pp100–101)* takes in still standing areas of ancient *hutongs*, some of which are undeniably tatty and some of which have been well renovated. It eventually weaves its way around the Back Lakes and their willow-fringed shores, home to myriad small bars and cafés. Despite the area's popularity it is always possible to step into a small alleyway and, for the time being at least, be immediately transported back into the past. If in places things moulder as they have done for centuries, on the walk around Pudu Si *(pp98–9)* the traditional has been rebuilt from the ground up, and you could cut your finger on the sharp edges of the 20th-century "Ming" brickwork. This walk sandwiches restored *hutongs* between a handful of historical imperial temples and modern-day shopping opportunities.

◁ Playing *mah jong* along the banks of the Hou Hai

A 90-Minute Walk East of the Forbidden City

This walk starts at the Imperial Ancestral Temple, a place often overlooked by visitors to the neighboring Forbidden City. Not far from these grand halls lie courtyard houses rebuilt from scratch (after leveling the originals and inserting an underground car park), which now serve as comfortable homes for officials with a taste for the traditional. The route also takes in the very much unpreserved and unreconstructed *hutong* residences of ordinary Beijingers, whose presence at the very heart of the city is surely unlikely to survive much longer. It ends on pedestrianized Wangfujing, the city's premier shopping street.

CourtYard restaurant ⑦

Tian'an Men, gateway to the Forbidden City ①

Park of the People's Culture

Make your way by subway to Tian'an Men Square. Facing the portrait of Mao that hangs on the **Tian'an Men** ①, turn right and walk east along the Imperial City wall. You soon arrive at an entrance overlooked by almost all. Go through this to the five-bay **Halberd Gate** ② and the Tai Miao, or **Imperial Ancestral Temple** ③, one of the most important in the city. A series of vast halls runs north in mimicry of the main sequence of "Harmony" halls inside the Forbidden City itself. Yet the entire site is usually deserted.

On reaching the canal at the rear of the temple, turn left to exit. This back way in to the complex was opened as a short cut ④ for the Qianlong emperor in his old age. Cross the canal, turn right and follow the dog-leg of the **moat** ⑤ round to the north to reach the **Dong Hua Men** ⑥, or east gate of the Forbidden City (closed to the public).

As you recross the moat by bridge, immediately on the left is the famed restaurant **CourtYard** ⑦ (not open for lunch) and its basement gallery. Although this is an ancient courtyard house, the interior has completely remodeled and internationalized.

Nan Chizi Dajie

Cross over at the first junction and head south down Nan Chizi Dajie. Take the first left into narrow Pudu Si Xi Xiang and follow it round to the right and south for instant relief from traffic noise. There are left turns to explore at whim, but continuing south soon brings you to the magnificent double-eaved hall of the **Mahakala Temple** ⑧, or

KEY

- • • • Walk route
- Ⓜ Subway station

Pudu Si, raised on a mound to the left. Back in the 15th century the temple was the home of a deposed Ming emperor, and later of the man who led Qing troops into Beijing in 1644. It became a lamasery in the 18th century, and housed a famous statue of Mahakala, whose cult the Qing had absorbed from the Mongols. In modern times its halls have echoed with the chanted lessons of primary

Entrance to the little visited Mahakala Temple, or Pudu Si ⑧ school children. The children are now gone, and the once sagging halls have been made shiny and new in preparation for their occupation by the land tax office.

Until recently much of the area around the temple was filled with the ramshackle residences of ordinary people. These have now been totally rebuilt in a reproduction of antiquity and house local government officials. Security guards patrol the alleys, ready to protect the haves from the have-nots.

Continue south down the east side of the underground car park (the west side will also do) looking for **old pillar bases** ⑨ set in the new grey

Children in the Changpu He Park ⑬

walls. At the end turn right into **Duanku Hutong** ⑩, the name of which – Satin Warehouse Alley – reveals the use to which the surrounding buildings were once put. Follow the alley round to the left; the odd surviving shop sign in green and white **Arabic lettering** ⑪ reveals that many in the cloth trade were Muslims. The alley jogs right again to rejoin Nan Chizi Dajie. Resume your progress south and you will encounter the old **Imperial Archive** ⑫ a little farther down on the left. Unfortunately, the main hall, which dates back to 1536, is not open but it is still an impressive complex to wander around. Neighboring halls sell made-for-tourist art that recycles the old clichés.

Da Tian Shui Jing Hutong

Continue south down Nan Chizi and you'll soon come to an area where the ancient housing has recently been removed to create the narrow but pleasant **Changhe Pu Park** ⑬. This park follows the eastward course of the stream that flows in front of the Tian'an Men. Turn left along the stream bank, passing 21st-century **pastiche Qing buildings** ⑭ on the left. The park ends at a main road: cross and head north, then turn right where the bicycle route is indicated. This takes you into **Da Tian Shui Jing Hutong** ⑮ (Big Sweetwater Well Hutong) – Beijing's wells were notoriously brackish and good water would have been worth noting.

For as long as it lasts, this is real *hutong* life, right in the heart of the city. The lane is filled with tiny restaurants advertising Chongqing-style hotpot (very spicy) and noodles, all for real Beijing prices – less than ¥5 per dish. After passing a group of video parlors the alley re-engages with modernity, emerging into **Wangfujing Snack Street** ⑯, a tourist-pleasing food market, where you'll pay five times as much for the same dish as back in the *hutong*.

Turn left to reach the pedestrianized shopping street of **Wangfujing Dajie** ⑰ (see p72), with its fashionable shops with permanent sales, and McDonald's and other imports. Those still with some walking in their legs can then enjoy some shopping.

TIPS FOR WALKERS

Length: 1.8 miles (3 km).
Getting there: Subway to Tian'an Men Dong.
Galleries at the Imperial Archive: Open 10am–noon & 1pm–6pm daily.
Stopping off points: There are Western and Chinese restaurants around the Nan Chizi crossroads near the CourtYard restaurant. In summer, stands around the Imperial Archive offer cold drinks for sale. The restaurants in Da Tian Shui Jing Hutong are grubby, but authentic and cheap. Otherwise, Wangfujing Dajie and its malls sport numerous Western and local fast food outlets and branches of coffee chains, as well as several superior Chinese and international restaurants.

0 kilometers 1

0 miles 0.5

HUAMEN DAJIE
DONG'ANMEN DAJIE
CAICHANG HUTONG
DARUANFU HUTONG
⑰
⑮ DA TIAN SHUI JING HUTONG
NANHEYAN DAJIE
⑯
HUALONG JIE
WANGFUJING DAJIE
XIAGONGFU JIE
CHENGYI LU
Wangfujing Ⓜ

Doorway to a courtyard home in
Duanku Hutong ⑩

A Two-Hour Walk around Hou Hai

Hou Hai (Back Lakes) is a cluster of three linked bodies of water just over a mile or so north of the Forbidden City. They lie at the heart of a district of labyrinthine old *hutongs* (alleys), studded with a handful of monuments of modest grandeur. This walk takes you through areas of mouldering housing to a renovated courtyard dwelling, and past abandoned mansions to one that has been largely preserved. It meanders through an area undergoing revitalization as a lively nightlife hub before winding up at a couple of ancient towers, which you can ascend to look back over the area which you have just explored.

Women exercise beside the lake shore at Hou Hai ⑩

Xinjiekou Bei Dajie
The walk starts at the Circle Line subway station of Jishuitan. Leave by exit C, turn left down Xinjiekou Bei Dajie, cross the road and continue south past **clothing and shoe shops** ①, all with prices far lower than home. The building set back from the road with a sign on top in green characters, is the **Xu Beihong Memorial Hall** ②. This is worth a look in for the lively watercolors

Xu Beihong statue ②

of horses that made Xu (1885–1953) internationally famous.
  Continue on south past lots more small shops and cross back to the east side of the road at the traffic signals. Note the **model shop** ③ on the corner of Hangkong Hutong with large supplies of hard to obtain plastic kits at cheap prices. Walk on past electric guitar shops and jewelers to take the next left turning but one into **Bai Hua Shen Chu** ④. The name

means "in the depths of many flowers," a reference to a time when the *hutong* was famous for its hothouses, which had carefully ducted steam to ensure that the flowers bloomed just in time for the major festivals and temple fairs. One of the biggest such fairs used to be held at the **Protect the Nation Temple** ⑤, or Huguo Si. Take the first right into Huguo Si Xi Xiang which leads down past ramshackle housing to the temple's sole surviving hall. This was formerly the home of a Yuan dynasty prince, banished for treason in 1355; it was turned into a temple a decade later. The institution was funded by imperial eunuchs and doubled as a retirement home for them. These haunting remains represent the sad state of historic conservation in Beijing: abandonment leading to eventual ruin.

Huguo Si Jie
At the bottom end of Huguo Si Xi Xiang turn left onto the busier main road of Huguo Si Jie. You pass take-away snack shops, vegetable and meat vendors, the odd internet café, and an art shop, before coming to the **Mei Lanfang Memorial Hall** ⑥. This is a traditional *siheyuan* (courtyard house) in a fine state of preservation, which shows what can be done with old Beijing when tourism income is anticipated. This was the home of Beijing Opera's greatest performer (1894–1961), *see pp30–31*. The rear rooms have been left with

Street entrance to the Mei Lanfang Memorial Hall ⑥

For hotels and restaurants in Beijing see pp178–82 and pp198–202

their traditional furniture, exactly as they were when Mei died. Other rooms contain hagiographic accounts of his life, diagrams of the stylized movements required by the form, and a video of Mei, already 61, but still playing the young girl roles for which he was famous.

Crossing the next junction, which is with busy Desheng Men Nei Dajie, look in the next gate on the left for a glimpse of part of a former **princely mansion** ⑦, which has not fared as well as Mei Lanfang's residence. Continue east, cross Songshu Jie, and

The Silver Ingot Bridge between Hou Hai and Qian Hai ⑪

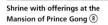

Shrine with offerings at the Mansion of Prince Gong ⑧

KEY

• • • Walk route

Ⓜ Subway station

turn left along the outer wall of the **Mansion of Prince Gong** ⑧ *(see p68)*. It is worth making time for a look around this extensive former royal residence with its beautiful gardens. The sad fact is that this is the last intact house of its kind in an area that once held several similarly grand mansions.

The Back Lakes
On exiting Prince Gong's mansion turn right and follow the compound wall around to the right and into **Da Xiang Feng Hutong** ⑨, looking for drum stones, carved panels, and door guardians adorning the fronts of the old houses. Just before the end of the *hutong* you'll catch a glimpse of the waters of **Hou Hai** ⑩ down a narrow left turn: head this way. You now hit tourist territory. The shores of the lake are hugely popular with both foreign visitors and locals and are lined with ersatz Western bars and restaurants. The hub of all activity is the bottleneck of the **Silver Ingot Bridge** ⑪, which arches over the narrow channel between the Hou Hai and Qian Hai, and gives modestly pretty views in two directions.

Once over the bridge go straight ahead and jink left then right into **Yandai Xiejie** ⑫, a terrifically vibrant small street with corner street-food sellers and an odd mix of gift

shops and bars mixed in with the practical, such as a bicycle repair shop. Look up for glimpses of finely carved wood here and there that belongs to ancient façades to which modern shop fronts have been attached. There is a former bathhouse here that's now a boutique and a temple that's now a café.

Turn left at the end onto main Di'an Men Wai Dajie, to see the **Drum Tower** ⑬ rearing up ahead; the **Bell Tower** ⑭ is just behind. The balconies of both give views back across the labyrinth you've just navigated.

TIPS FOR WALKERS

Length: 2.5 miles (4 km).
Getting there: Subway to Jishuitan.
Xu Beihong Memorial Hall: Open 9am–4pm Tues–Sun.
Mei Lanfang Memorial Hall: Open 9am–4pm Tues–Sun, but closed for a month in Jan–Feb.
Mansion of Prince Gong: Open 8:30am–4:30pm daily.
Bell Tower and Drum Tower: Open 9am–5pm daily.
Stopping off points: After turning left onto Huguo Si Jie, turn right at the next crossroads down Hucang Hutong, to find Jing Wei Lou on the right at the corner with the major avenue, Ping'an Da Dao. This is a bustling restaurant with a picture menu of dishes. Just before the entrance to Prince Gong's Mansion is Sichuan Fandian, one of Beijing's oldest restaurants, serving excellent fiery Sichuan food. Some bars along the lake shore offer dishes that faintly resemble the Western foods for which they are named.

SHOPPING IN BEIJING

From what is for now the world's second biggest shopping mall (the biggest is also in China) to thriving street markets where everything from counterfeit designer goods to reproduction antiques can be found, there is almost nothing you can't buy in Beijing. A new Ferrari? There has been a dealership in Beijing since 1994. Tiffany, the New York jeweler, opened its first branch in the city in 2001. But as with the likes of Japanese electronics and Swiss watches, severe import duties ensure these foreign products all cost substantially more than they would at home. Beijing should not be mistaken for the duty-free haven Hong Kong.

Chairman Mao lighter

Traditionally Wangfujing Dajie and its side turnings are the heart of Beijing's shopping, along with the more downmarket Dong Dan Bei Jie, which is parallel one block to the east. But Beijing's historic symmetry means there's a similar concentration west of the Forbidden City at Xi Dan. There are also department stores and markets scattered throughout the city's residential quarters, many with far better prices than the central locations.

SHOPPING ETIQUETTE

The frantic sanitization of Beijing has removed many of the traditional small side-street markets, and has driven all the better-known larger markets under the cover of purpose-built sites. If you do come across any surviving street markets on your travels – you may still encounter them in residential areas – then they are always worth browsing for cheap prices.

Always bargain hard, not just at markets, but also at supposedly fixed price shops too, just as the Chinese do. Beijing's economy is more fragile than it looks, and malls and stores attract far more window shoppers than big free spenders.

Wherever you go, shop with caution. If you are told that something is supposedly old, rare, or intrinsically

Caged birds for sale at a traditional Beijing street market

Stallholder selling silks and fabrics at Hong Qiao Market

expensive, it is most likely a fake. China is not the place to shop for valuable antiques, gems, or jewelry (including jade and pearls) unless you really are an expert. Nothing with an internationally traded value can be bought cheaply in either Beijing or Shanghai. Famous brand-name goods, from Louis Vuitton bags and Calvin Klein apparel to Apple iPods, are all commonly faked. At the very least with high-value locally-made items like carpets, considerable time should first be spent visiting carpet dealers and learning about quality, manufacturing methods, and prices.

At the end of the day if you like the item and it seems a reasonable deal to you, go ahead and buy it, but don't assume you have got a real bargain or something of great value cheaply.

ANTIQUES, CRAFTS, AND CURIOS

Genuine antiques are almost impossible to find, and all purchases should be made on the assumption that what is being bought is fake. Objects dating between 1939 and 1795 cannot officially be taken out of the country without a certificate, something any honest dealer with a genuinely ancient item would help you to acquire. Anything older may not be exported at all. The most interesting market for so-called antiques and curios is **Panjiayuan Market** in the southeast of town but even vendors admit that 80 percent of what is on sale is fake. However, there is nowhere better to do all your gift shopping in one go, although you may find yourself hoarse by the end of the day from bargaining for items such as Russian optical equipment, gramophones, stuffed deer heads, framed calligraphy, and bamboo-and-bone *mah jong* sets. Even for anybody who doesn't like shopping, Panjiayuan is worth visiting as a sight in its own right. Neighboring **Beijing Curio City** also has a vast array of ceramics, furniture, jewelry, and Tibetan art on several floors, although authenticity is equally suspect.

The large **Hong Qiao Market** near the Temple of Heaven has an odd range of clothing, souvenirs, and low quality (or fake) pearls up on the third and fourth floors. The **Friendship Store** on Jianguo Men Wai Dajie also has traditional craft objects, as well as everything else under the Chinese sun.

Visitors could spend a few hours browsing through the pleasant little shops of **Liulichang** *(see p61)*, which specialize in lacquerware, ceramics, paintings, and assorted crafts. China has a long tradition of making excellent furniture and **Huayi Classical Furniture** sells classical antique, restored, and reproduction furniture, some of which, at least, is clearly marked as being what it is.

Perhaps the most unusual curios are those connected with Beijing's four traditional pastimes of flowers, birds, fish, and insects *(hua, niao, yu, chong)*. While the animals can not be exported to your

Curios and reproduction antique furniture at Panjiayuan Market

home country, some of the associated paraphernalia – ornate bird cages, tiny feeding dishes, gourd homes for insects, and perhaps even tapes for teaching your mynah Mandarin – will certainly make excellent conversation pieces and are genuine souvenirs of Beijing. Even for those who don't do shopping, the **Huasheng Tian Qiao Market** offers a compelling aural and visual feast, as the chirrups and clicks of the insects compete with the wider ranging whistles of the birds. A similar experience can be had at the considerably smaller **Guanyuan Market**, a short walk north of Fucheng Men subway station on the west side of the Second Ring Road.

ART AND CALLIGRAPHY

Paintings done in traditional styles and of traditional subjects can be found at all curio markets and souvenir shops, and hundreds if not thousands of copies will be painted of anything foreigners find appealing. Modern painting in Western styles also tends to choose tourist-pleasing subject matter, attaching prices that show an

understanding of Western art markets – although such pieces could rarely be sold on for anything like the same price outside of China. There is tourist kitsch aplenty at the galleries in the **Imperial Archive** *(see p99)*; for more serious efforts, but still often conscious of Western preferences and beliefs about China, try the **Red Gate Gallery** *(see p73)*, the **CourtYard Gallery**, attached to the restaurant of the same name, and the small gallery at the **Green T. House**. Serious art shoppers should consider spending half a day visiting the dozens of artists' studios and galleries that make up the **798 Art District** *(see p85)*. Prices will be prohibitive to all but the most committed and deep-pocketed of collectors, but there is no charge for looking.

BOOKS

Take your own reading material when traveling to China, as the choice of imported and English-language fiction in Beijing is limited to say the least. The best selection is on the top floor at the **Foreign Languages Bookshop** on Wangfujing. On the other hand, English books on cultural and travel topics, as well as coffee-table photography books on Chinese themes, although often marked-up in price for the foreign market, are plentiful. The Foreign Languages Bookshop, **Wangfujing Bookshop**, and Beijing's largest bookshop the **Tushu Dasha** have selections, but specialist art bookshops can also be found in and around the **National Art Museum of China** *(see p72)*. For even more art books try **Timezone 8** in the 798 Art District area.

Hanging scroll painted with elegant script

Traditional-style painting on parchment – a popular souvenir

Detail from a traditional embroidered men's robe

CARPETS, TEXTILES, AND CLOTHING

Beijing's markets sell a variety of carpets from Tibet, Gansu, and Xinjiang. Try the **Qian Men Carpet Company**, which has antique, imitation antique, and new carpets for sale. It also arranges shipping. The **Beijing Silk Store** is the best starting point for silk and related fabrics at local prices. Tour groups are often taken to the popular **Yuanlong Silk Corporation**,

Modern decorative beaded purse

which has fabrics and a large selection of ready-made silk garments. What is known as the **Xiushui Silk Market**, is in fact almost entirely free of silk – its four floors of vendors mostly stock counterfeit designer goods at prices that indicate they know the ignorance of foreign shoppers. None of this stops it from reportedly being one of the city's biggest tourist attractions after the Forbidden City and Great Wall. Sanlitun's **Yaxiu Market** (sometimes written Yashow) also has four floors of clothes, fabric, and curios, plus a tailoring services for those who want a figure-hugging *qipao* (*cheongsam*).

For unique clothes by local designers, try **Na Li Market**, off Sanlitun's "Bar Street," and the neighboring, new **San Dian San (3.3)** fashion mall, both of which are home to numerous small, independent boutiques.

DEPARTMENT STORES AND SHOPPING MALLS

Wangfujing's two monster malls, **Oriental Plaza** and **Sun Dong'an Plaza** get most attention from visitors. Of the two, the Oriental Plaza is by far the more upscale. It boasts a glittering array of international names, from Paul Smith and Armani to an Apple computer store. The basement level has a large Watson's pharmacy, a supermarket, and an excellent Southeast Asian-style food court. There are also some surprisingly classy dining options including a branch of the excellent South Beauty chain, which specializes in Sichuan cuisine. At the Sun Dong'an, which is further north, the most accessible levels hold international fashion stores mixed in with branches of Hong Kong-originating retailers. Reasonable prices for clothing and shoes are to be found, although often only in sizes for the elfin. Tea, sweets and just about everything else from China is down in the basement, while the top floor hosts lots of cheap restaurants and a modern multi-screen cinema.

ELECTRONICS

Despite what you might think, China is not a good source of cheap electronics. If the equipment is imported then it is going to be much more expensive than in the West; if it is locally made then it usually comes with a Chinese operating system, pirated software, and a guarantee that is no use outside China. However, China is excellent value for accessories such as cables and converters, and media such as blank CDs, MDs, and DVDs. Zhongguang Cun in the northwest district of Haidian is the main place for all such things, but it is a long way to travel. A better option is the **Bai Nao Hui** computer market, which is conveniently central. Anywhere tourists go to shop or play, vendors will be found with fake DVDs of Hollywood movies. Setting aside legal issues, copies may be of foreign language versions with no English option, subtitles may be for a different film altogether, the disc may stop playing partway through, and copies of recent titles will have been made by placing a camera at the back of a cinema auditorium. The authorities in China keep making noises that they will crack down on

Wangfujing Dajie, Beijing's modern, mall-lined main shopping street

this piracy, and occasionally there are arrests and fines. But it is such a big industry and there is such a gap between the cost of legitimate goods and the average wage in China that the trade will be impossible to stamp out completely. At around as little as US$1 per disk, pirated DVDs are understandably still very popular.

TEA

Malian Dao Lu has all the teas in China, available from endless rows of tiny shops on either side of the street, and from the four stories of the **Malian Dao Cha Cheng** with dozens of stalls. Rare and expensive teas should be

Chinese children's kite

avoided unless you're an expert, but few foreigners come here, and most stalls have thimble-sized cups to give you a taste. Packaging is

often very attractive, and bricks of the cheapest tea, pounded into a mould with an assortment of patterns, make attractive if slightly heavy souvenirs.

TOYS

You can find everything from the Chinese edition of Monopoly to Gameboys, jigsaw puzzles, and radio-controlled cars, all at bargain prices under one roof at the **Hong Qiao Toy City**. Children's shoes, clothing, and more toys can be found in most department stores and at the **New China Children's World** on Wangfujing Dajie, with several floors of nothing but goods for tots to teens.

DIRECTORY

ANTIQUES, CRAFTS, AND CURIOS

Beijing Curio City
21 Dongsanhuan Nan Lu.
Tel (010) 6773 6098.

Friendship Store
17 Jianguo Men Wai Dajie.
Map 3 E5.
Tel (010) 6500 3311.

Guanyuan Market
Fucheng Men Bei Dajie.
Map 1 D3.

Hong Qiao Market
16 Hong Qiao Lu.
Map 5 E3.
Tel (010) 6711 7429.

Huasheng Tian Qiao Market
E of Shili He Bridge.

Huayi Classical Furniture
89 Xiaodian Dongwei Lu.
Tel (010) 8431 1836.

Panjiayuan Market
Panjiayuan Lu, off Dongsanhuan Nan Lu.

ART AND CALLIGRAPHY

CourtYard Gallery
95 Donghua Men Dajie.
Map 2 B5.
Tel (010) 6526 8882.

Green T. House
6 Gongren Tiyuchang Xi Lu, by west gate of

Workers' Stadium.
Map 3 E3.
Tel (010) 6552 8310.

Imperial Archive
Nan Chizi Dajie.
Map 2 B5.

Red Gate Gallery
Southeast Corner Watch-tower, off Jianguo Men Nan Dajie.
Map 5 F2.
Tel (010) 6525 1005.

798 Art District
2–4 Jiuxian Qiao Lu, Da Shan Zi.

BOOKS

Foreign Languages Bookshop
235 Wangfujing Dajie.
Map 2 B5.
Tel (010) 6512 6917.

National Art Museum of China
1 Wusi Dajie.
Map 2 B4.
Tel (010) 6400 1476.

Timezone 8
798 Art District, 4 Jiu Xian Qiao Lu.
www.timezone8.com

Tushu Dasha
17 Xi Chang'an Jie.
Map 4 B1.
Tel (010) 6607 8459.
www.bjbb.com.cn

Wangfujing Bookshop
Wangfujing Dajie.
Map 2 B5.
Tel (010) 6602 2589.

CARPETS, TEXTILES, AND CLOTHING

Beijing Silk Store
5 Zhubaoshi, off Qian Men Dajie.
Map 4 C2.
Tel (010) 6301 6658.

Na Li Market
Off Sanlitun Bei Lu.
Map 3 F3.

Qian Men Carpet Company
44 Xingfu Dajie.
Map 5 F3.
Tel (010) 6715 1687.

San Dian San (3.3)
33 Sanlitun Bei Lu.
Map 3 F3.
Tel (010) 6417 3333.

Xiushui Silk Market
Xiushui Dong Jie.
Map 3 E5.

Yaxiu Market,
58 Gongren Tiyuchang Bei Lu.
Map 3 F3.

Yuanlong Silk Corporation
15 Yongding Men Dong Jie.
Map 5 D4.
Tel (010) 6702 4059.

DEPARTMENT STORES AND MALLS

Oriental Plaza
1 Dong Chang'an Jie.
Map 2 B5.

Sun Dong'an Plaza
138 Wangfujing Dajie.
Map 2 B5.

ELECTRONICS

Bai Nao Hui
Chaoyang Men Wai Dajie.
Map 3 E4.

TEA

Malian Dao Cha Cheng
11 Malian Dao Lu.
Map 4 C2.
Tel (010) 6346 1811.

TOYS

Toy City
See Hong Qiao Market.

New China Children's Toy World
168 Wangfujing Dajie.
Map 2 B5.
Tel (010) 6512 0566.

ENTERTAINMENT IN BEIJING

Literary and cultured, but still too much under the thumb of a highly conservative government to be truly progressive, Beijing nevertheless offers entertainment that includes the tourist-pleasing, the traditional, and the reasonably recherché. This is, of course, the home of the world famous Beijing Opera, which continues to be performed at venues across the city on a nightly basis, although the majority of these shows cater for foreign visitors. The

Lurid Beijing cocktails

same is true of the various acrobatic performances. The rock and pop scene, on the other hand, is vibrant and wholly targeted at a young, local audience. Performing arts in general have received a shot in the arm thanks to the new National Theater. This vast, mercury bubble of a building, controversially designed by French architect Paul Andreu and opened in 2006, is worth a visit for the spectacle of the structure itself, regardless of the entertainment within.

PRACTICAL INFORMATION

For details of performances – from large-scale stadium rock concerts to dance troupes appearing on handkerchief-sized stages – see the listings in the expat-produced listings magazines such as *Beijing Talk, that's Beijing* and *Time Out Beijing*. These are available free in hotel lobbies and at many restaurants and bars. Only these weekly and monthly publications can hope to keep up with frantic schedules, rapid changes in fashion, and the may-fly existence of some venues that close almost as soon as they've opened.

Tickets are generally bought at the venue box offices and paid for in cash. At small music clubs, pay on the door. Most hotel concierges can usually help in securing seats.

The chinoiserie trappings of the World of Suzie Wong

One of the great number of Sanlitun "Bar Street" venues

BARS AND CLUBS

Sanlitun is the one district that all Beijing expats know intimately. Sanlitun Bei Lu, also known as "Bar Street" is lined with drinking dens, although the better bars are actually in the side streets, including long-standing favorite **The Tree**, which marries draught beer with wood-fired pizza.

A more picturesque alternative for a night out is the eastern shore of Hou Hai, where new bars and cafés are springing up all the time. Pick of the bunch is the under-stated and wholly original **No Name Bar**, which was the first bar to open in the area. It benefits from a wonderful waterside site just south of the Silver Ingot Bridge.

Across the lake on the western shore is Lotus Lane, which is a developer's

attempt to recreate Sanlitun, but the bars and clubs here are a little tawdry and suffer from a lack of inspiration. Instead, head north and east into the *hutongs*. Nearby Nan Luogu Xiang (South Drum and Gong Alley), just east of Hou Hai, has several attractive bars, including notably the **Pass By Café**, which also acts as a restaurant and book lending library, and has a charming courtyard.

Farther north, a couple of alleys up past the Bell Tower, **Bed Tapas and Bar** is a multi-courtyarded venue whose labyrinth of rooms is filled with Chinese-style four-posters and other beds. It is a wonderful fusion of the hip and the traditional, and delivers a truly Beijing-style bar experience. Similarly, the **World of Suzie Wong**, over in the east of town at Chaoyang Park, which employs padded and cushioned alcoves for a hint of Shanghai-style opium den chic. Also worth a look are **Souk**, another bar with beds, plus a pleasant court-yard, which is just a few doors away from Suzy Wong, and the **Stone Boat**, a small pub that "floats" in a corner of the Ri Tan Park lake.

Beer in a local bar can cost as little as ¥3, but in foreigner-frequented venues it will more commonly be anything from ¥15–¥30. You also pay inflated prices for imported pleasures such as cocktails, particularly if you take them in foreign-run places where they are done best, such as the currently fashionable **Centro** at the Kerry Center Hotel (whose deep-pocketed customers consume more Moët et Chandon between them than those of any other mainland venue, and go there to be seen doing it), the China World Hotel's woody **Aria** with its potent apple martinis, and the soothing sofa-filled **Red Moon** at the Grand Hyatt.

Night clubs tend to be derivative of the Western experience to the point where famous-name DJs are regularly imported to spin exactly what they spin elsewhere. Fashions come and go rapidly, but despite the occasional change of location **Banana** seems to have staying power, complete with waitresses in purple wigs, and tiers of glass-walled seating looking down on the rather small dance floor.

BEIJING OPERA

For most non-Chinese, Beijing Opera *(see pp30–31)* is a taste not easily acquired. Incomprehensible plots, unfamiliar sounds, and performances lasting up to three hours can make for uncomfortable viewing. However, there's no denying the acrobatic ability and dramatic splendor of the event, so everyone should try it once. Performances are best seen in the splendid Ming-dynasty **Zhengyici Theater** or Qing-dynasty **Huguang Guildhall**. During the warmer months, there are evening shows at the **Mansion of Prince Gong** *(see p68)* at 7:30pm. Given the choice, you should opt for any of these over the **Liyuan Theater** in the Qian Men Hotel, which is where tour groups are taken.

Beijing Opera star

CINEMA

Government-imposed restrictions mean that cinemas show a very limited number of imported English-language films. Instead try **Cherry Lane Movies** (www.cherrylanemovies.com.cn), an independent cinema club, where Chinese films and documentaries are shown with English subtitles on Friday and Saturday nights.

As the numbers of private cars grows, one entrepreneur has revived an institution almost completely forgotten in the West – the drive-in

Beijing Opera – difficult to follow, but the color is dazzling

movie. Unfortunately hiring a vehicle is likely to cost rather more than the tickets, and the presence of the driver might be a little off-putting. The **Feng Hua Yuan Drive-in** is also occasionally used for rock concerts during the summer, with no car required.

CLASSICAL CONCERTS

Take the chance to see and hear a Chinese orchestra, if at all possible. Sections of unfamiliar plucked string, bowed string, woodwind, and percussion instruments compete for attention in swirling arrangements.

The new **Beijing National Grand Theater**, just one block west of Tian'an Men Square, is a spectacular multi-purpose venue that puts on classical concerts, ballet, and opera, as well as providing space for art exhibitions. Its central location and impressive architecture alone certainly merit a visit.

Beijing National Grand Theater – or, as it is more commonly known, "the Egg"

Popstars performing an outdoor concert in Beijing

ROCK AND POP

The question of which city has the best tunes provokes regular shouting matches between the youth of Beijing and Shanghai, but there is no argument really: Beijing wins.

Beijing-based Cui Jian, the Bob Dylan-like old man of Chinese rock, became the first famous indigenous name in rock with his protest songs, including "Nothing to My Name," with its references to the events in Tian'an Men Square of June 1989. As a result he was forbidden to play large venues until 2006.

But the once lone voice of rock is now drowned out by the innumerable punk bands for which Beijing is famous, and Chinese versions of just about any kind of popular music you can think of. Most of the new generation think Cui Jian should retire, although he played small venues across North America in 2005, and was the support act for the Rolling Stones when they played Shanghai for the first time in 2006.

Many Chinese rock and pop musicians take Western music genres as a starting point, on to which they then overlay Chinese characteristics. Singing in Mandarin isn't enough: they will also perhaps add an electrified *erhu (see p31)* to the line-up, or use vocal styles from Chinese opera. The results range from appalling to appealing, but there's no lack of talent and enthusiasm. More than a few names would probably find some sort of following in the West if only they sang in English.

Sanlitun's **Workers' Stadium** is the usual venue for large-scale rock, filled regularly by Taiwanese and Hong Kong stars, but also by a few mainland pan-Asia mega-stars such as the infinitely talented Wang Fei (Faye Wong to her Cantonese-speaking fans). Tickets are always hard to get, and there is always a thriving trade for them on the black market.

Among the many smaller venues for live music, all with rosters of rock, blues, jazz, punk, and anything else that seems likely to bring in the masses, the **Yu Gong Yi Shan** bar is the current favourite for its cheap drinks and eclectic programing policy.

TEAHOUSES

China's long history of growing and drinking tea has led to considerable refinement in its production, preparation, and serving. A very elaborate tea ceremony may include the use of a sniffing cup into which a small amount of tea is poured and then emptied before the residual aroma is savored. In fact, most ceremonies involve a lot of filling and spilling, or tipping away – the aim is to provide a good number of exquisitely small cups of perfect tea, all at the same strength, from one pot of tea leaves. Teahouses such as the **Purple Vine** near the west gate of the Forbidden City, offer calm interiors with antique furnishings, and a respite from the city's bedlam. The **Xi Hua Yuan Teahouse**, which is across the street from Purple Vine, adds a Chinese-speaking mynah bird to the attractions. The **Confucian Teahouse**, which is across the lane from the Confucian Temple, is known for its particularly fine décor.

At such establishments the prices of various teas are clearly given on a menu, and a demonstration of the traditional preparation of tea is included in the cost of the more expensive ones.

Watch out for English-speaking Chinese who strike up conversations at tourist sites. Sometimes the visitor is asked whether they have ever seen a Chinese tea ceremony? A short walk to a tucked-away teahouse, and a few samples of tea later, a bill that is the equivalent of well over a hundred US dollars or more is presented. Your new Chinese friends will profess to be horrified, as they had no idea it would be so expensive, but of course they are party to the con.

The elaborate art of tea drinking

PUPPET THEATER AND ACROBATICS

When it comes to theater, language truly is a barrier. However, there is always traditional Chinese puppet theater. Plays with wooden puppets (*mu'ouxi*) involve elaborate and colorfully dressed marionettes. The fun is as much in admiring the craftsmanship and dexterity as attempting to work out the plot; see what's on at the **China Puppet Art Theater**.

Enterprising entrepreneurs have also put together performances of "teahouse art," which may include acrobatics, story-telling, singers, jugglers, and short

Chinese acrobatic troupe performing with bicycles

extracts from Beijing Opera. These bite-sized cultural morsels are usually served in recreated period atmosphere

with tea and a meal. Try the **Lao She Teahouse** (which has shows at 7:50pm daily), just south of Tian'an Men Square, and the **Tian Qiao Happy Teahouse**.

China has a worldwide reputation for its gymnasts who perform breathtaking routines that showcase their unnerving flexibility. Displays of balance often involve props such as chairs and plates, with one of the most popular tricks being to pile 20 or so acrobats on a bicycle. Venues include the **Chaoyang Theater** and **Tiandi Theater**, both with nightly shows, and occasionally the **Poly Theater**. All of these theaters are in the eastern district of Sanlitun.

DIRECTORY

BARS & CLUBS

Aria
China World Hotel,
1 Jianguo Men Wai Dajie.
Map 3 F5.
Tel (010) 6505 2266.

Banana
Scitech Hotel, 22 Jianguo
Men Wai Dajie.
Map 3 F5.
Tel (010) 6528 3636.

Bed Tapas and Bar
17 Zhangwang Hutong,
off Jiu Gulou Dajie.
Map 2 A2.
Tel (010) 8400 1554.

Centro
Kerry Center Hotel,
1 Guanghua Lu.
Map 3 F5.
Tel (010) 6561 8833.

No Name Bar
Qianhai Dong Yan, S. of
Silver Ingot Bridge.
Map 2 A2.
Tel (010) 6401 8541.

Pass By Café
108 Nan Luogu Xiang, off
Di'an Men Dong Dajie.
Map 2 B2.
Tel (010) 8403 8004.

Red Moon
Grand Hyatt Hotel,
Oriental Plaza, 1 Dong
Chang'an Jie.
Map 2 B5.
Tel (010) 6510 9366.

Souk
West gate of Chaoyang
Park, behind Annie's
restaurant.
Tel (010) 6506 7309.

Stone Boat
Southwest corner of
Ri Tan Park.
Map 3 E5.
Tel (010) 6501 9986.

The Tree
43 Sanlitun Bei Lu, behind
Poachers Inn.
Map 3 F3.
Tel (010) 6415 1954.

World of Suzie Wong
West gate of Chaoyang
Park.
Tel (010) 6593 7889.

Yu Gong Yi Shan
Gongren Tiyucheng Bei
Lu, opposite N. gate of
Workers' Stadium
Map 3 E3.
Tel (010) 6415 0687.

BEIJING OPERA

Huguang Guildhall
3 Hufang Lu.
Map 4 B3.
Tel (010) 6351 8284.

Mansion of Prince Gong
14 Liuyin Jie, off Hou Hai
Nan Yan.
Map 2 A2.
Tel (010) 6616 8149.

Zhengyici Theater
220 Xiheyan Dajie.
Map 4 B2.
Tel (010) 8315 1649.

CINEMA

Cherry Lane Movies
E. of 21st Century Theater,
Liang Ma Qiao Lu.
Tel (0139) 0113 4745.

Feng Hua Yuan Drive-in Cinema
East of Yansha Bridge,
East Third Ring Road.
Tel (010) 6432 9884.

MUSIC

National Grand Theater
Xi Chang'an Jie, W. of
Great Hall of the People.
Map 4 C1.
Tel (010) 6606 4705.

Workers' Stadium
Gongren Tiyuchang Bei Lu.
Map 3 E3.
Tel (010) 6501 6655.

TEAHOUSES

Confucian Teahouse
28 Guozi Jian Lu, off
Yonghe Gong Dajie.
Map 2 C2.
Tel (010) 8404 8539.

Purple Vine
2 Nan Chang Jie.
Map 2 A5.
Tel (010) 6606 6614.

Xi Hua Yuan Teahouse
Bei Chang Jie, across from
the west gate of the
Forbidden City.
Map 2 A5.
Tel (010) 6603 8534.

PUPPET THEATER AND ACROBATICS

Chaoyang Theater
36 Dongsanhuan Bei Lu.
Map 3 F4.
Tel (010) 6506 8849.

China Puppet Art Theater
A1 Anhua Xi Li.
Tel (010) 6424 3698.

Lao She Teahouse
3 Qian Men Xi Dajie.
Map 4 C2.
Tel (010) 6301 7454.

Poly Theater
Poly Plaza, 14 Dong Zhi
Men Nan Dajie.
Map 3 D3.
Tel (010) 6500 1188.

Tiandi Theater
10 Dong Zhi Men Nan
Dajie.
Map 3 D3.
Tel (010) 6416 9893.

Tian Qiao Happy Teahouse
1 Bei Wei Lu.
Map 4 C3.
Tel (010) 6304 0617.

BEIJING STREET FINDER

The map references given with all sights, hotels, restaurants, shops, and entertainment venues described in this chapter refer to the following maps. The first figure of the map reference indicates which map to turn to, and the letter and number that follow are the grid reference. The key map below shows which parts of Beijing's city center are covered in this Street Finder. A complete index of street names follows the maps. Note that there are different ways of presenting Chinese names, so, for example, the main street Jianguo Men Nai Dajie might appear on signs in Beijing as Jianguomennai Dajie. For more on street names see page 168. Modern Beijing has extended a long way beyond the main city center zone depicted below and outlying areas are shown on the Beijing Farther Afield map on page 87.

KEY TO STREET FINDER

▣	Major sight	ℹ	Tourist information
▣	Place of interest	✚	Hospital
▢	Other important building	⊠	Post office
▤	Train station	▥	Temple
▤	Long-distance bus station	✝	Church
Ⓜ	Subway station	Ⓒ	Mosque
▥	City bus station		

SCALE OF MAP ABOVE

0 kilometers   2

0 miles   2

SCALE OF MAPS 1–5

0 meters   500

0 yards   500

Beijing Street Finder Index

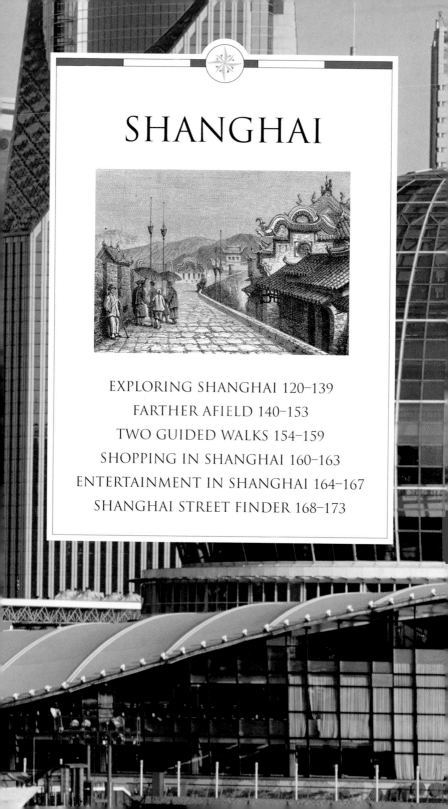

SHANGHAI

Exploring Shanghai

Shanghai has three main areas of interest to the visitor. The Old City is typically Chinese, with alleys, markets, and temples. It is also home to the very lovely Yu Gardens (Yu Yuan). The former concession areas, once under the direct rule of the French, British and Americans, boast the Bund, the riverside avenue lined with grand colonial buildings, as well as the city's two main shopping streets, Nanjing Lu and Huaihai Lu. Pudong, Shanghai's newest district, on the Huangpu's east bank, is an immense business zone, with a clutch of museums and some of the highest buildings in the world.

LOCATOR MAP

SEE ALSO

• *Where to Stay* pp182–7

• *Where to Eat* pp202–7

SIGHTS AT A GLANCE

Historic Buildings, Sites, and Neighborhoods
The Bund pp122–3 ❶
Bund Sightseeing Tunnel ❷
French Concession ❽
Jinmao Tower ❶
Longhua Cemetery
of Martyrs ❷
Nanjing Lu ❷
Oriental Pearl TV Tower ❶
Shanghai Exhibition Center ❾
Site of the First National
Congress of the Chinese
Communist Party ❻
Song Qingling's Former
Residence ❶

Temples and Churches
Jade Buddha Temple ❶
Jing'an Temple ❶
Xujiahui Catholic Cathedral ❶

Parks and Gardens
Century Square ❶
Fuxing Park ❼
Hongkou Park ❶
People's Park & Square ❸
*Yu Gardens & Bazaar
pp130–31* ❺

Museums
Shanghai Museum pp126–9 ❹
Shanghai Ocean Aquarium ❶

Towns
Song Jiang ❷

Areas of Natural Beauty
She Shan ❷

KEY

▨	Street-by-Street area: *see pp130–31*
✕	Domestic airport
✈	International airport
🚊	Train station
Ⓜ	Subway station
🚌	Bus terminus
⛴	Ferry terminal
⛴	Riverboat pier
ℹ	Tourist information
✚	Hospital
⊠	Post office
✝	Church
═	National highway
▬	Major road
—	Railroad

GETTING AROUND

The subway is the best way to get around Shanghai. At the time of writing there are three lines but the network is rapidly expanding *(see pp226–7)*. Taxis are also convenient, cheap, and plentiful. Buses tend to be extremely crowded and slow due to traffic congestion, especially during the morning and evening rush hours. A road tunnel links the east and west banks of the Huangpu River but it's more fun to take a ferry.

GREATER SHANGHAI

SHANGHAI-NANJING EXPRESSWAY

Hongqiao Airport

Huangdu

Pudong International Airport

Pudong

17
18
19
20
16

Qingpu

Xinzhuang

Zhou

21

Wujing

Huangpu

SHANGHAI-HANGZHOU EXPRESSWAY

22

Minhang

The Bund ❶
外滩

Lion, symbol of colonial power

Some places are forever associated with a single landmark and in the case of Shanghai it is surely the Bund. Also known as Zhongshan Lu, the Bund was at the heart of colonial Shanghai, flanked on one side by the Huangpu River and on the other by the hotels, banks, offices, and clubs that were the grandiose symbols of western commercial power. Most of the old buildings are still in place and a walk along here can easily absorb a couple of pleasant hours.

The Bund, at its peak the third biggest financial center in world

★ Hong Kong & Shanghai Bank
Built in 1921, it was vaunted to be the most beautiful building in Asia. Inside there are some delightful restored murals.

Customs House
The entrance hall is decorated with some handsome marine mosaics.

The bronze lions' paws and head are rubbed for good luck.

Russo-Asiatic Bank Building

Former Bank of Communications

★ River promenade
On the river side of the Bund is a wide pavement, a wonderful place for watching the river traffic and, in the early morning, locals practising tai ji quan (tai chi).

STAR SIGHTS

★ River promenade

★ Hong Kong & Shanghai Bank

★ Peace Hotel

★ Views of Pudong

For hotels and restaurants in Shanghai see pp182–7 and pp202–7

★ Peace Hotel
The most distinctive building on the Bund was built in 1930 by the millionaire, Sir Victor Sassoon. Something of a pre-war atmosphere lingers in the form of its Old Jazz Band.

Bank of China
Blending 1920s American and traditional Chinese styles, this impressive block was built by a rival of Sassoon, H.H. Kung.

Former Palace Hotel
The Palace Hotel was built in 1906 and was for a long time one of the best hotels in Shanghai until it became part of the Peace Hotel in 1949.

Chartered Bank Building of India, Australia, and China.

Former Bank of Taiwan

North China Daily News Building

★ Views of Pudong
In the evening the Bund throngs with people enjoying the river breeze and the spectacular lights of Pudong's modern skyline.

Chen Yi's statue
The bronze statue looking down the Bund is not Chairman Mao but Chen Yi, revolutionary commander and first mayor of Shanghai after 1949.

Nanjing Lu ❷
南京路

Map 1 D3/E3/F2 & 2 A2/B2/C2. Ⓜ
Henan Zhong Lu (for Nanjing Dong Lu), Shimen Yi Lu (for Nanjing Xi Lu).

Nanjing Lu has traditionally been Shanghai's foremost shopping street, although since the 1990s it has faced increasing competition from Huaihai Lu in the French Concession. The street is divided into two distinct halves: Nanjing Dong (East) Lu stretches between the Bund and People's Park; Nanjing Xi (West) Lu runs from People's Park out past Jing'an Temple. Together the two parts total close to six miles (10 km).

The "shopper's paradise" has always been **Nanjing Dong Lu**. Before 1949, all the major stores were located here. One of them, the Sun Department Store, is now the **Shanghai No. 1 Department Store**, which continues to attract 100,000 customers every day with its exotic window displays. Many of the other department stores are looking decidedly tawdry these days, but it is worth a walk down the street by night because, when the sun goes down, Nanjing Dong Lu

Statues on Nanjing Dong Lu

resembles a Chinese Las Vegas with its shop fronts illuminated by a multitude of garish neon signs.

Nanjing Xi Lu once went by the charming name of Bubbling Well Road, after the well near Jing'an Temple *(see p134)*. A grand relic of those times survives in the **Park Hotel**, across from People's Square, which when built in 1934 was the tallest building in Shanghai – a record it held until as recently as 1988 – not to mention, one of the most fashionable addresses in the Park, **Huanghe Lu** is a great place for street food. The same is true of **Wujiang Lu**, which loops off Nanjing Lu west of People's Square; visit for *xiao long bao*, the dumplings for which Shanghai is famed.

Beyond the point at which it is rejoined by Wujiang Lu, Nanjing Xi Lu is lined by a series of exclusive shopping and commercial centers such as the Westgate Mall, CITIC Square and Plaza 66 *(see p162)*, all filled with multiple levels of designer shops, including names such as Armani, Louis Vuitton and Cartier, with prices even higher than at home. A little farther along is the **Shanghai Center**, one of the earliest such developments, with several good restaurants, a popular bar, and airline offices clustered around the Portman Ritz-Carlton Hotel.

Birds for sale at the Fish & Flower Market on Jiangyin Lu

People's Park & Square ❸
人民广场

Nanjing Xi Lu. **Map** 2 A2 & A3.
Ⓜ *Renmin Park & Renmin Square.*

What used to be a racecourse *(see p125)* is now occupied by the pleasantly landscaped People's Park (Renmin Gong Yuan) in the northern half, and People's Square and the **Shanghai Museum** *(see pp126–9)* in the southern section. Locals visit the park to walk, gossip, exercise, or fly kites but, in addition to the museum, there are several other sights and cultural monuments to attract the visitor. Quite literally over-shadowed by the gleaming new glass and steel sky-scrapers that surround it, **Mu'en Tang**, the Merciful Baptism Church, lies on the eastern side of the square. It was built in 1929 as the American Baptist Church. An inter-denominational survivor of China's many revolutions, it is open to all, although the services are in Chinese only.

On the northeast side of the square, the building with four inverted tents for a roof is the **Urban Planning Exhibition Center**. The Yangzi River delta is the world's fastest-growing urban area and that is reflected here with the world's largest model. The model, which can be viewed from a gallery above, sprawls across 100 square meters, and depicts the Shanghai of the not-too-distant future. This,

The Park Hotel, formerly one of the most fashionable addresses in town

For hotels and restaurants in Shanghai see pp182–7 and pp202–7

unsurprisingly, takes the form of a forest of skyscrapers, all lovingly detailed at a scale of 1:2000. Other floors have maps of more construction to come, and exhibitions on the city's signature *shikumen* housing and colonial-era Shanghai. The top floor houses a quiet café.

The newest arrival in the park itself is the elegant glass box of **MOCA Shanghai**, the Museum of Contemporary Art. Opened in late 2005, it resembles a designer greenhouse. Its two floors house regularly changing exhibitions of cutting-edge art and design.

At the northwest corner of the park, the rather more dowdy **Shanghai Art Museum** occupies the lower floors of the rather elegant old racecourse clubhouse. The collection is composed of a great many excellent traditional Chinese paintings, along with some officially approved – and hence quite dull – experimental works. However, it is the lavish marbled interiors of the 1930s Neo-Classical building that are of most interest. On the top floor, and accessed by the main clocktower entrance, is an excellent bar-restaurant, **Kathleen's 5**, which boasts marvelous views over the park from its roof terrace. On your way up the stairs, look out for

THE OLD RACECOURSE

The old racecourse was the center of Shanghai social life in the early 20th century, and its Race Club was one of the most profitable corporations in China. It also boasted a swimming pool and a cricket pitch. After the Communists came to power in 1949, the course became a symbol of Western decadence, and was turned into a park and an adjacent square that was used for political rallies. It was later landscaped to accommodate the Shanghai Museum. With the grandstand becoming the Shanghai Art Museum, all that remains of the racecourse is its old grandstand clock on the park's west side.

A view of Shanghai's racecourse prior to 1949

the horses' heads worked into the decoration of the bannisters.

Behind the Art Museum is the striking new **Shanghai Grand Theater** made almost entirely of glass and topped by a spectacular convex roof. It is definitely worth a visit, for a meal with a view or just to look around; official tours are also available.

🚩 Mu'en Tang
315 Xizang Zhong Lu. ⬜ *five daily services, see entrance for times.*

🏛 MOCA Shanghai
People's Park, 231 Nanjing Xi Lu. ⬜ *10am–6pm Sat–Thu.* ● *1pm–10pm Wed.* 🈂 🚫

🏛 Shanghai Art Museum
People's Park, 325 Nanjing Xi Lu. ⬜ *9am–5pm daily.* 🈂 🚫

🎭 Shanghai Grand Theater
People's Square. ⬜ *9am–11am, 1pm–4pm daily.* 🈂 🎟

🏛 Urban Planning Exhibition Center
100 Renmin Da Dao. ⬜ *9am–4pm Mon–Thu, 9am–5pm Fri–Sun.* 🈂 ¥30.

Ornamental flower display in the beautifully maintained People's Park, at the heart of Shanghai

Shanghai Museum **❹**
上海博物馆

**Bronze coin
(AD 927–51)**

With a collection of over 120,000 pieces, the Shanghai Museum displays some of the best cultural relics from China's neolithic period to the Qing dynasty, a span of over 5,000 years. While the highlights are the bronze ware, ceramics, calligraphy, and painting, it also has excellent displays of jade, furniture, coins, and Chinese seals or "chops." The museum was established in 1952, and the current building opened in 1995 with a design that recalls some of the exhibits and symbolizes "a round heaven and a square earth."

**Shanghai Museum, reminiscent of a
Shang-dynasty bronze *ding* pot**

Calligraphy
To the Chinese, calligraphy is more than mere communication, it is one of the highest art forms. This cursive script (see pp18–19) was painted by Huai Su (AD 737) in typically wild movements that combine delicate and forceful strokes.

Third floor

★ Sancai pottery figures
The major technical advance of the Tang dynasty (618–907) in ceramics was the development of sancai (three-color) pottery. This grave figure is a superb piece of polychrome pottery.

Celadon ware
Celadon's simple beauty and strength made it highly desirable. This example of Longquan ware from the Southern Song dynasty (1127–1279) elegantly captures the movement of the coiled dragon.

Second floor

KEY TO FLOORPLAN

☐	Bronzes		
☐	Sculpture	☐	Jade
☐	Ceramics	☐	Furniture
☐	Zande Lou ceramics	☐	Coins
☐	Paintings	☐	Ethnic minorities gallery
☐	Calligraphy	☐	Temporary exhibitions
☐	Seals	☐	Non-exhibition space

Zande Lou ceramics
is a privately donated collection of 130 pieces and includes some outstanding Qing imperial items.

Fourth floor

Ming & Qing furniture gallery

Liangtuxuan is a privately donated collection of paintings and calligraphy.

The Seal Gallery displays examples of virtuoso carving and calligraphy.

Back entrance

Main entrance

The Sculpture Gallery holds a collection of ancient and mainly religious pieces.

VISITORS' CHECKLIST

201 Renmin Da Dao, People's Square. **Map** 2 A3. *Tel* (021) 6372 3500. Renmin Square. 9am–5pm daily (last entry one hour before closing). **www**.shanghaimuseum.net

Jade gallery
Sculpture in jade, the quintessential Chinese stone, reached its peak in the Qing dynasty (1644–1911) as exemplified by this exquisite jade gu (wine vessel).

★ Landscape paintings
Chinese painting owes a great deal to Daoist philosophy. Accordingly, Wang Meng's (1308–85) picture Retreat in the Qingbian Mountain *tries to capture the powerful, almost animate essence of nature.*

★ Shang bronzes
This jia (wine vessel), a burial gift from the mid-15th–13th century BC, shows great skill and craftsmanship in its sophisticated animal mask design or taotie.

GALLERY GUIDE
The calligraphy and painting exhibits are changed frequently for their own protection. As well as the permanent collections, the museum often shows exhibits from other major museums around the world.

STAR SIGHTS

★ *Sancai* pottery figures

★ Landscape paintings

★ Shang bronzes

Exploring the Shanghai Museum

Eleven galleries display a selection of the museum's permanent collection and three others are used to show temporary exhibitions from around the world. The scope and quality of the exhibits mean that one visit may not be enough for the interested visitor. The displays and interpretation are probably the best in China and, as such, should be savored. There's also an excellent shop within the museum with one of the best selections of books on China that you are likely to find anywhere.

Bronze *ding* (food vessel), mid Western Zhou (10th century BC)

BRONZES

China's Bronze Age (18th to 3rd century BC) is represented by an extraordinary collection of wine vessels, three-legged *ding* (cooking vessels), and bells, all cast in bronze using ceramic moulds. Particularly attractive are the *zun* wine vessels, such as one in the shape of a sturdy ox, 2,500 years old, complete with horns and nose-ring and covered in incised decoration. The intricacy of the metal-work – quite impractical for everyday items – is evidence that these beautiful works of art were used for ritual offerings of food and wine, and that the society that created them was possessed of a sophisticated level of technology. It would also have taken powerful rulers, great organization, and vast amounts of manpower to mine, transport, and refine such large amounts of metal ore and then create these wonderful pieces, setting a precedent for Chinese societies to come.

SCULPTURE

Buddhism's arrival in China and its gradual absorption into the mainstream is reflected in over 120 pieces of bronze, wood, stone, and pottery dating from around 475 BC to AD 1644, the end of the Ming dynasty. Gradually, the high-cheekboned slender figures of a North Indian and Central Asian aesthetic take on the plumper, moon-faced shapes of the Chinese. There are also legions of tomb figurines from different dynasties, and fine examples of the polychrome equestrian figures that characterize sculpture during the Tang dynasty period.

Gilt bronze Buddha

PAINTING

A lighting system in each display cabinet that only comes on as visitors approach helps to protect the 120 delicate exhibits on display in the museum's third-floor painting gallery. Some of the pieces date back as far as the Tang dynasty (618–907). Despite the concrete and bedlam of modern Shanghai just outside, here's a reminder of the Chinese delight in nature and wildlife that goes back centuries. Waterfalls plunge down mountains topped with gnarled pines and inhabited by pheasants and other wild birds. Notable treasures include the only surviving original painting by Sun Wei of the Tang dynasty, showing seven hermits disporting themselves in a bamboo forest.

CALLIGRAPHY

Calligraphy in China is said to have already atttained maturity by the time of the Eastern Zhou dynasty (770–221 BC). However, the art's greatest exponent is often said to be Wang Xizhi (c. AD 303–361), who is known as the "Sage of Calligraphy". Few Chinese these days can understand much of the classical script of these scrolls, and perhaps the foreign visitor's appreciation of their beauty is enhanced because it is undistracted by any flashes of meaning, allowing concentration on the shapes alone. Stylistic differences can be identified even by the non-specialist, such as the difference between the running style and the more flamboyant cursive style, while the characters adorning the seals seem from another language altogether.

Hermits, a hand scroll by Sun Wei, Tang dynasty (AD 618–907)

Polychrome glazed pottery, Tang dynasty (AD 618–907)

CERAMICS

The museum is particularly proud of its display of 500 pieces from all over China, which together illustrate 8,000 years of ceramic production. Some are incredibly rare and were deemed too delicate for public presentation until the current modern facility was built. It is visibly a long journey from the clumsy solidity of some of the early pots displayed here to the *famille verte* of the Qing Kangxi emperor's era, delicately painted with traditional scenes, and the *famille rose* of his successors with their flowery over-decoration and rococo elements designed to pander to the Orientalism of European markets. Better than either is the fine, white-glaze porcelain of the Jin dynasty. Also notable are the delicate celadon hues of Song dynasty wares and the charm of the underglaze paintings of fish and flowers in blue or red of the Ming dynasty. This one gallery alone makes a visit to Shanghai worthwhile.

JADE

The precious substance most closely linked with China, at least by foreigners, is jade, a word the Chinese use to describe a variety of different stones of various hues, but principally the bluish green nephrite and jadeite. Never particularly abundant in China, stocks are now largely exhausted. Some of the jade objects here are described as dating back to the 51st century BC. These early examples were symbols of status, as the dense stone requires a great deal of effort to shape. In the late Zhou period, around 2,500 years ago, jade's symbolic value was augmented by an appreciation of its beauty. The stone began to be used for ornaments such as wine cups and brooches. The museum's collection includes examples carved into dragons, turtles, and tigers of marvellous delicacy.

Porcelain vase of Jingdezhen origin

FURNITURE

Up on the topmost floor of the museum is the furniture gallery, where Ming-dynasty constructions of elegant simplicity sit alongside over-elaborately decorated later Qing pieces. Should any of these items take your fancy, most can be found copied in "antique" furniture stores in both Shanghai and Beijing. Two beautiful brick-floored rooms contain recreations of the layouts of studies of both eras. Perhaps best of all are the miniature wooden furniture sets, together with a procession of wooden figurines, retrieved from Ming tombs.

SEALS

Seals, or chops, as they are also known, remain essential when important documents are signed, even in modern China. They are easily purchased, coming in straightforward plastic and rubber forms. But those in the museum's collection of more than 500 include miniature works of art in ivory, jade, and soapstone. Some are in the shapes of animals or mythical creatures, and some are carved with tiny landscapes. This is rightly regarded as the best such collection in China, although anyone visiting Hangzhou may also want to visit the Museum of the Seal Engravers Society (see p153).

OTHER DISPLAYS

Other displays include pottery, costume, embroidery, and lacquerware from a few of the 55 or so ethnic minorities that make up the peoples of China. Also as one of the first countries to systematically use coins and then notes there's an extensive collection of these items from throughout China's history.

Sandalwood Qing-dynasty throne chair with carved cloud and dragon design

Yu Gardens and Bazaar ❺
豫园

Chinese
lion statue

The old-style buildings of the Yu Gardens bazaar are not really old, but the fanciful roofs are nevertheless very appealing. The shops here peddle everything from tourist souvenirs to traditional medicines and, despite inflated prices, the area is incredibly popular. It is best to arrive early and go straight to the beautiful and relatively peaceful Ming-dynasty Yu Gardens (Yu Yuan). A dumpling lunch, before the restaurants get too busy, will set you up for a hectic afternoon of shopping and haggling, followed by a cup of tea in the quaint Huxinting teahouse.

Yu Gardens Bazaar, modern shops in old-fashioned buildings

Restaurants surround the lake – you can see the dumplings being made in the morning.

Yu Gardens Bazaar
Despite being a bit of a tourist trap, there is plenty of fun to be had wandering among the stalls and haggling over prices.

Street performers
Every now and then a colorful troupe of performers appears bearing young children on top of poles to entertain the thronging crowds.

Shanghai Old Street (Fangbang Lu) and an entrance to the Bazaar

★ City God Temple
Dating back to the Ming era, the temple once housed the patron god of Shanghai and encompassed an area as large as the bazaar. Now this small restored temple is very popular with tourists.

STAR SIGHTS

★ City God Temple

★ Huxinting Teahouse

★ Huge rockery, Yu Gardens

★ Huxinting Teahouse
This charming building, built in 1784 by cotton merchants, only became a teahouse in the late 19th century. The zigzag bridge protects the structure, as evil spirits can't turn corners.

★Huge rockery
Reputed to be one of the best Ming rockeries, it is surely one of the largest. The rockery recalls the peaks, caves, and gorges of southern China.

Garden entrance

Dragon wall
The white walls in the garden are topped by an undulating dragon. Note it only has four claws and not five like an imperial dragon, so as not to incur the emperor's wrath.

Yu Gardens scenic areas
The walls divide the garden into six scenic areas, which makes it feel like a maze and seem larger than it really is. As a result, the garden gets very busy in the afternoon and on weekends.

Entrance, First National Congress of the Chinese Community Party

Site of the First National Congress of the Chinese Communist Party ❻
中共一大会址纪念馆

374 Huangpi Nan Lu. **Map** 2 A4. Ⓜ
Huangpi Nan Lu. ◯ 9am–4pm. 🖼

This house in the French Concession was the venue for a historic meeting, where representatives of China's communist cells met to form a national party on July 23, 1921. Officially, there were 12 participants including Mao Zedong, but it is believed that many others also attended. The police discovered the meeting and the delegates were forced to escape to a boat on Lake Nan, in Zhejiang. The house has a reconstruction of the meeting, with the original chairs and teacups used by the delegates. The exhibition hall tells the history of the Chinese Communist Party.

Fuxing Park ❼
复兴公园

Fuxing Zhong Lu. **Map** 1 F4. Ⓜ
Huangpi Nan Lu. **Sun Yat Sen Memorial Residence** 7 Xingshan Lu. **Tel** (021) 6437 2954. ◯ 9am–4:30pm daily. 🖼 **Zhou Enlai's Former Residence** 73 Sinan Lu. ◯ 9am–4pm daily. 🖼

The French bought this private garden, located in the French Concession, in 1908. It was known then as the

"French Park," and has elements of a formal Parisian *jardin*, with meandering paths flanked by cherry trees. It was renamed Fuxing, meaning "revival," in 1949.

Close by on Xiangshan Lu is the **Sun Yat Sen Memorial Residence**, a typical Shanghai villa where the leader and his wife, Song Qingling, lived between 1918 and 1924. The interior is just as it was in Sun's time, with many of his personal items such as his gramophone and books. South of the park, 73 Rue Massenet (now Sinan Lu) was the **Former Residence of Zhou Enlai**, who lived here when he was head of the city's Communist Party in the 1940s. It is furnished in a spartan style and is another excellent example of a European-style Shanghai villa.

French Concession ❽
法国花园

Ⓜ *Shaanxi Nan Lu.* **Map** 1 E4.

The former French Concession, stretching from the western edge of the Old City to Avenue Haig (Huashan Lu), comprises boulevards,

Statue of Sun Yat Sen, Sun Yat Sen Memorial

shops, and cafés, and its residents were mainly White Russians and Chinese. It had its own electrical system, judiciary, and police force, whose highest ranking officer "Pockmarked Huang," was the leader of the infamous Green Gang which controlled the opium trade.

Today, the Concession is centered on **Huaihai Lu** – a vibrant street lined with boutiques, candy stores, hair salons, and bars – and the stylish **Jinjiang Hotel**. The hotel's compound includes the Grosvenor Residence, pre-war Shanghai's most exclusive property. The VIP Club, in the hotel's old wing, retains its 1920s architecture. The surrounding streets, especially Julu Lu and Maoming Nanlu, come alive at night with lively bars and clubs (*see pp164–7*). Another interesting building is the **Ruijin Guesthouse** at the corner of Fuxing Zhong Lu and Shaanxi Nanlu. This Tudor-style manor is now an inn set in a quiet compound. **The Children's Palace** at the western end of Yan'an Lu was part of an early-1920s estate, and is now a children's arts center. The tourist office arranges tours to watch its singing and dancing shows.

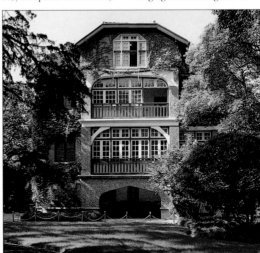

The European-style villa that was Zhou Enlai's former residence

The Huangpu River

The Huangpu River is a mere 68 miles (110 km) in length from its source, Dianshan Lake, to its junction with the Yangzi River, 17 miles (28 km) downstream from Shanghai. As a spectacle, however, it is fascinating and there is much for the eye to take in, from the majestic but elderly waterfront at the Bund, and burgeoning modern metropolis on Pudong,

Cargo ships, Huangpu River

to the bustling docks that line the Huangpu all the way to the wide, windblown mouth of the Yangzi. The boat departs from the wharves on the Bund between Nanjing Lu and Yan'an Lu (*see pp120–21*). The one-hour trip takes visitors as far as the Yangpu Bridge, but there is also the longer three-and-a-half hour trip, all the way to the Yangzi River.

The Yangzi River ⑦
The color of the water changes markedly here, as the oily Huangpu meets the muddy and turbulent Yangzi. A lighthouse marks the confluence of the two.

Shanghai Docks ④
The Shanghainese proudly claim that nearly a third of all China's international trade enters via the perennially busy Huangpu river.

Wusong Fort ⑥
The site of a decisive battle against the British in 1842, it consisted of a crescent-shaped fort with ten imported cannons.

Yangpu Bridge ③
Built in 1993, this is one of the world's longest cable-stay bridges – cables are anchored to each tower.

Gongqing Forest Park ⑤
This large and pleasantly landscaped park was reclaimed from marshland and is popular with the Shanghainese on weekends.

Huangpu Park ②
At the northern tip of the Bund, this park is home to the Monument to the People's Heroes.

Huangpu River

| 0 km | | 6 |
| 0 miles | 3 | |

Pudong

The Bund ①
The best way to enjoy the Bund's grandiose skyline is from a boat, which also gives the visitor a view of the city that would have greeted all expatriates on their arrival here before 1949.

TIPS BOX

Length: 37 miles (60 km).
One-hour trip: 10 miles (16 km).
Boat trips: The boats vary in size and facilities, so make sure you know what you are getting. The more expensive ones do food and even entertainment of sorts.
Times: 9am, 2pm, 7pm Mon–Fri; 11am, 3:30pm, 8pm Sat–Sun. The one-hour trips leave more frequently (times can vary).

Façade of the Soviet-style Shanghai Exhibition Center

Shanghai Exhibition Center ❾
上海展览中心

1000 Yan'an Zhong Lu. **Map** 1 E3. *Tel* (021) 6279 0279. **M** *Jing'an Temple.* ◯ *9am–4pm daily.*

The enormous Shanghai Exhibition Center is one of the few reminders of the influence the Soviet Union once had in Shanghai. Built in 1954, it was known as the Palace of Sino-Soviet Friendship, and was designed as a place for exhibiting China's technological and agricultural advances since the founding of the People's Republic in 1949. Ironically, the building stands on the site of the estate of millionaire Silas Hardoon – Shanghai's biggest capitalist in the 1920s. The Center is worth seeing for its grimly florid Soviet-style architecture. It has an impressively ornate entrance, with columns decorated with red stars, and a gilded spire. Today, it is a gigantic mall, filled with shops selling furniture and a variety of souvenirs.

Nearby on Xinle Lu, in the former French Concession, is the old **Russian Orthodox Church** with its distinctive onion-shaped domes. It served thousands of refugees from the Russian Revolution in 1917. The area around Julu Lu and Changle Lu, nearby,

has a number of interesting Art Deco and early 20th-century villas and mansions constructed by Shanghai's wealthy residents.

Jing'an Temple ❿
静安寺

1686 Nanjing Xi Lu (near Huashan Lu). **Map** 1 D3. **M** *Jing'an Temple.* ◯ *7:30am–5pm daily.*

Located opposite the attractive Jing'an Park, which contains the old Bubbling Well Cemetery, Jing'an Temple (Temple of Tranquility) is one of the city's most revered places for ancestor worship. Originally founded in the Three Kingdoms Period, its current structure dates to the Ming and Qing dynasties. In the 1930s, it was Shanghai's wealthiest Buddhist temple, headed by the influencial abbot Khi Vehdu, who was also a gangster with a harem of concubines and White Russian bodyguards. It is said that his bodyguards went with him everywhere, carrying bulletproof briefcases as shields in the event of an attack. The temple was closed during the Cultural Revolution, but has reopened to become one of the best examples of an active Buddhist shrine in the city. It is a popular place to offer coins and pray for financial success.

Jade Buddha Temple ⓫
玉佛寺

170 Anyuan Lu. **Map** 1 D1. *Tel* (021) 6266 3668. **M** *Hanzhong Lu then taxi.* ◯ *8:30am–4:30pm daily.*

The most famous of Shanghai's temples, Jufo Si lies in the northwest part of the city. It was built in 1882 to enshrine two beautiful jade Buddha statues that were brought from Burma by the abbot Wei Ken. The temple was originally located elsewhere, but shifted here in 1918, after a fire damaged the earlier structure. After being closed for almost 30 years, it reopened in 1980, and today has some 100 monks. Built in the southern Song-dynasty style, it has sharply curved eaves and figurines on the roof. Its three main halls are connected by two courts. The first hall is the **Heavenly King Hall**, where the four Heavenly Kings line the walls. The **Grand Hall of Magnificence** houses three incarnations of the Buddha, while the **Jade Buddha Chamber** contains the first jade statue – that of a large reclining Buddha. The finer of the two statues, however, lies upstairs. Carved from a single piece of jade, this jewel-encrusted seated Buddha is exquisite. Visitors should note that photography is forbidden here.

Wall detail, Jade Buddha Temple

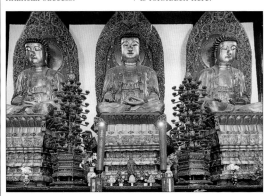

Golden Buddhas in the Jade Buddha Temple

For hotels and restaurants in Shanghai see pp182–7 and pp202–7

Old Shanghai

Until 1842 Shanghai was a minor Chinese river port, worthy of a protective rampart but otherwise undistinguished. In that year the Chinese government capitulated to western demands for trade concessions resulting in a number of ports along China's eastern seaboard, including Shanghai, becoming essentially European outposts. Their key feature was that of extra-territoriality – foreign residents were answerable only to the laws of their own country. Thus the

Calendar girls, 1930s

Americans, British, and French had their own "concessions" – exclusive areas within the city with their own police forces and judiciary – a situation that attracted not only entrepreneurs, but refugees, criminals, and revolutionaries. This mix was a potent one and Shanghai's reputation for glamor and excess derives from the politically combustible period between the two world wars. It all came to an end in the 1940s when foreigners gave up their rights in the face of growing Chinese opposition.

The Bund, *also known as Zhongshan Lu, was the wide thoroughfare running along Huangpu River. This was where all the major players in Shanghai commerce built their offices and created the distinctively grandiose skyline that still greets the river-going traveler today.*

The Great World *was a quintessential Shanghai creation, a mixture of freakishness, fashion, sex, and theater under one roof, owned by the gangster Pockmarked Huang.*

The Race Course, *located in the area of today's People's Park, was an indispensable part of expatriate life, where, just as in the numerous clubs and institutions for non-Chinese, expats were able to socialize as if they were at home.*

Opium, trafficked commercially *with claims for free-trade by British companies like Jardine Matheson, was the foundation of Shanghai's prosperity and dens dotted the city. When the mercantile veneer was jettisoned, opium became the currency of Shanghai's gangster underworld.*

Nanking Road, *as it was then known, was, and still is, Shanghai's retail hub. Divided in two parts (the western end then known as Bubbling Well Road), it was home to China's first department stores, where Chinese and expatriates mixed on an equal footing.*

Pudong's Oriental Pearl TV Tower lit up at night, as seen from the Jinmao Tower

Bund Sightseeing Tunnel ⑫
外滩观光随道

The Bund at Beijing Dong Lu, and near the foot of the Oriental Pearl TV Tower in Pudong. **Map** 3 D2. **Tel** (021) 5888 6000. Ⓜ *Henan Zhong Lu (Bund) or Lujiazui (Pudong).* ◯ *8am–10:30pm daily (8am–10pm winter).* 🖬

Part high-tech, computer-controlled subway ride, part low-tech, fairground haunted house, and wholly ridiculous, the oddly named Sightseeing Tunnel offers a brief but surreal 2,132-ft (650-m) jaunt beneath the Huangpu river. Passenger cars zip down a tunnel assailed en route by a neon and laser light show,

The psychedelic experience that is the Bund Sightseeing Tunnel

with inflatable figures and an accompanying soundtrack. Official government promotional materials imaginatively describe the experience as *pavonine* (peacock-like). You may just consider it kitsch. However, it is a very Shanghai experience and something that should be done at least once. For the return journey, consider taking the ferry: at ¥2 it costs a fifteenth of the fare on the Sightseeing Tunnel and it delivers rather better sightseeing opportunities.

Oriental Pearl TV Tower ⑬
东方明珠广播电视塔

1 Shiji Dadao. **Map** 3 D2. **Tel** (021) 5879 1888. Ⓜ *Lujiazui.* �In 🚗 ◯ *Tower and Shanghai History Museum 8am–9pm daily.* 🖬 🍴 🖳

One of the first modern towers to rise above the rubble of the peasant homes that once fringed the river on the Pudong side, when it was completed in 1994 the 1,500-foot (457-m) Oriental Pearl instantly became China's most recognizable modern icon. Despite all the high-rises that have gone up since, it is still one of the most striking buildings in Shanghai. It houses an assortment of entertainments, including

viewing platforms at various heights reached by express elevators, rotating restaurants, and, in the basement, the **Shanghai History Museum**. This excellent museum appears rather more down-to-earth, but with ingenious use of technology it conjures up recreations of long-vanished city life. Models of early Shanghai street scenes ring with the traditional cries of vendors, and projected figures re-enact episodes of Shanghai domestic life. The museum also displays the original bronze lions made to guard the Hong Kong and Shanghai Bank *(see p122)* – the pair you see on the Bund today are replicas.

Shanghai Ocean Aquarium ⑭
上海海洋水族馆

158 Yincheng Bei Lu, east of the Oriental Pearl TV Tower. **Map** 3 E2. **Tel** (021) 5877 9988. Ⓜ *Lujiazui.* 🚗 ◯ *9am–6pm daily.* 🖬 🍴 🖳 🛈

Rated by enthusiasts as one of the best in the world, this vast, US$55 million aquarium features more than 10,000 temperate and tropical fish representing more than 300 species, as well as turtles and other sea creatures. But more impressive than these statistics are the 480 feet (150 m) or so of underwater, clear viewing tunnels that even include a submarine escalator, which puts visitors right among everything, from the pretty to the predatory. There are careful recreations of different aquatic environments from around the world including Antarctica, Africa, and the Amazon, as well as displays highlighting the endangered aquatic species native to China. Feeding times, which occur mid-morning and mid-afternoon, are especially good times to visit.

Viewing tunnel at the Shanghai Ocean Aquarium

Jinmao Tower 🅯
金茂大厦

88 Shiji Dadao. **Map** 3 E2. **Tel** (021) 5047 5101. Ⓜ Lujiazui. 🚌 🚐 🕘 8:30am–9pm daily (observation deck). 🌐 🍴

American architects Skidmore, Owings & Merrill get credit for the finest tower in Pudong, the US$540 million, 88-story, 1,379-foot (421-m) Jinmao Tower. For now it is the tallest building in China and one of the tallest in the world, with a basement food court, 42 floors of offices, and the luxurious Grand Hyatt hotel between the 53rd and 87th floors. This is topped by an 88th-floor enclosed viewing gallery. The silvery exterior, wrapped with rails, narrows in steps, pagoda-like, to a sharp point. According to the architects, the building is a pen, the curved roof of the attached exhibition hall a book, and the Huangpu itself the ink. Express elevators to

THE MAGLEV TRAIN

This is, for the moment at least, the fastest you'll ever travel without flying. The German-built "magnetically levitated" train travels the roughly 18.6 miles (30 km) from Shanghai's eastern suburbs to Pudong Airport in under eight minutes, briefly reaching a speed in excess of 267 mph (430 kph) with

A super-fast Maglev train slows as it approaches the terminus

considerable smoothness and limited noise. A counter in each carriage tells you how fast you are actually going. However, lower than expected passenger numbers due to high ticket prices, the rather limited service, and the inconvenient location of the Shanghai terminus – you still need a taxi to get into the city – mean that the trains travel half-empty most of the time.

Despite a projected project cost of around US$3.75 billion, the Shanghai authorities announced plans in February 2006 to extend the line to a total length of 105 miles (169 km), running all the way to the lake-side city of Hangzhou. With maximum speeds of 450kph (279 mph) the journey time will be only about 27 minutes including three stops on route.

the viewing gallery are reached via the basement, but equally breathtaking is the view up the 33-story interior atrium from the Hyatt's 56th-floor reception. Sometime early in 2008 the Jinmao will be surpassed in height by its neighbor, the 1,509-foot (460-m) Shanghai World Financial Center, whose upper floors will also house a luxury Hyatt. A hole like a needle's eye near the top of the building will provide an open-air promenade.

The skyscraping, silvery, pagoda-like form of the Jinmao Tower

Century Square 🅰
世纪广场

Shiji Dadao and Yanggao Zhong Lu intersection. Ⓜ Shanghai Kejiguan Zhan. 🚌 **Science and Technology Museum** 🕘 9am–5pm Tues–Sun (last ticket sold at 3:30pm). 🌐

Shanghai's largest square is dominated by a giant sculpture called "Oriental Light" that features an arrow piercing a disk that looks a bit like a sundial; it is meant to signify time. The square is graced by flower beds spelling out the characters of its name – Shiji Guangchang, in Chinese – as well as assorted sculpture and water features. It is flanked by local government buildings, the new and striking **Oriental Arts Center**, designed in the form of a blooming magnolia (the city flower of Shanghai), and the ultimately disappointing **Science and Technology Museum**. The latter is well-intentioned but the lack of clear interpretation or a coherent purpose to the museum renders most exhibits baffling. The museum also has two IMAX cinemas and an IWERKS 4-D theater.

Brightly colored boats alongside the lake pier at Hongkou Park (Lu Xun Park)

Hongkou Park 🕗
虹口公园

146 Dong Jiangwan Lu.
Ⓜ *Hongkou.* ◯ *daily.* 🖼

To the north of Suzhou
Creek and Waibaidu
Bridge lies the
Japanese section
of the former
International
Settlement, which
once had a Zen
temple, a Japanese
school, and specialist
Japanese shops. The
area's most
interesting spot is
Hongkou Park, which
is a pleasant place to pass the
time and watch the Chinese
taking boat rides on the lake,
playing chess, practising *tai ji
quan* or simply relaxing. It is
also known as Lu Xun Park
due to its strong associations
with the great Chinese
novelist Lu Xun (1881–1936),
who lived nearby. His most
famous work is *The True Story
of Ah Q*, which lampooned
the Chinese national
character. Lu Xun was also
an early proponent of the
baihua or plain speech
movement, which championed
the simplification of the
Chinese script and the use of
spoken Chinese in literature.
Lu Xun's Tomb, where his
ashes were interred in 1956 to
mark the 20th anniversary of
his death, is also in the park.
To the right of the park's
main entrance lies a **Memorial
Hall** dedicated to the novelist,
where visitors can view early
editions of his work and his
correspondence with various
intellectuals including George
Bernard Shaw. Just south of

**Statue, Lu Xun's
Tomb**

Hongkou Park is **Lu Xun's
Former Residence**, where the
novelist spent the last three
years of his life at a house on
Shanyin Lu. It is an interesting
example of a typical 1930s
Japanese-style residence, but
is perhaps even more
sparely furnished than
other houses of the
time. Lu Xun's rattan
chairs and writing
desk are also on
display.

🏛 **Lu Xun's Former
Residence**
9 Dalu Xincun, Shanyin Lu.
◯ *9am–4pm daily.* 🖼

Song Qingling's
Former
Residence 🕘
宋庆龄故居

1843 Huaihai Zhong Lu.
Ⓜ *Hengshan Lu.* ◯ *9–11am
& 1pm–4:30pm daily.* 🖼

At the southwestern edge of
the city is the fine villa that
was the residence of Song
Qingling, wife of the

revolutionary leader Dr. Sun
Yat Sen. All the Song siblings
– three sisters and a brother
– came to wield a lot of
influence in China. Of the
three sisters, Song Meiling
married Chiang Kai Shek,
the head of the Nationalist
Republic of China from 1928
to 1949; Ailing married H.H.
Kung, the director of the Bank
of China, and Song Qingling
married Sun Yat Sen. Her
brother, known as T.V. Song,
became Chiang Kai Shek's
finance minister. Song Qingling
stayed in China once the
Communists took over and
became an honorary
Communist heroine. She lived
in Shanghai after her husband's
death, initially in the house
they had shared in the former
French Concession (*see p132*),
before moving to this villa. She
died in Beijing in 1981.

The house is a charming
example of a mid-20th-
century Shanghai villa. It
has some wonderful wood
paneling and lacquerwork.
Her limousines are still
parked in the garage, and
some of her personal items
are also displayed.

Song Qingling's Former Residence – a charming early 20th-century villa

For hotels and restaurants in Shanghai see pp182–7 and pp202–7

Xujiahui Catholic Cathedral ⓳
徐家汇堂

158 Puxi Lu. **Tel** *(021) 6438 2595.*
Ⓜ *Xujiahui.* ◯ *1pm–4pm Sat, Sun.*

The red brick Gothic Cathedral
of St. Ignatius that stands at a
southwestern corner of
Shanghai has long been
associated with foreign
nationals. The land originally
belonged to a member of the
Xu clan, Xu Guangqi (1562–
1633), who was converted to
Catholicism by Matteo Ricci.
Upon his death, Xu left land
to the Jesuits for the building
of a church, seminary, and
observatory. The cathedral,
with its 164-ft (50-m) twin
towers, was built in 1906. It
was partly destroyed during
the Cultural Revolution, but
was rebuilt, and now holds
Sunday services attended by
over 2,000 worshipers. The
interior is an interesting mix of
traditional Catholic decoration
and Chinese embellishment.
Xu Guangqi is buried nearby
in Nandan Park.

Longhua Cemetery of Martyrs ⓴
龙华烈士陵园

2887 Longhua Lu. Ⓜ *Shanghai
Stadium then taxi.* **Tel** *(021) 6468
5995.* 🚌 *No. 41.* ◯ *6am–4:30pm
daily.* 🏛 **Longhua Si** *2853 Longhua
Lu.* ◯ *7am–4:30pm daily.* 📷

This site honors those who
died for the communist cause
before the People's Republic
was established in 1949. At
the center is a Memorial Hall,
while many commemorative
sculptures dot the park. The
cemetery is situated on the
site of the Nationalist Party's
execution ground, where
several hundred Communists
were put to death by Chiang
Kai Shek.
  Nearby is **Longhua Temple**
and an octagonal pagoda. A
temple has existed on this site
since AD 687, and a pagoda
since AD 238–251. The
foundations of the current
pagoda, with its upturned
eaves, date to AD 977, while

Commemorative statue at the Longhua Cemetery of Martyrs

the temple buildings were built
during the late Qing era. The
temple has several halls and
is very active. The surrounding
area is pretty in spring, when
the peach trees are in bloom.

She Shan ㉑
佘山

22 miles (35 km) SW of Shanghai.
🚌 *from Wenhua Guangchang bus
stop or Xi Qu bus station in Shanghai.*

She Hill or She Shan is a mere
328-ft (100-m) high, and is
surmounted by a grand, red-
brick Catholic church, **Our
Lady of China**. In the 1850s,
European missionaries built a
small chapel here. Later, a
bishop took refuge in the area
and vowed to build a church.
The basilica was built between
1925–35. Services, often in

**Exterior of the grand She Shan
church, Our Lady of China**

Latin, take place on Christian
holidays and particularly in
May, when pilgrims stream
here in their hundreds. The
impressive cathedral is worth
a closer look. The route to
the top represents the Via
Dolorosa (The Way of
Suffering), the road that Christ
took to his crucifixion. It is a
pleasant walk past bamboo
groves, but there is a cable
car that goes to the summit.
The hill also has an ancient
observatory that houses an
ingenious earthquake-
monitoring device of a jar
with dragon heads around
the outside and a pendulum
inside. Each dragon has a steel
ball in its mouth. When an
earthquake occurred, the
pendulum would swing, knock
a dragon, causing its mouth to
open and a ball to drop out
and thereby point out the
quake's direction.

Song Jiang ㉒
松江

25 miles (40 km) SW of Shanghai. 🚌
from Xi Qu bus station in Shanghai.

Situated on the Shanghai-
Hangzhou railway line, Song
Jiang is a small county town
with a handful of sights.
These include a Song-dynasty
square pagoda, and close by,
a 13-ft (4-m) high and 20-ft
(6-m) long Ming screen wall,
decorated with carvings of
legendary beasts that
represent human failings.
West of Song Jiang is an old
mosque, part of which dates
to the Yuan dynasty and is
said to be one of the oldest
Islamic buildings in China.
It is still a place of worship.

FARTHER AFIELD

Despite Shanghai's vast sprawl, it is not too difficult to escape to greener and more pleasant spots. The spongy landscape of the surrounding region is laced with canals and dotted with picturesque towns and villages, each claiming to be the "Venice of China." The best known and largest of these canal towns is Suzhou, which is a short train or bus ride from Shanghai. Once a favored abode of retired scholars and officials, it combines the attractions of boat rides and ornamental gardens with centuries of history. Suzhou was also once a center for the production of one of China's most famous exports – silk. The trio of nearby, smaller canal towns of Tongli, Wuxi, and Zhouzhuang all boast pleasant waterways as well. The last named of these was shown off to good effect in the movie *Mission: Impossible III.*

Hangzhou, the delight of poets for centuries, perhaps now lacks the peace they once associated with it, and even boasts a sprinkling of noteworthy modern buildings, not to mention showrooms for the likes of Ferrari sports cars. But the real joy of the poets was around the West Lake, where narrow causeways still provide today's visitor with tranquility. And there is always the option of escape onto the water – with a few sweeps of the oars of a hired boatman, the roar of traffic becomes no more than a gentle murmur.

SIGHTS AT A GLANCE

Towns and Cities
Hangzhou *pp150–51* **6**
Suzhou *pp144–5* **5**
Tongli **1**
Wuxi **3**
Zhouzhang **2**

Lakes and Areas of Natural Beauty
Tai Hu **4**

KEY
City limits
✈ International airport
☒ Domestic airport
━ National highway
━ Major road
═ Minor road
— Railroad
-- Shanghai Province border

◁ Waterside pavilion in the Humble Administrator's Garden, Suzhou

Houses fronting canals in Zhouzhuang's old town

Tongli ❶
同里

16 miles (25 km) SE of Suzhou.
👣 45,000. 🚌

A pretty little water town
typical of the region, Tongli
gives visitors a good idea of
what Suzhou must have been
like in its heyday. All its
houses open out on to a
network of canals that are
spanned by dozens of stone
bridges and are busy with
transportation and trading
boats. Some of its buildings
are open to the public, such
as **Jiayin Hall**, the former
home of Liu Yazi, an early
20th-century actor renowned
for his rather bizarre
collection of gauze caps. The
other interesting sight is **Tuisi
Yuan**, a classical garden dating
from the late Qing period.

🌸 **Tuisi Yuan**
🕐 7:45am–5:30pm daily. 🎫

**Sightseeing boats on one of Tongli's
numerous canals**

Zhouzhuang ❷
周庄

12 miles (20 km) W of Shanghai.
👣 32,000. 🚌 Shanghai, Suzhou.
🚤 to Tongli. **Old Town** tickets from
Quangong Lu. **Tel** (0512) 6721 1655.

A small town on the Jinghang
Canal, which links Suzhou
and Shanghai, Zhouzhuang
was once a flourishing port,
specializing in silk, pottery,
and grain. It attracted scholars
and officials who built fine
bridges and houses between
the Yuan and Qing eras. The
charming **Old Town** can be
explored on foot or via a boat
tour on the canals. Among the
sights are the Ming-era Hall
of Zhang Residence with 70
rooms, and the Hall of Shen's
Residence, with 100 rooms
connected to the main hall.
The Chengxu Temple, located
near the museum, is a Song-
dynasty Daoist shrine.

Wuxi ❸
无锡

25 miles (40 km) NW of Suzhou.
👣 4,320,000. 🚌 🚌 🚤 services
to Hangzhou & Suzhou. 🛈 88
Chezhan Lu. **Tel** (0510) 401 6081.

The highlights of a trip to
Wuxi are the scenic Tai Hu
(Lake Tai) and the Grand
Canal. According to legend,
the town was established
3,500 years ago as the capital
of the Wu Kingdom and was
a center for the production of
tin. When the mines ran dry
(Wuxi means "without tin"),
the capital moved west, but
Wuxi remained significant

due to its location on the
Grand Canal. **Xihui Park** in the
west of town was established
in 1958, and houses the
Jichang Yuan garden. At the
park's entrance, a path leads
to the Dragon Light Pagoda
on top of Xi Shan. A cable car
connects Xi Shan to nearby
Hui Shan. The **Wuxi Museum**
has exhibits dating back 6,000
years, and includes some
Qing-dynasty cannons.

🌸 **Xihui Park**
Huihe Lu. 🕐 6am–6pm daily. 🎫
🏛 **Wuxi Museum**
71 Huihe Lu. 🕐 9am–4pm daily. 🎫

**The scenic cable car ride, Xihui
Park, Wuxi**

Tai Hu ❹
太湖

3 miles (5 km) SW of Wuxi.

One of China's largest lakes,
Tai Hu is famous for its rocks,
an indispensable feature of a
traditional garden (see pp28–
9). The lake's northern shores
are fringed with scenic spots
including **Mei Yuan** (Plum
Garden), spectacular in spring
when its 4,000 fruit trees
blossom. **Yuantou Zhu** (Turtle
Head Promontory) is a
favorite with the Chinese,
with tea houses and pretty
lake views. Nearby, **Sanshan
Island** is a former bandit's
haunt with temples and tall
Buddha statues. However,
none is as tall as the 289-ft
(88-m) Lingshan Buddha on
Ma Shan peninsula, a short
bus ride from the other sights.
The area also has a handful
of lakeside theme parks.

🌸 **Mei Yuan & Yuantou Zhu**
🕐 7am–5pm daily. 🎫

For hotels and restaurants in this region see p187 and p207

The Grand Canal

Boat for canal cruises

The Grand Canal, started in 486 BC, was built in sections over the next one thousand years, with the aim of linking the Yangzi with the Yellow River, and one capital with another. It remains the world's largest man-made waterway. The earliest northern section was built for military reasons but large-scale construction began in the 7th century under the Sui Wendi emperor, involving over 5 million conscripted males aged between 15 and 55, supervised by a vast and brutal police force. Linking the comparatively populous north with the southern rice-producing region, it reached Beijing only in the 13th century. In the early 20th century, a combination of the altered course of the fickle Yellow River and the rise of the railways saw its gradual demise.

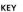

This map *shows the route of the 1,112-mile (1,900-km) canal from Beijing to Hangzhou. Crossing the traditional battlefields between north and south, the canal supplied food throughout the empire. The hilly terrain led to the first recorded use of double locks in AD 984.*

KEY

▬ Grand Canal

The Sui Yang Di emperor *is said to have celebrated the completion of his work by touring the canal with a flotilla of dragon boats hauled by the empire's most beautiful women.*

Tourist boats *are now the only way to enjoy a journey on the canal as road and rail transport is favored by the locals. Regular tourist boats operate overnight services between Hangzhou and Suzhou or Wuxi, whilst boats can also be chartered for day-trips between the major tourist stops.*

Barges splutter *their way along the canal laden with agricultural produce and factory supplies. The busiest sections are in the south and north of the Yangzi to the border with Shandong.*

The canal banks *are lively with people performing domestic tasks. Families, even if they have houses, may live on board the boats when they are working.*

Suzhou ⑤
苏州

Milefo Buddha at the base of Beisi Ta

A network of canals, bridges, and canal-side housing characterizes the city of Suzhou. Its history dates back to the 6th century BC, when the first canals were built to control the area's low water table. The construction of the Grand Canal *(see p143)*, 1,000 years later, brought prosperity as silk, the city's prized commodity, could be exported to the north. During the Ming dynasty, Suzhou flourished as a place of refinement, attracting an influx of scholars and merchants, who built themselves numerous elegant gardens. The city has plenty of sights, and is dissected by broad, busy roads laid out in a grid.

🔲 Beisi Ta

1918 Renmin Lu. **Tel** *(0512) 6753 1197.* ◯ *8am–6pm daily.* 🎫

The northern end of Renmin Lu is dominated by the Beisi Ta (North Pagoda), a remnant of an earlier temple complex, which has been rebuilt. The pagoda's main structure dates from the Song dynasty, but its foundations supposedly date to the Three Kingdoms era (AD 220–265). Towering 249 ft (76 m) high, it is octagonal in shape, and has sharply upturned eaves. Visitors can climb right to the top, from where there are good views of the city, including Xuanmiao Guan and the Ruiguang Pagoda.

The octagonal Beisi Ta

🏛 Suzhou Silk Museum

2001 Renmin Lu. **Tel** *(0512) 6753 6505.* ◯ *9am–4:30pm daily.* 🎫

The Suzhou Silk Museum is a pleasure to visit, mainly because its exhibits are well-documented with English captions. It traces the history of silk production and its use from its beginnings in about 4000 BC to the present day. Exhibits include old looms with demonstrations of their workings, samples of ancient silk patterns, and a section explaining the art of sericulture. The museum's most interesting exhibit is its room full of live silk worms, eating mulberry leaves and spinning cocoons.

🏛 Suzhou Museum

204 Dongbei Jie. **Tel** *(0512) 6754 1534.* ◯ *9am–4pm daily.* 🎫

The municipal museum is housed in the villa which was formerly part of the adjoining Humble Administrator's Garden. The villa was occupied by Li Xiucheng, one of the leaders of the Taiping Heavenly Kingdom Rebellion in 1860. This rather dry museum has no English captions, and concentrates on Suzhou's association with canal production and silk production. Some of the exhibits, especially the early maps, are of interest, but are difficult to appreciate properly without captions.

🪷 Humble Administrator's Garden

See pp146–7

🪷 Shizi Lin

23 Yuanlin Lu. ◯ *daily.* 🎫

The Lion Grove Garden is considered by many the finest in Suzhou. However, visitors unfamiliar with the subtleties of Chinese garden design may find it rather bleak, as rocks are its main feature. Ornamental rocks were a crucial element of classical gardens, and symbolized either the earth or China's sacred mountains. Dating to 1342, the garden was originally built as part of a temple. The large pool is spanned by a zigzag bridge and buildings with unusually fine latticework, while part of the rockery forms a labyrinth.

🪷 Ou Yuan

Cang Jie. ◯ *8am–5pm daily.* 🎫

The Ou Yuan (Double Garden) is not as busy as many of the city's other classical gardens, and is a pleasure to visit. It takes its name from its two garden areas, separated by buildings and corridors. A relaxing place, Ou Yuan has rockeries, a pool, and a fine, open pavilion at its center, which is surrounded by several tea-houses. It is situated in a charming locality filled with some of the most attractive houses, canals, and bridges in the city.

The charming Ou Yuan Garden

Mural in the Hall of Literary Gods, Xuanmiao Guan

🏛 Museum of Opera & Theater

14 Zhongzhangjia Xiang. **Tel** (0512)
6727 3334. 🕐 9am–4pm daily. 🈸
Housed in a beautiful Ming-
dynasty theater of latticed
wood, the Museum of Opera
and Theater (Xiqu Bowuguan)
is a fascinating and highly
visual museum. Its display
halls are filled with examples
of old musical instruments,
delicate hand-copied books
of scores and lyrics, masks,
and costumes. It also exhibits
other paraphernalia including
a life-size orchestra and vivid
photographs of dramatists and
actors. Traditional Suzhou
Opera, known as *kun ju*, is
renowned as the oldest form
of Chinese opera, with a
history of about 5,000 years.
The museum is the venue
for occasional performances,
while the adjacent teahouse
stages daily shows of *kun*-
style opera and music.

🔲 Xuanmiao Guan

Guanqian Jie. **Tel** (0512) 6777 5479.
🕐 8:30am–4:30pm daily. 🈸
The Daoist Temple of Mystery
was founded during the Jin
dynasty but like many
Chinese temples, has been
rebuilt many times. The Hall
of the Three Pure Worshipers
dates to the Song dynasty,
and is the largest ancient
Daoist hall in China. The
intricate structure of the
roof in particular is worth
scrutiny. Located in Suzhou's
commercial center, the temple
was associated with popular
street entertainment, and
although the musicians and
jugglers have gone, it retains
a casual atmosphere.

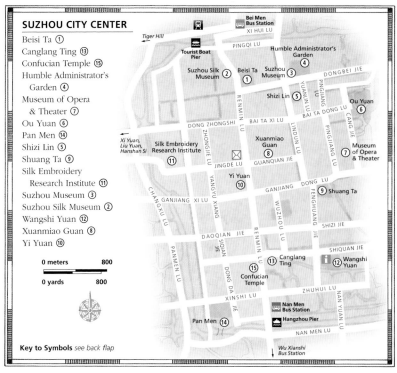

SUZHOU CITY CENTER

0 meters 800
0 yards 800

Key to Symbols see back flap

Humble Administrator's Garden
拙政园

Tai Hu rock
display

Suzhou's largest garden, Zhuozheng Yuan, the Humble Administrator's Garden is also considered the city's finest. It was established in the 16th century by a retired magistrate, Wang Xianchen, and developed over the years as subsequent owners made changes according to the fashion of the day. A 16th-century painting shows that originally the garden was less decorative than it is now. The garden is separated into three principal parts, east, central, and west. The eastern section has colorful flowers but is of less interest than the other two. There is also a museum that explains the history and philosophy of Chinese gardens.

Covered walkway – a way to enjoy the garden even in the hot sun

Western section of the garden

★ **Mandarin Duck Hall**
Split into two equal rooms, this arrangement allowed visitors to enjoy the cooler north-facing chamber in summer, and the warmer south-facing one in winter.

The Wavy Corridor rises up and down over the water as if going over waves.

The central part of the garden imitates the scenery of China south of the lower Yangzi.

STAR SIGHTS

★ Fragrant Isle

★ Mandarin Duck Hall

★ Hall of Distant Fragrance

★ **Fragrant Isle**
This pavilion and terrace is supposed to resemble the deck and cabin of a boat. As it projects out over the water, it gives excellent views of the garden from all sides.

THE HUMBLE ADMINISTRATOR'S GARDEN

☐ Area illustrated below

① Entrance
② Eastern Garden
③ Garden Museum
④ Penjing Nursery *(see p29)*

0 meters 100
0 feet 300

VISITORS' CHECKLIST

178 Dongbei Jie, Suzhou City.
Tel (0512) 6751 0286. 🚌
🕐 8am–5:30pm daily (last
admission 5pm). 🎟 *includes
the Garden Museum.* 📷 🛍
www.szzzy.cn

Orange Pavilion
*Artificial mountains
were an important
element in Chinese
gardens and were ideal
for contemplation.*

**Little Flying
Rainbow
Bridge**

**Entrance to the
central section**

**Secluded Pavilion of Firmiana
Simplex and Bamboo**
*The most famous view of the
garden, the "borrowed view"
(see p29) of Beisi Ta, the
Northern Pagoda reflected in
the water, is visible from here.*

★ Hall of Distant Fragrance
*The main hall of the garden,
is named after the perfume of
the large lotus pond nearby
that delicately wafts in.*

The octagonal Song dynasty twin pagodas, Shuang Ta

🔢 Shuang Ta
Dinghui Si Xiang. 🕐 daily. 📷
Once part of a temple, these 98-ft (30-m) high twin pagodas date to the early Song era. According to a recently discovered inscription, they were first built in AD 982 by the students Wang Wenhan and his brother in honor of their teacher, who helped them pass the imperial civil service exams. Twin pagodas are commonly found in India but are a rarer feature of Chinese temples, as pagodas were largely built as single edifices.

🍀 Yi Yuan
343 Renmin Lu. 🕐 7:30am–4:30pm daily. 📷
The Garden of Happiness is one of Suzhou's newer gardens, dating from the late Qing dynasty. It was built by a government official, who utilized rocks and landscape designs from other abandoned gardens. The garden appears to have originally covered a larger area; today its central feature is a pool encircled by rockeries and spanned by a zigzag bridge. The best

viewpoint is from the Fragrant Lotus Pavilion, while another pavilion that juts into the pool is known for catching cooling breezes. Look out for the calligraphy by famous scholars and poets.

🏛 Silk Embroidery Research Institute
280 Jingde Lu. 🕐 daily. 📷
Housed in the Huan Xiu Shan Zhuang (Surrounded by Majestic Mountains) Garden, this institute creates exquisitely fine silk embroidery, work that is mainly done by women. In order to produce the painting-like effect of their designs, the women sometimes work with silk strands that are so fine, they are almost invisible. They specialize in double-sided embroidery – for example, a cat with green eyes on one side and blue on the other.

🍀 Wangshi Yuan
11 Kuojiatou Xiang. Tel (0512) 6529 3190. 🕐 7:30am–5pm daily. 📷
It is said that the Master of the Nets Garden was named after one of its owners – a retired official who wished to become an accomplished

fisherman. Dating to 1140, it was completely remodeled in 1770 and for many people, is the finest of all Suzhou's gardens. Although exceptionally small, it succeeds, with great subtlety, in introducing every element considered crucial to the classical garden (see pp28–9). It includes a central lake, discreet connecting corridors, pavilions with miniature courtyards, screens, delicate latticework, and above all, points which "frame a view", as if looking at a perfectly balanced photograph. The best known building is the Pavilion for Watching the Moon, from where the moon can be viewed in a mirror, in the water, and in the sky. Regular evening performances of Chinese opera, including local kun ju, take place here.

🍀 Canglang Ting
3 Canglang Ting Jie, Renmin Lu. Tel (0512) 6519 4375. 🕐 daily. 📷
The Dark Blue Wave Pavilion Garden – whose name is suggestive of a relaxed and pragmatic approach to life – is perhaps Suzhou's oldest garden, first laid out in 1044 by a scholar, Su Zimei, on the site of an earlier villa. His successor, a general in the imperial army, enlarged it in the 12th century, and it was rebuilt in the 17th century. It is known for its technique of "borrowing a view", allowing the scenery beyond the garden's confines to play a role in its design. Here, it is

The Pavilion for Watching the Moon, Wangshi Yuan

Gateway to the Confucian Temple

achieved by lowering walls on the north side of some of the pavilions, allowing views across water; elsewhere the southwest hills can be seen. The central feature is a mound that is meant to resemble a wooded hill. Gardens were ideal places for contemplation and writing poetry, a fact demonstrated by the engravings of verses dotting Canglang Ting.

Pan Men Scenic Area

2 Dong Da Lu. ☐ 8am–5pm daily.

This area has been extensively restored but it still contains some of the city's most interesting historical sights. Pan Men is a unique fortified gate that controlled access to the city by both land and water nearly 700 years ago, although most of the present construction is more recent. Other highlights include the graceful Wu Men Bridge and the views of the city from the 140-ft (43-m) high Ruigang Pagoda. The bridge and pagoda both date back to the Song dynasty, although each has been rebuilt since.

Confucian Temple

45 Renmin Lu. ☐ daily.

The original Song-dynasty temple was rebuilt in 1864 after it was destroyed in the Taiping Rebellion. Its main hall, dating from the Ming dynasty, has several stone carvings including China's oldest surviving city map, depicting Suzhou, or Pingjiang as it was known in 1229. Also on display is a star chart dating from 1247 that

maps the positions of stars and celestial bodies in the heavens. It is one of the earliest surviving maps of its kind.

Tiger Hill

Huqiu Lu. **Tel** (0512) 6723 2305.
☐ 7:30am–5pm daily.
In the city's northwest is the popular Tiger Hill (Huqiu Shan), the burial place of He Lu, the King of Wu and founder of Suzhou. His spirit is said to be guarded by a white tiger, which appeared three days after his death and refused to leave.

The main attraction is the Song-dynasty leaning pagoda (Yunyan Ta or Cloud Rock Pagoda), built in brick, which leans more than 7 ft (2 m) from the perpendicular at its highest point. Some 10th-century Buddhist *sutras* and a record of the year that it was constructed (959–961) were

Ceremonial urn, Tiger Hill

discovered during one of the attempts to prevent it from falling. The park is quite large, with pools and flowerbeds filled with blooms in spring and early summer. One of the many boulders is split in two, allegedly the result of He Lu's swordsmanship. He is supposedly buried nearby along with 3,000 swords.

Hanshan Si

24 Hanshansi Long. **Tel** (0512) 6533 6634. ☐ 8am–5pm daily.
First constructed in the Liang dynasty, the Cold Mountain Temple was named after a Tang-dynasty poet-monk. A stone rendition of him and his fellow monk, Shi De, is to be seen here. The temple was rebuilt in the 19th century, after it was destroyed during the Taiping Rebellion. Located close to the Grand Canal, it was immortalized by the Tang-dynasty poet Zhang Ji, who arrived here by boat and anchored nearby. His poem "Anchored at Night by the Maple Bridge" is inscribed on a stone stele, and contains the lines that made Hanshan Si famous: "Beyond Suzhou lies Hanshan Temple; at midnight the clang of the bell reaches the traveler's boat." The bell alluded to here was subsequently lost, and the temple's current bell was presented by Japan in 1905. Nearby, a beautiful arched bridge offers views along the Grand Canal.

Incense burners in the grounds of Hanshan Si

Hangzhou ❻
杭州

Renowned in medieval China as an earthly paradise, Hangzhou became the splendid capital of the Southern Song dynasty between 1138 and 1279. Later, when the conquering Mongols chose what is now Beijing as their new capital, Hangzhou continued to be a thriving commercial city. Its glories were extolled by Marco Polo *(see p153)*, who allegedly visited Hangzhou at the height of its prosperity and described it as "the City of Heaven, the most magnificent in all the world." Although most of the old buildings were destroyed in the Taiping Rebellion, the attractive West Lake and its surrounding area are still worth visiting.

Statue of Yue Fei

Entrance archway to Yue Fei Mu (Tomb of Yue Fei)

🛕 Yue Fei Mu
Bei Shan Lu. *Tel (0571) 8796 9670.* ⏲ 7:30am–5:30pm daily. 📷

Just north of the West Lake lies the tomb of the Song general, Yue Fei, a popular Chinese hero revered for his patriotism. His campaigns against the invading Jin were so successful that his Song overlords began to worry that he might turn against them. He was falsely charged with sedition and executed, only to become a martyr whose exploits were widely celebrated in painting.

The Yue Fei Temple is a late 19th-century construction, and the tomb lies beside it. Leading to the tomb is a small avenue of stone animals. The central tumulus belongs to Yue Fei, while the smaller one is his son's, who was also executed. The kneeling figures in iron represent his tormentors – the prime minister, his wife, a jealous general, and the prison governor. It was customary to spit on them, but this is no longer encouraged.

🌸 Huanglong Dong Park & Qixia Shan
North of West Lake (Xi Hu).

This hilly area, crisscrossed with paths, has several sights of interest. Huanglong Dong Park, nestling in the hills, is very attractive with its teahouses, ponds, and flowers, and a pavilion where musicians perform traditional music in summer. To the east is **Baoshu Ta**, a 20th-century rebuild of a Song-era pagoda. Looming close by is Qixia Shan (Lingering Clouds Mountain), with the **Baopu Daoist Temple** located halfway up its slopes. This active temple has services on most days. It makes an interesting stopover, where visitors can watch pilgrims, priests, and perhaps even one of the frequent ancestral worship ceremonies.

Wood panel carving at Baopu Daoist Temple

🏛 Hu Qingyu Tang Museum of Chinese Medicine
95 Dajing Xiang. *Tel (0571) 8702 7507.* ⏲ 8:30am–5pm daily. 📷

This interesting museum is housed in a beautiful old apothecary's shop. It was established by the merchant Hu Xueyan during the Qing dynasty and traces the history of traditional Chinese medicine, which goes back thousands of years. It is still an active dispensary and pharmacy.

🌸 West Lake
See pp152–3.

🏛 Tea Museum
Longjing Lu. *Tel (0571) 8796 4232.* ⏲ 8:30am–4:30pm daily. 📷

Tracing the history of tea production, the Tea Museum has lots of interesting information regarding the different varieties of tea, its cultivation, and the development of tea-making and tea-drinking vessels. Fortunately, many of the captions are in English.

🏘 Longjing Village
SW of Tea Museum. 📷

The village of Longjing (Dragon Well) produces one of China's most famous varieties of green tea. Visitors can wander around the tea terraces, catching glimpses of the different stages of production – cutting, sorting, and drying – and also buy the tea, which varies in price according to its grade.

Inside the main hall of the Hu Qingyu Tang Museum of Chinese Medicine

🏛 Lingyin Si

1 Fayun Long, Lingyin Lu. **Tel** *(0571) 8796 8665.* ⬤ *6am–6pm daily.* 🎫

The hill area known as Feilai Feng (The Peak that Flew Here) is home to some of the city's main sights, including Lingyin Si. Founded in AD 326, this temple once housed 3,000 monks who worshiped in more than 70 halls. Though now much reduced in size, it is still one of China's largest temples. It was damaged in the 19th-century Taiping Rebellion, and then again by fire in the 20th century. It is said to owe its survival to Zhou Enlai, who prevented its destruction during the Cultural Revolution. Still, some parts of the temple are ancient, such as the stone pagodas on either side of the entrance hall, which date from AD 969. Behind this hall is the **Great Buddha Hall**, with an impressive 66-ft (20-m) statue of the Buddha carved in 1956 from camphor wood.

The **Ligong Pagoda** at the entrance was built in honor of the Indian monk, Hui Li, who gave the mountain its eccentric

Buddha sculptures at Feilai Feng

VISITORS' CHECKLIST

75 miles (120 km) SW of Shanghai. 🏙 *6,115,000.* ✈ 🚆 *Train Station, East Train Station.* 🚌 *East Bus Station, North Bus Station, West Bus Station, CAAC (buses to airport).* ⛴ *Ferry to Suzhou & Wuxi.* 🚩 *1 Bei Shan Lu, (0571) 96123.*

name. Hui Li thought it was the spitting image of a hill in India and asked whether it had flown here. Feilai Feng is known for the dozens of Buddhist sculptures carved into the rock, many dating from the 10th century.

🏛 Six Harmonies Pagoda

16 Zhijiang Lu. **Tel** *(0571) 8659 1401.* ⬤ *6:30am–5:30pm daily.* 🎫

Standing beside the railway bridge on the northern shore of the Qiantang River, Liuhe Ta is all that is left of an octagonal temple first built in AD 970 to placate the tidal bore, a massive wall of water that rushes upstream during high tide. Over 197-ft (60-m) high, it served as a lighthouse up until the Ming dynasty.

HANGZHOU CITY CENTER

Hu Qingyu Tang Museum of Chinese Medicine ③
Huanglong Dong Park & Qixia Shan ②
Lingyin Si ⑦
Longjing Village ⑥
Six Harmonies Pagoda ⑧
Tea Museum ⑤
West Lake ④
Yue Fei Mu ①

North Bus Station, Ferry Terminal

East Train Station, East Bus Station

CAAC Airport

West Bus Station
TIANMUSHAN LU
SHUGUANG LU
TIYUCHANG LU

Huanglong Dong Park & Qixia Shan ②
QINGCHUN LU
Yue Fei Mu ①
JIEFANG LU
Lake Tours Jetty
City Government Office
⑦ Lingyin Si
West Lake ④
Art Institute
HEFANG JIE
XINCHENGZHAN LU
Train Station
Chinese Medicine Museum ③
Tea Museum ⑤
Huagang Gongyuan
Lin Biao's Former Residence
⑥ Longjing Village
MANJUELONG LU
Zoo
Hupaomeng Quan Gongyuan
Six Harmonies Pagoda ⑧
FUXING DA DAO
Qiantang River

0 km   1
0 miles   1

Key to Symbols *see back flap*

West Lake
西湖

Metal work, Xiaoying Island

Long considered one of the scenic wonders of China, covering over three square miles (8 sq km), West Lake (Xi Hu) is situated at the heart of Hangzhou. Surrounded by gentle green hills, the lake's willow-shaded causeways and fragrant cover of lotus blossoms have long been an inspiration for artists. Originally the lake was an inlet off the estuary of the Qiantang River, becoming a lake when the river began to silt up in the 4th century. The lake had a tendency to flood, so several dykes were built, including the Bai and Su Causeways. Hiring a private boat from the eastern shore for an afternoon on the water is highly recommended, as is a leisurely stroll along the shady causeways.

★ Three Pools Reflecting the Moon
Three small stone pagodas rise from the waters near Xiaoying Island. At full moon candles are placed within and their openings are covered in paper to create reflections resembling the moon.

XI LI HU

Huagang Garden
This garden is intended as a place for viewing fish. Designed by a Song-dynasty eunuch, its pools are filled with shimmering goldfish in a restful setting of grasses and trees.

STAR FEATURES

★ Xiaoying Island

★ Three Pools Reflecting the Moon

★ Su Causeway

★ Xiaoying Island
Often called San Tan Yin Yue Island, referring to the three moon-reflecting pagodas off its shores, Xiaoying Island consists of four enclosed pools fringed by pavilions first built in 1611. The zig-zagging Nine Bend Bridge was built in 1727.

VISITORS' CHECKLIST

Hangzhou. 🚄 regularly from
eastern shore near Hubin Lu.
Boats for hire on Gu Shan Island.
Zhejiang Provincial Museum
25 Gushan Lu. **Tel** (0571) 8798
0281. ○ 1pm–4pm Mon, 9am–
4pm Tue–Sun. 💷

★ Su Causeway
*The longer of the two causeways takes its name from the
Song-dynasty poet, Su Dongpo, who also served as governor.
Linked by six stone bridges, the causeway is a peaceful
thoroughfare running along the lake's western edge.*

Bridge to Quyuan Garden
*This bridge leads to a stunning
garden surrounded by lotus flowers.
It is considered one of the ten
prospects from where the lake
can be seen to best advantage.*

**The Seal Engravers
Society** is open in
the summer months.

GU SHAN

Zhejiang
Provincial
Museum

XI HU

BEI LI HU

MARCO POLO

Whether Marco Polo ever visited China
is much disputed. However, according to
the book he dictated to a ghost writer who
embroidered it substantially, Polo became
governor of nearby Yangzhou for three
years during the Yuan dynasty. He describes
Hangzhou as paradise and the finest city in
the world, with fascinating markets, pleasure
boats, and prostitutes.
Hangzhou was indeed a
cosmopolitan city, ever
since the Southern Song
dynasty made it their
capital. *The Travels of
Marco Polo*, however,
may be based on
earlier journeys by his
father and uncle, and
stories from other
merchants.

**Engraving of Marco
Polo, 1254– 1324**

Bai Causeway
*Named after the 9th-century poet-governor
Bai Juyi, this dyke leads to Gu Shan, an
island first landscaped during the Tang
dynasty, and now containing a tea house
and the provincial museum.*

TWO GUIDED WALKS

After the grandiose sweep of the Bund, the best walking in Shanghai is through the areas where the *shikumen*, or stone-gate houses, of ordinary people stand next to the vast European-styled villas and mansions erected in the early years of the 20th century for foreign business magnates.

Although the city is best known for its foreign influences, something even Shanghainese highlight first when talking about their home town, the Chinese side of Shanghai should not be forgotten. After the Opium Wars of the 1840s and 1850s, the original modest walled city became surrounded by swathes of foreigner-controlled territory. But it is in what survives of the Old City that the remnants of more traditional Chinese culture can still be found.

The first walk begins at the heart of this district, taking in temples and the scant remains of the original city fortifications. It ends with a look at a successful modern attempt to recycle the city's traditional buildings with the shiny new shopping, dining, and

Art Deco detailing

entertainment district of Xin Tiandi ("New Heaven and Earth"), which makes striking use of old housing.

West of Xin Tiandi, the French Concession offers some of the best of the surviving colonial-era villas and mansion blocks. Some are now hotels, or restaurants and bars, and some have been preserved through the accident of having at some point been occupied by those the ruling Communist Party promotes as "Great Men."

The second walk visits some of the more notable examples of Concession architecture. It traces a century's worth of history written in brick and stone, from the party town that was Shanghai in its 1930s heyday, through the rather more dour Party decades post 1949, to the rebirth of the city, as most visibly exemplified by the high-end international retailers now crowding fashionable Huaihai Lu. For good measure, the walk also includes a hint of the good old-fashioned seediness for which the city was formerly famed, in the shape of Maoming Lu Bar Street.

KEY

··· Walk route

◁ One of the villas in the French Concession's Ruijin Guesthouse complex, now home to the Face bar

A 90-Minute Walk through the Old City

Although the city walls of the original Chinese settlement were pulled down early last century, their former path is still clearly visible on maps, marked by a perfect circle of road. Within this ring you'll find everything from bustling produce markets full of pyjama-clad vendors and shoppers, to some delightful old timber and brick architecture. The Old City is also home to the famous Yu Gardens, and to places of worship of every shape, size, and religious persuasion. After time spent observing back-street reminders of Shanghai's history, the walk ends with the ultra-fashionable, rebuilt oldness of Xin Tiandi.

Dajing Lu food market ⑦

Fangbang Zhonglu ②

Fangbang Zhonglu

The walk begins on Fangbang Zhonglu at the southern entrance to the Yu Gardens and Bazaar complex. Just inside is the **City Temple** ①. Once much larger, the temple is now squeezed by tall mock-traditional department stores, but it remains a popular place of worship and is fascinating to visit. After seeing the temple, return to **Fangbang Zhonglu** ② and walk west past dealers in "antiques," along with sellers of tea, furniture, peasant art, and traditional blue-and-white batik-style cloth. The shops are worth browsing, but they are also prone to over-charging anyone who does not know better.

Where the bazaar comes to an end turn right and head north towards the large **decorative gate** ③, or *pailou*. However, before reaching it turn left and then take the first right; this will take you

by the long, mustard-colored wall of the **Chengxiang Ge Buddhist Temple** ④. Turn left at the top of the alley and dodge the enthusiastic pearl vendors whose shops cluster near the temple entrance. The three large halls that make up

the complex remain home to a sizeable community of nuns.

Continue west a short distance to the **Fuyou Lu Mosque** ⑤, Shanghai's oldest place of Islamic worship (1868) – a green sign indicates its location down a tiny alley.

Dajing Lu

At Henan Nan Lu turn left and pass beneath another gaudy **reconstructed arch** ⑥.

The courtyard of the Chengxiang Ge Buddhist Temple ④

KEY

• • •   Walk route

Ⓜ   Subway station

Dajing Tower museum ⑧

Xin Tiandi – old architecture put to new uses ⑭

chunk of original **city wall** ⑨ – it's on the right-hand side of the street and is invariably obscured by laundry flapping on bamboo poles.

Dongtai Lu

Busy **Renmin Lu** ⑩ follows the line of the walls that formerly encircled the Old City. Despite Shanghai's growing number of cars it still resembles a cycle track in rush hour. Leave it to turn right into Kuaiji Lu, cross main Xizang Nan Lu, and continue along Liuhekou Lu, where there's an indoor **bird and flower market** ⑪, full of cricket enthusiasts (the insect, not the game), who gather with their jars of twitching creatures. A little further on is **Dongtai Lu Market** ⑫, optimistically called an "antiques market," but in view of the unlikelihood of finding any authentic treasures, it is more accurately described as a flea market.

Xin Tiandi

Head north up Dongtai Lu and turn left on Chongde Lu, following the street until it turns right into Taicang Lu. This borders **Huahai Park** ⑬ for a bit, and then a few hundred yards farther west is **Xin Tiandi** ⑭, an area of *shikumen* (stone tenements) redeveloped into a smart shopping and restaurant complex. The exteriors are original, but all the internal walls have been removed to make way for new interiors. This is now said to be the most popular tourist sight in Shanghai for out-of-town Chinese, and a model for redevelopments across China.

TIPS FOR WALKERS

Length: 2 miles (3.2 km).
Getting there: Take a taxi to the Yu Gardens Bazaar.
Yu Gardens: Open 8:30am–5pm daily.
Chengxiang Ge: Open 7am–4pm daily.
Dajing Tower: Open 9am–4pm daily.
Bird and Flower Market: Open 8am–6pm daily.
Dongtai Lu Antiques Market: Open 9am–5pm daily.
Stopping off points: Huxinting Teahouse in the Yu Gardens is the most famous spot for tea and snacks, and the Nanxiang Steamed Bun Restaurant has possibly Shanghai's best dumplings, but both may have long queues. At Xin Tiandi, try Crystal Jade for a dim sum lunch, the Paulaner for German beer, Visage for coffee and cake, or T8 for a reasonably priced set lunch.

Continue south for a little while before turning right into Dajing Lu, which soon becomes a bustling **food market** ⑦. Depending on the time of day, you'll see groups of wizened ladies sorting through leafy piles of greens, chefs tossing blackened woks full of noodles and traditional Shanghai dumplings, and fishmongers scaling the catch of the day. Stay on this road until you reach the junction with Renmin Lu, which is where you'll find the **Dajing Tower** ⑧. Originally part of the city's defences and then an active temple, the tower now houses a small museum with a model of the old city walls and an exhibition of black-and-white photos. If you backtrack slightly from the tower, you might be able to find the only surviving

Dongtai Lu Antiques Market ⑫

A 90-Minute Walk around the French Concession

In 1854, the British negotiated a deal with the Chinese that led to the creation of the International Concession, a zone of self-rule for foreign powers in Shanghai. The French, however, declined to join. They made a separate deal to found their own concession, beginning with a narrow finger of land between the old Chinese city and what is now Yan'an Lu, and later spreading to cover a large area to the west. Redevelopment is constantly removing the old villas and apartment buildings that formerly made this area of Shanghai resemble a typical French provincial town, but there remains much to see and this is a very walkable part of town.

cafés, craft shops, boutiques, and galleries. Side turnings are lined with fine examples of *shikumen*, the houses with stone-framed entrances that are this city's counterpart to Beijing's *siheyuan* dwellings.

Si Nan Lu
At the top of the alley turn right along Jianguo Zhong Lu, then left into Si Nan Lu, past mansions with hints not only of

Taikang Lu Art Street ⑥

Ruijin Er Lu and Taikang Lu
Start by taking a taxi to 27 Shaoxing Lu for morning coffee or Chinese tea at the **Old China Hand Reading Room** ①. This is a quiet café with elegant period furnishings that also sells books on the old architecture of Shanghai and elsewhere produced by the team of American-born but long-time Shanghai resident Tess Johnston and local photographer Deke Erh.

From the café head off east along Shaoxing Lu, and turn right at the end down **Ruijin Er Lu** ②. On this street look above the modern shop fronts for hints of the city's Art Deco past, and other oddities such as the particularly **Germanic mansion** ③ at No. 152. Cross the junction with Jianguo Zhong Lu and take the next left into **Taikang Lu** ④, which is lined with art shops with foreigner-pleasing watercolors, and tailors happy to make a traditional *qipao* dress to fit the foreign form. At Zui Zhu Zhai (No. 322) framed calligraphy by a living master is available from about ¥600 – much cheaper than in Xin Tiandi or elsewhere.

Cross over the road for a fascinating **wet market** ⑤, full of live fish, frogs, eels, and snakes, then return to pass under an arch leading into what's known as **Taikang Lu Art Street** ⑥. This is a narrow alley lined by

Café-cum-bookshop-cum-library: Old China Hand Reading Room ①

France, but Spain and Germany too. These were spacious enough to attract senior figures from both the rival Nationalist and Communist parties in their day. On the right you come to the **Former Residence of Zhou Enlai** ⑦ (*see p132*), Premier and Foreign Minister under the People's Republic, while farther along is the **Sun Yat Sen Memorial Residence** ⑧

Cafés and bicycles on Maoming Nan Lu ⑬

Sun Yat Sen, founder of
the Nationalist Party ⑧

| 0 meters | 500 |
| 0 yards | 500 |

KEY

• • • Walk route

Ⓜ Subway station

TIPS FOR WALKERS

Length: *2.4 miles (4 km).*
Getting there: *Taxi to the Old China Hand Reading Room.*
Old China Hand Reading Room: *Open 9:30am–midnight daily.*
Taikang Lu wet market: *Open 6am–4pm daily.*
Stopping off points: *There's a "French Bakery" at the corner of Jianguo Zhong Lu and Ruijin Er Lu, with cakes and bread to take away. Otherwise, there are cafés and restaurants among the boutiques and galleries in the Taikang Lu Art Street. For something more substantial, the 1931 restaurant at Maoming Lu 112 does excellent Shanghainese food. The Face bar is a terrific place to wind up with a stiff drink, and it has a very decent Southeast Asian restaurant upstairs in the La Na Thai.*

(see p132). Both are supposedly left furnished much as they were at the time, Zhou's proletarian credentials reinforced by the spartan interior of his house, while Sun's more middle-class origins are betrayed by the house's treasures and trinkets.

Huaihai Zhong Lu

Immediately east of the Sun Yat Sen residence is the French-created **Fuxing Park** ⑨ *(see p132),* which is certainly worth a quick detour, before returning to Si Nan Lu via Gaolan Lu – and another quick detour for the onion-domed former **Russian Orthodox Church of St. Nicholas** ⑩, built in 1933 and dedicated to the last Tsar.

Continuing north brings you eventually to **Huaihai Zhong Lu** ⑪. Once the French Concession's main boulevard, it's now the city's premier shopping street, mixing international big brand names with an appealing array of smaller boutiques. Walking west, after a short time you'll see the splendid, spire-topped Art Deco exterior of the **Cathay Theater** ⑫ over on the north side of the road. Built in the 1930s it is still in use as a cinema showing predominantly Western movies subtitled with Chinese. Turn left here into **Maoming Nan Lu** ⑬.

This is a charming street, shaded by trees, typically filled with bicycles, and lined with small boutiques, cafés, and restaurants. However, the southern end has quite a different character – here it becomes **Bar Street** ⑭, home to a strip of loud neon-lit bars favored by expats.

For more salubrious entertainment look for the gateway on the left side of the street that leads into the grounds of the **Ruijin Guesthouse** ⑮. This is a glorious city center estate developed by a newspaper magnate. The main villa is now a striking hotel, while various satellite buildings, all set among beautifully manicured lawns now house a variety of dining and drinking venues, including Face *(see p165).*

Former Residence of Zhou Enlai ⑦

SHOPPING IN SHANGHAI

Intricate paper cut, found in craft stores

Where Beijing boasts a thousand-plus years of imperial history and asssociated monuments, Shanghai reigns supreme when it comes to the modern passions of eating and shopping. With the latter, the enticements begin with the likes of Chinese cotton slippers, sold two pairs for a dollar at the street market, and run all the way up to high-fashion labels such as Chloé, Lanvin, and YSL, loading the racks at Three for Women, part of the lifestyle complex that is Three on the Bund. The former main shopping street of Nanjing Dong Lu remains stuck in the socialist era, with its flagship the No. 1 Department Store, where you can buy Mao-label tea and cigarettes in a packet emblazoned with a golden Oriental Pearl TV Tower. Instead, the new breed of Shanghai shoppers throng Huaihai Lu, which is lined with high-gloss malls at its eastern end and boutique shopping farther west. Markets are generally thinner on the ground than in Beijing but, even so, only the most morose opponent of consumerism could fail to find fun shopping in Shanghai.

PRACTICAL INFORMATION

Most shops are open seven days a week from around 10am through until 9pm or even later. Markets will start and finish earlier. Credit cards are not as widely accepted as you might expect; some places only take local cards and many don't take any form of plastic at all. You need to carry cash. If you run short, ATMs are not hard to find.

SHOPPING ETIQUETTE

When bargaining at any market that sees plenty of foreign shoppers – Fangbang Lu or Dongtai Lu, for example – don't listen to advice that says half or one third of the first offer made by the vendor is reasonable. This first-named price may easily be five, ten or even fifteen times what

A Western fashion house advertises in the windows of a Shanghai mall

any local would consider a reasonable sum. A counter-offer of only half the vendor's price marks you down as easy prey. Offer far less – maybe as little as 10 percent of the price you were quoted. Your first counter-offer says, "I'm not as stupid as you think. And maybe I'm not that interested anyway." It's hard to make an offer that's too low, and you also have nothing to lose. Either the vendor will dramatically lower his or her price, or he or she will let you walk away, in which case you can improve your offer. Your second offer should be no more than a fraction higher than your first.

It is worth remembering that since there is nothing original or truly antique in Shanghai's markets, there is little that is unique either.

You should always try your luck with a number of vendors before settling on any purchase.

Always do everything in a friendly way and with a smile.

Refunds are impossible, so be certain that you have what you want before you pay.

ANTIQUES

There aren't any true antiques on sale in Shanghai and if there were you'd need special permission to export them anyway. What there is, however, is lots of Mao-era memorabilia. The place for this is **Dongtai Lu**, which is just east of the Xin Tiandi complex. Referred to as an antiques market, the stalls that line this fairly short street are in fact filled with an assortment of Communist Party kitsch and other

Modern twists on classic Chinese fashion at Shanghai Tang

miscellaneous junk, much of which is grossly overpriced. Still, it is fun to browse, and you never know when a foot-high, pewter Mao figurine is going to come in handy. There are similar pickings on **Fuyou Lu** (open Sunday only), and **Fangbang Lu**. Fangbang Lu's **Hubao Building Basement Market**, which is part of the busy Yu Gardens Bazaar complex, is the city's largest indoor antiques market.

Over in the French Concession, **Madam Mao's Dowry** is a curiosity store of odd bits and pieces of recent heritage collected by its magpie owners, from vintage clothing to Socialist-Realist posters. Everything here is the genuine article – no repros.

Other stores worth a visit include the state-run **Shanghai Antique & Curio Shop**, just off the Bund, which is something of an antique itself, having been around for over a hundred years, while over in the Hongkou district **Duolun Lu** has a row of shops selling antiques and curios.

Antique radio for sale at a street market

ART

The Shanghai equivalent of Beijing's 798 Art District is **Mogan Shan Lu**. This is a street north of Jing'an, not far from the train station on the west bank of Suzhou

Creek. Here, an area of light industrial buildings has been taken over by artists' ateliers and workshops, as well as a number of commercial galleries. These include the well-respected **ShanghART**, which also has a branch at Fuxing Park in the French Concession. Also in the French Concession is **Art Scene China**, which represents more than 20 of China's leading contemporary artists. Its main gallery is in a European-style villa just around the corner from the US Consulate.

For something less polished, **Taikang Lu Art Street** is an attempt to foster an arts and crafts district based around a former candy factory. The project has yet to mature but there are a handful of art galleries, plus some handicraft workshops and a few interesting small jewelry and ethnic clothing boutiques in the surrounding alleys. It is a pretty area to explore with interesting architecture and a handful of pleasant cafés and bars; it is visited as part of one of the Shanghai Guided Walks (see p158).

BOOKS

Shanghai beats Beijing hands down for English-language books. Like its counterpart in the capital, the state-run

Mao's "Little Red Book" – still widely available in Shanghai

Foreign Languages Bookstore has a reasonable selection of English-language novels, as well as plenty of souvenir picture books. Far better though is **Chaterhouse Booktrader**, a branch of a Hong Kong bookstore that stocks a phenomenal range of English-language fiction and non-fiction, plus international magazines and newspapers. **Garden Books**, at the heart of the French Concession, combines bookselling with a pleasant café and ice-cream counter, while the **Shanghai Museum Shop** is as good as it gets when it comes to books about not just Shanghai, but China as a whole.

The **Confucius Temple** in the Old City has a book market every Sunday that makes for fun browsing.

CHINESE PHARMACIES

If you know your Chinese medicine, speak Chinese, or are just plain curious, **Tong Han Chun** is a venerable example of a traditional Chinese medicine store – one reputedly established in 1783. Claiming even older roots, **Lei Yun Shang Pharmacy** first opened in Suzhou in 1662 but is a relative newcomer to Shanghai, having arrived only in 1860. It still maintains its old-fashioned wooden interior. In both of these shops you will find shelves of large glass jars filled with the likes of dried seahorses and dried placentas, both good for the kidneys, apparently.

Browsing for antiques and trinkets on Dongtai Lu

Boutique clothes store on Huaihai
Zhong Lu, French Concession

CLOTHES & TEXTILES

Most major clothing brand
names from Europe, the US,
and Japan are represented in
Shanghai. Prices in the stores
are slightly cheaper than you
would find at home, which is
to be expected given that a
large percentage of clothing
sold the world over now
originates in factories in
China. The main shopping
streets are **Huaihai Lu** in
the French Concession and
Nanjing Lu west of People's
Square, which is where
you find modern, high-end
malls such as **CITIC Square**
and **Plaza 66**.

For something a bit
different, tree-lined **Changle
Lu**, particularly between
Shaanxi Nan Lu and Fumin
Lu, has the best boutiques in
the city. Styles are Western,
although sizes are Eastern
(small). Many of these places
specialize in factory seconds
of items by well-known
international designers.

For original designer items,
with price tags to match, the
place to go is Three on the
Bund, where **Three for Women**
stocks clothes and accessories
by some of the most exclusive
names, including the Asian-
inspired creations of Vivienne
Tam. Maoming Lu has a
branch of **Shanghai Tang**, the
glamorous retro-Asian, Hong
Kong high-fashion store.

The city has also revived
its tradition of fine tailoring.
W.W. Chan & Sons Tailor Ltd. is
noted for high quality at fair

prices. Fabrics by the meter
or the bolt are sold at the
**Shanghai Nan Waitan (South
Bund) Textile Market**. Filling
four floors, it resembles a
provincial shopping mall, but
it sells only fabric. Most stalls
also have a resident tailor
ready to whip up made-to-
measure cashmere coats,
cotton shirts, or silk dresses.
They can follow any pattern
provided, or even make
copies from fashion pictures
clipped from a magazine.
It typically takes a week for
garments to be made but rush
jobs can be done for a little
more. A shirt will cost the
equivalent of around $10,
trousers $20.

CRAFTS

It is never good practice to
shop near sites with a high
volume of tourist traffic,
and as you might
imagine there is a
lot of trash for
sale at the shops
around the **Yu
Gardens Bazaar** (see
pp130–31). But even
Shanghainese visit the
quieter corners of the
complex for items
such as tea, teapots, and tea
sets. For porcelain in general,
some of the best buys are the
fine reproductions of classic
designs available at the
Shanghai Museum Shop (see
pp126–9). The shop also has
lots of other beautiful items,
from calligraphy to carved
jade, jewelry, and silk slippers.
Although expensive, the work
sold here is of better quality
than almost anything else
on the market.

Silk embroidered
coasters

Handicrafts made by some
of China's myriad ethnic
minorities, as well as by
people of neighboring
countries, including Nepal,
are available at shops dotted
along Nanjing Lu.

DEPARTMENT STORES
& MALLS

Avoid the outmoded
Friendship Store, a leftover
from the days when peanut
butter was only available
when specially imported for
foreigners, and which now
exists largely to overcharge
tourists. Relics such as this
have been superseded by the
likes of Japanese department
store **Isetan**, which has two
branches in Shanghai.

The Shanghainese have also
caught the mall craze. Nanjing
Xi Lu has three in a
row: six-story **CITIC
Square**, the plush
Plaza 66, and the
more egalitarian
Westgate Mall. All
these places are
full of luxury-
brand Western
goods (at significantly
higher than Western
prices) of the kind that
you used to find faked at the
main city market.

Now that the municipality
has shut down the fake
market, and the old fabric
market has moved under
cover, Shanghai is severely
lacking in open-air commerce.
The most colorful alternative
is the **Hong Kong Shopping
Center**, a warren of passages
beneath Renmin Square filled
with hundreds of small fashion
and accessories stores.

Plaza 66, one of three adjacent modern malls on Nanjing Xi Lu

ELECTRONICS

There are no bargains to be had on computers or other electronic items. Most everything is imported and so costs as much, if not more than, in the US or Europe. There are a few exceptions such as Sony shortwave radios, made in China for export, which may be bargained down to decent prices. Cheap Chinese MP3 players or DVD players are often multi-lingual and multi-voltage, but there's no warranty except with a very few global Chinese brands. Accessories and media such as disks, tapes, leads, and

Nanjing Dong Lu, once Shanghai's main shopping street

convertors, all made in China, are cheaper than the identical item packaged up for sale at home, and these can all be

found at **Bai Nao Hui** in the district of Xuhui, which has several floors of audio-visual and computing bits and pieces.

PEARLS & JEWELRY

Jewelry shops abound all over the city, particularly in the Old City around the Yu Gardens Bazaar and along pedestrianized Nanjing Dong Lu. Pearls are a specialty, both fresh- and saltwater. One of the best known places is Nanjing Lu's **Shanghai Pearl City**. Prices are competitive, but you do need to know what you are looking at.

Directory

ANTIQUES

Dongtai Lu Antiques Market
Dongtai Lu, off Chongde Lu, near Xin Tiandi.
Map 2 B4.

Fuyou Lou Market
Cangbao Lou, Fangbang Zhong Lu 457, Old City.
Map 2 C4.

Hubao Building Basement Market
Fangbang Lu, Old City.
Map 2 C4.

Madam Mao's Dowry
70 Fuxing Xi Lu, by Yongfu Lu, French Concession.
Tel (021) 6437 1255.

Shanghai Antique & Curio Shop
218–226 Guangdong Lu, by Jiangxi Zhong Lu, Huangpu District.
Map 2 C3.
Tel (021) 6321 4697.

ART

Art Scene China
No. 8 Lane, 37 Fuxing Xi Lu, by Wulumqi Lu, French Concession.
www.artscenechina.com

ShangART
50 Mogan Shan Lu, off Xisuzhou Lu, Putuo District.
www.shangart.com

BOOKS

Chaterhouse Booktrader
Times Square, 93 Hauihai Zhong Lu, French Concession.
Map 2 B4.
Tel (021) 6391 8235.

Confucius Temple Book Market
215 Wenmiao Lu, Old City.
Map 2 B5.

Garden Books
325 Changle Lu, French Concession.
Map 1 E4.
Tel (021) 5404 8728.

Foreign Languages Bookstore
390 Fuzhou Lu, Huangpu District.
Map 2 B3.
Tel (021) 6322 3200.

Shanghai Museum Shop
201 Renmin Da Dao, People's Square.
Map 2 A3.
Tel (021) 6372 3500.

CHINESE PHARMACIES

Lei Yun Shang
2 Huashan Lu, Jing'an District.
Map 1 D3.
Tel (021) 6217 3501.

Tong Han Chun
20 Yuyuan Xin Lu, by Jiuxiao Lu, Old City.
Map 2 C4.
Tel (021) 6355 0308.

CLOTHES AND TEXTILES

Shanghai Nan Waitan (South Bund) Textile Market
399 Lujiabang Lu, Huangpu District.

Shanghai Tang
59 Maoming Nan Lu, by Changle Lu, French Concession.
Map 1 E4.
Tel (021) 5466 3006.

Three for Women
Three on the Bund, 3 Zhongshan Dong Yi Lu, Huangpu District.
Map 2 C3.
www.threeonthebund.com

W.W. Chan & Sons Tailor Ltd.
129 Maoming Nan Lu, by Huaihai Zhong Lu, French Concession.
Map 1 E4.
Tel (021) 5404 1469.

CRAFTS

Shanghai Museum Shop
See **Books** above.

Yu Gardens Bazaar
Fuyou Lu, Old City.
Map 2 C4.

DEPARTMENT STORES & MALLS

CITIC Square
1168 Nanjing Xi Lu, Jing'an District.
Map 1 E3.

Friendship Store
65 Yan'an Dong Lu, by Jiangxi Lu, Huangpu District.
Map 2 C3.
Tel (021) 6337 3555.

Hong Kong Shopping Center
Beneath People's Square.
Map 2 A3.

Isetan
527 Huaihai Zhong Lu, French Concession.
Map 1 F4.

Plaza 66
1266 Nanjing Xi Lu, Jing'an District.
Map 1 E3.

Westgate Mall
1038 Nanjing Xi Lu, Jing'an District
Map 1 E3.

ELECTRONICS

Bai Nao Hui
11 Cao Xi Bei Lu, Xuhui District.

PEARLS & JEWELRY

Shanghai Pearl City
558 Nanjing Dong Lu, Huangpu District.
Map 2 C2.

ENTERTAINMENT IN SHANGHAI

It is frequently said that Beijing produces the art and culture, and Shanghai sells it. There is some truth in this. Beijing has the happening music scene; its film academy has produced almost every director of note of recent times; and it is the home of traditional art forms such as Beijing Opera. But in the last decade Shanghai has pulled ahead in building arts and entertainments venues, including theaters, concert halls, and galleries. However, because the city prides itself on being cosmopolitan, such

Sax player on bar balcony

places are more likely to be hosting *Cats* or Pavarotti, rather than any home-grown talent.

Shanghai's modern nightlife exists in the shadow of the reputation of the famously wild 1920s and 1930s. Many of the hotel bars at one end, and the seedier expat hang-outs of Maoming Lu and Julu Lu at the other, play on this reputation, with female wait staff dressed in the figure-hugging *qipao* (dresses) of old, live jazz, and cocktails. The scene offers far more variety than Beijing, but prices are correspondingly higher.

Shanghai Grand Theater, the city's premier venue for performing arts

PRACTICAL INFORMATION

For details of what's on in town pick up one of the local English-language listings magazines, such as *Shanghai Talk* and *that's Shanghai*. These are available free in hotel lobbies and at many restaurants and bars.

Tickets are generally bought at the venue box offices and paid for in cash. At small music clubs, pay on the door. Most hotel concierges can usually help with securing seats at the theaters.

CLASSICAL MUSIC AND THE PERFORMING ARTS

The major theaters – which include the **Shanghai Grand Theater**, **Lyceum Theater**, **Majestic Theater**, and the

Shanghai Center – put on large-scale concerts of Chinese and foreign music, including Hong Kong stagings of Western musical hits such as *Rent*, as well as some home-grown dance and musical spectaculars. Other theaters put on more traditional Chinese Opera performances, notably the **Tianchan Yifu Theater**.

Shanghai is most famous for its acrobatic shows. Although most performances are now constructed with tourists in mind, complete with theatrical lighting and sequined costumes, this makes them no less valid or spectacular. Lissom adults and children who seem more fluid than solid make towers out of themselves and assortments of tables, chairs, and

umbrellas, and disappear into the objects the same size as carry-on luggage.

BARS AND PUBS

Shanghai's image in the West links it inextricably to the cocktail, and certainly there are now many suitably luxurious locations in which to drink one. Hotel bars such as the Grand Hyatt's dizzying 88th-floor **Cloud Nine**, the Shangri-La's supremely chic 36th-floor **Jade**, and the Radisson's 47th-floor **Sky Dome** with its live jazz are among those offering views that may quickly induce the slightly colonial feeling of being master of all you survey. Nearer to ground level is the Grand Hyatt's glittering **Pu-J's**, while down in the basement at the Shangri-La is **B.A.T.S.**, with a nightly roster of professional bands working up the crowd's enthusiasm.

International sophistication spreads well beyond the big hotels. **Bar Rouge**, with snooty patrons awash in Veuve Cliquot, is one of the very few places in China where a dress code is enforced. If you're anything less than "smart casual" look elsewhere, although it's a shame to miss the terrace overlooking the Huangpu. Upstairs at **Park 97** has a mixed Chinese and expat clientele looking to meet Mr. or Miss Right over cocktails in

The blue façade of the Blue Frog on Maoming Lu

a velvety interior with a background of live soul music. **Face**, in the lush grounds of the Ruijin Guesthouse, offers a rare bit of green space to go with your G&T, while **Barbarossa** offers a North African theme with sequined pillows and a terracotta-tiled rooftop terrace overlooking a small lake in central Renmin Park.

Most chic of all perhaps is **Glamour Bar**, the cocktail venue attached to restaurant M on the Bund. It boasts regular live acts, which range from the eccentric to the internationally renowned; it is a place for a pre-dinner martini, a post-dinner liqueur, or simply to spend the whole evening wallowing in glam.

As an alternative to the cocktail scene, there is no shortage of more down-to-earth pubs. **O'Malley's** is possibly the best – by a leprechaun's nose – of the city's many Irish pubs. It has the usual Celtic clutter on the walls, international sport on large screens, and Guinness at prices that reflect how far it has traveled. By contrast, black beer from the Xinjiang Autonomous Region of northwest China is only ¥10 at local student haunt **Windows Scoreboard**, and goes down well with a ¥10 burger in between games of pool. Is this really China? **Blue Frog** with its clean, modern design is known for

The logo of stylish bar Face

its rack of shots, with plenty of draft beer or white wine available as alternatives. The **Paulaner Brauhaus** brews its own ale, with schnitzels and wurst to help it down, and views of the lights coming on along the Bund in the early evening. **Cotton's** is a big old house with rooms galore, each furnished with a grand fireplace.

The Maoming Lu and Julu Lu areas are crowded with further options, such as **Buddha Bar**, **Goodfellas**, **Judy's Too** and the smart **California Club** in Fuxing Park. To the west, Hengshan Lu's popular **Bourbon Street** offers live bands and dancing. Just north of Nanjing Xi Lu, Tongren Lu has the American-style bar, **Malone's**. Upscale Xin Tiandi has an good selection of pubs including the stylish **Le Club at La Maison**.

CLUBS

You're unlikely to travel to China just to go clubbing, but Shanghai regularly attracts big-name foreign DJs and hip-hop acts. Again, see the local English-language press for details. If you have ever wondered what Shanghainese rap sounds like, then you can join crowds of baggy-jeaned locals and foreign students at **Pegasus** to find out. Hong Kong and Taiwanese DJs appear at long-standing favorite **Guan Di** in Fuxing Park, playing trance, house, and hip hop at high volumes, while VIPs recline on the fringes drinking Chivas and green tea (and that's in the same glass). Smart city-center **Club dkd** booms out young Shanghai's favorite trance with plenty of guests from overseas. Many nights out end at late-opening **Mint**.

FILM

Cinemas in Shanghai suffer the same handicaps as movie houses in Beijing, namely heavy censorship, a strict limiting of the number of foreign movies that can be screened, and the fact that you can get any new release on DVD for less than a dollar long before it reaches the big screen. For all these reasons, Shanghai possesses far fewer cinemas that you would expect for a city of its size. The most modern and high-tech venue is the **Paradise Warner Cinema City**, a fairly new multiplex in the Xujiahui

The giddy heights of Cloud Nine, a bar 88 floors above street level

The foyer of the Cathay Theater, one of Shanghai's 1930s cinemas

district. However, probably more convenient for most visitors is the **UME International Cineplex** in Xin Tiandi. For a taste of cinema-going of old, visit the 1930s Art Deco **Cathay Theater** in the French Concession. It often screens international movies with Chinese subtitles.

Shanghai is also the venue for an international film festival, held every June *(see p35)*. Films screenings are open to the public and the movies shown are not subject to the usual censorship.

JAZZ

The last living relic of the "Whore of the Orient" era, the nonagenarian band at the **Peace Hotel Jazz Bar**, is more novelty act than any kind of serious musical proposition, although concierges and guide books will usually direct you to them. Serious jazz lovers would do better to head for the **Cotton Club**, which, while nowhere near as venerable as the Peace Hotel Jazz Bar, has been around long enough to garner a good reputation and is typically packed weekends. Try also **Club JZ**, a regular venue for visiting overseas jazzers and sessions of improvization. It is also where you

may see famous local singer Coco. The **House of Blues and Jazz**, in a small stone villa on the Maoming Lu Bar Street, is bluesier, and also features many touring bands from overseas. Drink prices at all these venues tend to be high. Foreign jazz acts also appear in residence at **Pu-J's**, and at some other cocktail venues, including the **Glamour Bar** and **Sky Dome**.

ROCK AND POP

Beijing claims the crown when it comes to live contemporary music, but Shanghai is trying hard to catch up. **Shuffle** features an even mix of local

Shanghainese and expat bands, with an emphasis on indie rock, but otherwise everything from flamenco guitar to Britpop. As in the Shanghai of old, some of the foreign players wouldn't make it on stage anywhere else, but cheap drinks help dull the pain.

Xin Tiandi, the Hong Kong-financed rebuild of *shikumen* housing into a playground for the well-heeled, is where you'll find **ARK Live House**, a sort of rock warehouse, with nightly performances ranging from Japanese glam rock to Nanjing punk, although with drinks unfortunately at Xin Tiandi prices. At the other end of the scale, **Harley's** is for Chinese biker wannabes with either mohawks or long greasy locks a-plenty, pogoing to heavy metal, punk, and anything from the noisier end of the scale.

TEAHOUSES

Normally the traditional Chinese tea house offers a respite from the crowds, but Shanghai's most famous, the **Huxinting** or "mid-lake pavilion," is set amid the bedlam of the Yu Gardens and its attendant shopping, and is anything but calm. However, its 200-year-old willow pattern looks, with access only via a ghost-thwarting zig-zag bridge (ghosts can only travel in straight lines) makes it the most popular place to experience a Chinese tea ceremony. Past visitors have included Queen Elizabeth II, Bill Clinton and other heads of state.

Fangbang Zhong Lu, the street that runs to the south of the Yu Gardens complex, has several similar operations of greater modernity, most selling tea as well as providing a place to drink it.

The Peace Hotel, home of Shanghai's oldest jazz band

DIRECTORY

CLASSICAL MUSIC AND THE PERFORMING ARTS

Lyceum Theater
57 Maoming Nan Lu, French Concession.
Map 1 E4.
Tel (021) 6217 8530.

Majestic Theater
66 Jiang Ning Lu, Jing'an District.
Map 1 E2.
Tel (021) 6217 4409.

Shanghai Center
1376 Nanjing Xi Lu, Jing'an District.
Map 1 E3.
Tel (021) 6279 8600.

Shanghai Grand Theater
300 Renmin Da Dao, Renmin Square.
Map 2 A3.
Tel (021) 6351 4668.

Tianchan Yifu Theater
701 Fuzhou Lu, Huangpu District.
Map 2 B3.
Tel (021) 6386 8686.

BARS, PUBS, AND CLUBS

ARK Live House
House 15, North Block, Lane 181, Xin Tiandi.
Map 2 A4.
Tel (021) 6326 8008.

Barbarossa
Nanjing Xi Lu 231, inside People's Park.
Map 2 A3.
Tel (021) 6318 0220.

Bar Rouge
7th Floor, 18 Zhongshan Dong Yi Lu, the Bund.
Map 2 C2.
Tel (021) 6339 1199.

B.A.T.S.
Pudong Shangri-La, 33 Fucheng Lu, Pudong.
Map 3 D3.
Tel (021) 6882 8888 ext. 24.

Blue Frog
207 Maoming Nan Lu, French Concession.
Map 1 E5.
Tel (021) 6445 6635.

Bourbon Street
191 Hengshan Lu, French Concession.
Tel (021) 6473 6662.

Buddha Bar
172 Maoming Nan Lu, French Concession.
Map 1 E5.
Tel (021) 6415 2688.

California Club
2A Gaolan Lu, Fuxing Park, French Concession.
Map 1 F4.
Tel (021) 6318 0785.

Cloud Nine
Grand Hyatt, Jinmao Tower, Pudong.
Map 3 E3.
Tel (021) 5049 1234.

Club dkd
438 Huaihai Zhong Lu, French Concession.
Map 1 E4.
Tel (021) 6359 9999.

Club JZ
46 Fuxing Xi Lu, French Concession.
Tel (021) 6431 0269.

Cotton Club
1428 Huaihai Zhong Lu, French Concession.
Map 1 E4.
Tel (021) 6437 7110.

Cotton's
132 Anting Lu, Xuhui District.
Tel (021) 6433 7995.

Face
Ruijin Guesthouse, 118 Ruijin Er Lu, French Concession.
Map 1 F5.
Tel (021) 6466 4328.

Glamour Bar
M on the Bund, 6th Floor, 20 Guangdong Lu, the Bund.
Map 2 C3.
Tel (021) 6350 9988.

Goodfellas
907 Julu Lu, French Concession.
Map 1 D4.
Tel (021) 6467 0775.

Guan Di
2 Gaolan Lu, inside Fuxing Park, French Concession.
Map 1 F4.
Tel (021) 5383 6020.

Harley's
265 Nandan Dong Lu, French Concession.
Tel (021) 5424 7317.

House of Blues and Jazz
158 Maoming Nan Lu, French Concession.
Map 1 E5.
Tel (021) 6437 5280.

Jade
Pudong Shangri-La, 33 Fucheng Lu, Pudong.
Map 3 D3.
Tel (021) 6882 8888.

Judy's Too
176 Maoming Nan Lu, French Concession.
Map 1 E5.
Tel (021) 6473 1417.

Le Club at La Maison
North Block, House 23, Xin Tiandi.
Map 2 A4.
Tel (021) 6326 0855.

Malone's
255 Tongren Lu, Jing'an District.
Map 1 D3.
Tel (021) 6247 2400.

Mint
333 Tongren Lu, Jing'an District.
Map 1 D3.
Tel (021) 6247 9666.

O'Malleys
42 Taojiang Lu, French Concession.
Map 1 D5.
Tel (021) 6474 6166.

Park 97
2A Gaolan Lu, Fuxing Park, French Concession.
Map 1 F4.
Tel (021) 5383 2328.

Paulaner Brauhaus
Binjiang Da Dao, by Pudong Shangri-La.
Map 3 D3.
Tel (021) 6888 3935.

Peace Hotel Jazz Bar
20 Nanjing Dong Lu, the Bund.
Map 2 C2.
Tel (021) 6321 6888.

Pegasus
Golden Bell Plaza, 98

Huaihai Zhong Lu, French Concession.
Map 1 F4.
Tel (021) 5385 8187.

Pu-J's
Grand Hyatt, Jinmao Tower, Pudong.
Map 3 E3.
Tel (021) 5049 1234.

Shuffle
137 Xingfu Lu, French Concession.
Tel (021) 6283 2768.

Sky Dome
Radisson Hotel, 88 Nanjing Xi Lu, People's Square.
Map 2 A2.
Tel (021) 6359 9999.

Upstairs at Park 97
2A Gaolan Lu, Fuxing Park, French Concession.
Map 1 F4.
Tel (021) 5383 2328.

Windows Scoreboard
681 Huaihai Zhong Lu, French Concession.
Map 1 E4.
Tel (021) 5382 7757.

FILM

Cathay Theater
Huaihai Zhong Lu 870, French Concession.
Map 1 E4.
Tel (021) 5404 2095.

Paradise Warner Cinema City
6th Floor, Grand Gateway, 1 Hong Qiao Lu, Xuhui District.
Tel (021) 6407 6622.

UME International Cineplex
2nd Floor, Lane 123, Xingye Lu, Xin Tiandi.
Map 2 A4.
Tel (021) 6373 3333.

TEAHOUSES

Huxinting
257 Yu Yuan Lu, Old City.
Map 2 C4.
Tel (021) 6355 8270.

SHANGHAI STREET FINDER

The map references given with all sights, hotels, restaurants, shops, and entertainment venues described in this chapter refer to the following maps. The first figure of the map reference indicates which map to turn to, and the letter and number that follow are the grid reference. The key map below shows which parts of Shanghai's city center are covered in this Street Finder. A complete index of street names follows the maps. In street names, the suffix "jie" meaning street, or "lu" meaning road are often interchangeable. Therefore, when asking directions, note that Tian Tian Jie may also be known as Tian Tian Lu. Many streets are also called "dajie" or avenue. Directionals such as "zhong" (central), and the four cardinal points – "dong" (east), "xi" (west), "bei" (north), and "nan" (south) are often added to street names.

KEY TO STREET FINDER

▦	Major sight	🛈	Tourist information
▦	Place of interest	✚	Hospital
▢	Other important building	⊠	Post office
Ⓜ	Subway station	✝	Church

SCALE OF MAP ABOVE

0 kilometers   2

0 miles   1

SCALE OF MAPS 1–3

0 meters   500

0 yards   500

Shanghai Street Finder Index

A

Anfu Lu	1 D4
Anlan Lu	2 B5
Anping Jie	2 C3
Anqing Lu	2 B1
Anren Jie	2 C4
Anyuan Lu	1 D5
Anyi Lu	1 D3

B

Baidu Lu	3 D5
Baihe Lu	2 A2
Beihai Lu	2 B3
Beijing Dong Lu	2 C2
Beijing Xi Lu	2 A2
Beishijia Long	3 D5
Beishipi Long	2 C4
Beisuzhou Lu	2 B1
Bund see Zhongshan Dong Yi Lu	

C

Chang'an Lu	1 F1
Changde Lu	1 D1
Changhua Lu	1 E1
Changle Lu	1 D4
Changping Lu	1 D1
Changshu Lu	1 D4
Changyi Lu	3 F3
Changzhi Lu	3 D1
Chengdu Bei Lu	1 F1
Chengdu Nan Lu	1 F4
Chenxiangge Lu	2 C4
Chongde Lu	2 B4
Chongqing Bei Lu	2 A3
Chongqing Nan Lu	2 A4
Cixi Lu	1 F2

D

Dagu Lu	1 F3
Daji Lu	2 B5
Dajing Lu	2 B4
Dalin Lu	2 B5
Daming Lu	3 D1
Danfeng Lu	3 D4
Danshui Lu	2 A4
Daochuan Long	2 C5
Datian Lu	1 F2
Datong Lu	2 A1
Daxing Jie	2 B5
Dianchi Lu	2 C2
Dong Jie	3 D4
Dongchang Lu	3 E4
Dongchangzhi Lu	3 E1
Dongdaming Lu	3 E1
Donghanyang Lu	3 E1
Donghu Lu	1 D4
Dongjiadu Lu	3 D5
Dongma Jie	2 C4
Dongmen Lu	3 D4
Dong Ping Lu	1 D5
Dongqinglian Jie	2 B4
Dongtai Lu	2 B4
Doushi Jie	3 D5

E

Ernei Lu	3 D1

F

Fangbang Zhong Lu	2 B4
Fangxie Lu	2 B5
Fengyang Lu	2 A2
Fenyang Lu	1 D5
Fucheng Lu	3 D3
Fujia Jie	2 C4
Fujian Bei Lu	2 B1
Fujian Nan Lu	2 B3
Fujian Zhong Lu	2 B3
Fumin Jie	2 C4
Fumin Lu	1 D3
Fuxing Dong Lu	2 C4
Fuxing Zhong Lu	2 A5
Fuyou Lu	2 C4
Fuzhou Lu	2 B3

G

Gangu Jie	2 C4
Gansu Lu	2 B1
Gaojia Long	2 C4
Gaolan Lu	1 F4
Gongping Lu	3 F1
Guang Dong Lu	2 B3
Guangfu Lu	1 E1
Guangqi Lu	2 C4
Guangqi Nan Lu	2 C5
Guangxi Bei Lu	2 B3
Guling Lu	2 A2
Guoqing Lu	2 A1

H

Haichang Lu	1 F1
Haifang Lu	1 D1
Hailing Lu	2 B1
Haixin Lu	3 E3
Hankou Lu	2 C2
Hanyang Lu	3 D1
Hanzhong Lu	1 F1
Hefei Lu	2 A5
Henan Bei Lu	2 C1
Henan Nan Lu	2 C4
Henan Zhong Lu	2 C2
Hengfeng Lu	1 F1
Hengtong Lu	1 F1
Houjia Lu	2 C4
Huai'an Lu	1 E1
Huaihai Dong Lu	2 A4
Huaihai Zhong Lu	1 D4
Huanghe Lu	2 A2
Huangjia Lu	2 C5
Huangpi Bei Lu	2 A3
Huangpi Nan Lu	2 A5
Huangpu Lu	3 D2
Huashan Lu	1 D3
Huasheng Lu	1 F1
Huating Lu	1 D4
Huaxing Lu	2 B1
Huayuanshiqiao Lu	3 E3
Hubei Lu	2 B3
Huqiu Lu	2 C2

J

Jiande Lu	1 F5
Jiangning Lu	1 E2
Jianguo Dong Lu	2 A5
Jianguo Xi Lu	1 E5
Jianguo Zhong Lu	1 F5
Jiangxi Bei Lu	2 C1
Jiangxi Nan Lu	2 C3
Jiangxi Zhong Lu	2 C2
Jiangyin Jie	2 B5
Jiaozhou Lu	1 D3
Jiashan Lu	1 E5
Jimo Lu	3 F2
Jinan Lu	2 A4
Jingxiu Lu	2 B5
Jinjia Fang	2 B4
Jinling Dong Lu	2 B3
Jinling Xi Lu	2 A4
Jinling Zhong Lu	2 A4
Jinxian Lu	1 E4
Jinyuan Lu	2 A1
Jiucang Jie	2 C4
Jiujiang Lu	2 C2
Jiujiaochang Lu	2 C4
Jiulong Lu	3 D1
Julu Lu	1 D4

K

Kaifeng Lu	2 A1
Kangding Lu	1 D2
Kangle Lu	2 B1
Kongjia Long	2 B4
Kuaiji Lu	2 B4
Kunshan Lu	2 C1

L

Laobaidu Nan Lu	3 E5
Laoshan Xi Lu	3 F5
Laotaiping Long	3 D4
Laoxin Jie	3 D5
Liling Lu	3 D1
Lingji Jie	2 C5
Linyin Lu	2 B5
Lishui Lu	2 C4
Liuhekou Lu	2 B4
Liujiang Jie	2 C5
Liulin Lu	2 B4
Liyang Lu	3 D1
Lu Xiangyuan Jie	2 B4
Luhe Lu	2 B2
Lujiabang Lu	2 A5
Luziazui Xi Lu	3 E3

M

Machang Lu	3 D1
Madang Lu	2 A4
Maojia Lu	3 D5
Maoming Bei Lu	1 F3
Maoming Nan Lu	1 E4
Meijia Jie	2 C5
Meiyuan Lu	1 F1
Menggu Lu	2 A1
Menghua Jie	2 B5
Miezhu Lu	3 D5
Minli Lu	1 F1

N

Nanbei Gaojia Lu	1 F3
Nanchang Lu	1 E4
Nanhui Lu	1 E2
Nanjing Dong Lu	2 C2
Nanjing Xi Lu	2 A3
Nansuzhou Lu	2 A1
Nanxing Lu	2 A1
Nanxun Lu	3 D1
Nanyang Lu	1 D3
Ningbo Lu	2 C2
Ninghai Dong Lu	2 B3
Ninghai Xi Lu	2 A3
Ninghe Lu	2 C5
Niuzhuang Lu	2 B2

P

Penglai Lu	2 B5
Pengze Lu	2 C1
Pucheng Lu	3 F5
Pudong Jie	3 F3
Pudong Nan Lu	3 F2
Puji Lu	1 E1
Pumin Lu	3 E3

Q

Qiaojia Lu	2 C5
Qinghai Lu	1 F3
Qinglian Jie	2 B4
Qipu Lu	2 B1
Qixia Lu	3 F3
Qufu Lu	2 A1
Qufu Xi Lu	2 A1

R

Rehe Lu	2 B1
Renhe Jie	1 D1
Renmin Lu	2 C3
Riverside Promenade	3 D2
Ruijin Er Lu	1 F5
Ruijin Yi Lu	1 F4
Rushan Lu	3 F4

S

Sanpailou Lu	2 C4
Shaanxi Bei Lu	1 D1
Shaanxi Nan Lu	1 E4
Shandong Nan Lu	2 B3
Shandong Zhong Lu	2 C3
Shangcheng Lu	3 E4
Shanghaiguan Lu	1 F2
Shangqiu Lu	3 E1
Shangwen Lu	2 C5
Shantou Lu	2 B3
Shanxi Bei Lu	2 B1
Shanxi Nan Lu	2 B2
Shaoxing Lu	1 E5
Shiji Dadao (Century Avenue)	3 E3
Shimen Er Lu	1 F2
Shimen Yi Lu	1 F3
Shipi Long	2 C4
Shouning Lu	2 B4
Shunchang Lu	2 A4
Sichuan Bei Lu	2 C1

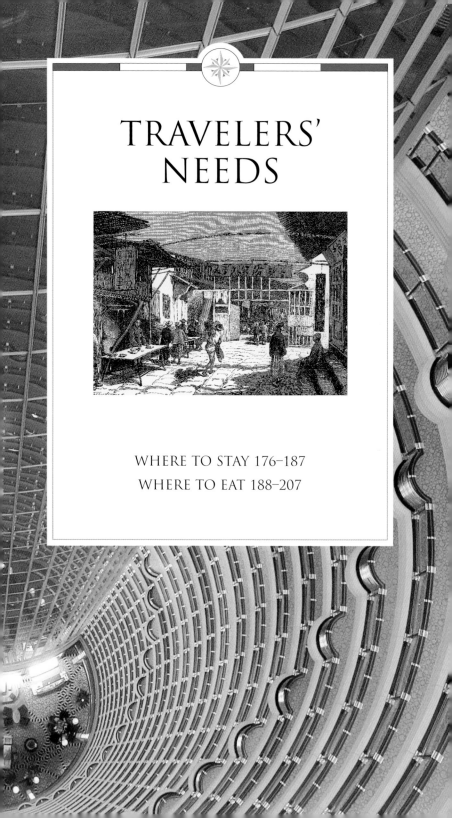

TRAVELERS'
NEEDS

WHERE TO STAY

Traditional red lantern

Beijing and Shanghai together offer the most glamorous hotels in mainland China, and some of the most historic too. Four- and five-star hotels, many belonging to foreign chains, are plentiful. Boutique hotels have yet to make an appearance, however Beijing does have a number of "court-yard" hotels, which are conversions of traditional old Chinese homes. There are plenty of other comfortable mid-range choices, and for budget travelers dirt-cheap need not mean dirty. Whatever your preference, it is recommended that you book your accommodations well in advance.

The courtyard of Beijing's Lu Song Yuan Binguan Hotel

INTERNATIONAL AND CHINESE-RUN HOTELS

Visitors in search of international standards of comfort and service should stick either to five-star hotels managed by familiar Western chains, or the Singapore- and Hong Kong-based luxury companies.

Chinese-run hotels do their best to emulate Western operations. However, while the published rack rates of Chinese four- and five-star hotels are indeed comparable, the level of service in Chinese hotels does not match their Western counterparts.

The Chinese star system of grading hotels is largely meaningless, since no star is ever lost once it has been given, despite sometimes dramatic deterioration. Rather than be involved in the star-rating system, some international hotels choose to go starless, but can be far superior to neighboring Chinese-run, five-stars. As a general rule for Chinese-run hotels, the newer the hotel, the better the facilities.

BUDGET HOTELS & OTHER TYPES OF ACCOMMODATIONS

Beijing has ample budget accommodations, including a new breed of sparkling hostels. In Shanghai things are more difficult, although dormitory beds can still be had for ¥50 or less.

Neither city has any sort of official camping grounds, and camping at random may lead to arrest.

BOOKING A HOTEL

In China, the real price of a hotel room is what the customer is willing to pay. Locals will always ask for a discount and you should too.

For most foreign-run hotels, the best available price will be on the hotel's own website. Prices can drop nearer to the planned day of stay, but it can be risky to wait too long as demand at international hotels is often high, particularly in Shanghai.

Websites for Chinese hotels will almost always quote a wildly inflated rack rate. Specialist websites often claim to offer huge discounts but, while they can sometimes offer good prices for advance bookings, you should be able to do better by turning up to book in person. Discounts of 10 to 20 percent are standard, 30 to 40 percent very common, and even 50 percent is not unheard of.

Sometimes only Chinese versions of well-known credit cards are accepted, so check before checking in. Foreign exchange facilities in hotels (available to guests only) are becoming less reliable, and holders of travelers' checks, in particular, may be sent to the nearest large branch of the Bank of China. Particularly in more modest Chinese hotels, always be prepared to pay in local currency.

HIDDEN COSTS

The prices quoted by major international hotels do not include their service charges. Many Chinese-run, upper-end hotels have begun to levy service charges of between

Luxurious bedroom at the Portman Ritz-Carlton, Shanghai

five and 15 percent. Since this is a new practice, most Chinese customers refuse to pay the charges, and hotels rarely insist, but ask before you check in. Note that minibar contents are as overpriced in China as they are elsewhere in the world. However, only a modest service charge is added on top of the cost of international phone calls made from your hotel room.

SEASONAL DEMAND

The busiest travel periods are during the week-long national holidays, around May 1 and October 1, and during the Spring Festival or Chinese New Year (see p34). But most of the travel is away from the big cities, and so demand for hotel rooms in Beijing and Shanghai isn't usually any higher than at most other times of the year. Exhibitions and conferences pose more of a problem – and dates are mostly unpredictable – but these tend to affect upper-end accommodations only, although the October dates of Shanghai's Formula One Grand Prix should be avoided. During the May and October holidays,

Reception at the courtyard Bamboo Garden Hotel, Beijing

accommodations in Suzhou and Hangzhou may be very hard to find.

GENERAL OBSERVATIONS & PRECAUTIONS

It is common for Chinese-run hotels to request payment for the room in advance. Check-out is usually noon, but you can pay half the nightly rate to keep the room until 6pm.

Many hotels in China advertise facilities such as night clubs and karaoke bars, but these are often fronts for prostitution. Be wary of unexpected telephone calls to your room offering massage.

It is nearly always a mistake to arrange transportation through your hotel, as it often costs four times as much as it would if you found a taxi on your own. Taxis hovering near the doors of upmarket hotels should also be approached with caution. Stop one in the street.

FACILITIES FOR CHILDREN & THE DISABLED

Most hotels allow under-12s to stay with their parents free of charge. Most will also add an extra bed for an older child for a nominal (and negotiable) fee.

In general, China is not a suitable destination for the disabled. Only the newest and best international hotels make any serious effort to provide wheelchair access, or fully adapted rooms.

TIPPING

Traditionally there is no tipping in China, but because of the increasing number of visitors that do tip regardless, this is starting to change. This is most particularly true in hotels in heavily touristed areas and in more upmarket establishments.

DIRECTORY

HOTEL CHAINS

Crowne Plaza
Tel 1-800 227 6963 (US).
0800 8222 8222 (UK).
www.ichotelsgroup.com

Grand Hyatt
Tel 1-888 591 1234 (US).
0845 888 1234 (UK).
1-800 481 034 (Ireland).
www.hyatt.com

Hilton
Tel 1-800 445 8667 (US).
08705 909 090 (UK).
www.hilton.com

Holiday Inn
Tel 1-800 465 4329 (US).
0800 405 060 (UK).
www.ichotelsgroup.com

Howard Johnson
Tel 1-800 446 4656 (US).
www.hojo.com

Hyatt Regency
Tel 1-888 591 1234 (US).
0845 888 1234 (UK).
www.hyatt.com

InterContinental
Tel 1-800 424 6835 (US).
0800 1800 1800 (UK).
www.ichotelsgroup.com

Marco Polo
www.marcopolohotels.com

Marriott
Tel 1-888 236 2427 (US).
0800 221 222 (UK).
www.marriott.com

Novotel
Tel 1-800 666 0835 (US).
www.novotel.com

Park Hyatt
Tel 1-888 591 1234 (US).
0845 888 1234 (UK).
www.hyatt.com

Peninsula
Tel 1-866 382 8388 (US).
0800 2828 3888 (UK).
www.peninsula.com

Radisson
Tel 1-800 201 1718 (US).
0800 374 411 (UK).
1-800 557 474 (Ireland).
www.radisson.com

Ramada
Tel 1-800 828 6644 (US).
0808 100 0783 (UK).
www.ramada.com

Regent
Tel 1-888 201 1806 (US).
0800 917 8795 (UK).
www.regenthotels.com

Ritz-Carlton
Tel 1-800 241 3333 (US)
0800 234 000 (UK).
1-800 145 004 (Aus).
www.ritzcarlton.com

St. Regis
Tel 1-877 787 3447 (US).
0800 3254 5454 (UK).
www.starwood.com

Shangri-La
Tel 1-800 942 5050 (US).
020 8747 8485 (UK).
www.shangri-la.com

Sheraton
Tel 1-800 325 3535 (US).
0800 3253 5353 (UK).
www.starwood.com

Sofitel
Tel 1-800 763 4835 (US).
08706 090 964 (UK).
1300 656 565 (Aus).
www.sofitel.com

Westin
Tel 1-800 228 3000 (US).
0800 3259 5959 (UK).
www.starwood.com

Choosing a Hotel

The hotels in this guide have been selected across a wide range of price categories for the excellence of their facilities, location, or character. The chart below lists the hotels in price categories within the chapters of the book. Many hotels have business facilities, gyms, and swimming pools, but only the best have been listed.

PRICE CATEGORIES
The following price ranges are for a standard double room (or single dorm bed) and taxes per night during the high season. Breakfast is not included.

Ⓨ under ¥200
ⓎⓎ ¥200–¥400
ⓎⓎⓎ ¥400–¥800
ⓎⓎⓎⓎ ¥800–¥1400
ⓎⓎⓎⓎⓎ Over ¥1400

BEIJING

Downtown Backpackers (Dongtang Qingnian Lüshe)
85 Nan Luogu Xiang **Tel** (010) 8400 2429 **Rooms** 20   **Map** 2 B2

Good value in the heart of one of Beijing's *hutong* neighborhoods, minutes from the imperial lakes, Drum and Bell Towers, and myriad restaurants and bars. Offers clean single rooms, doubles with attached bath, and 6–8 bed dorms, plus bike hire and laundry facilities.

Saga Hostel (Shizhu Qingnian Lüshe)
9 Shijia Hutong **Tel** (010) 6527 2773 **Fax** (010) 6524 9098 **Rooms** 30   **Map** 2 C4

Tranquil if slightly inconvenient *hutong* location south-west of Chaoyang Men subway. Featuring spotless doubles, triples, and dorm rooms, a communal kitchen and café, and a roof-top patio. Helpful English-speaking management organize bike hire, ticket bookings, and tours.

Sweet Garden Hostel (Tianyuan Qingnian Lüguan)
19 Dong Si Qi Tiao **Tel** (010) 6405 1538 **Rooms** 13   **Map** 2 C3

Peaceful, family-run hostel in a converted courtyard residence close to Dong Si Shi Tiao subway offers simple single, double, and 4–6 bed dorm rooms. Management speak little English but arrange bike hire, booking services, and even airport pick-up. Rates include Chinese breakfast.

Beijing City Youth Hostel (Beijing Chengshi Guoji Qingnian Lüshe)
1–5 Beijing Zhan Qian Jie **Tel** (010) 6525 8066 **Fax** (010) 6525 9066 **Rooms** 200   **Map** 5 F1

Good value budget accommodations and extremely convenient for those with early morning trains from Beijing Station. Reasonably priced twin rooms and dorms are relatively new and clean, and there are also cooking facilities and a 24-hour shop on site.

Dexinju Binguan
78 Dong Si Liu Tiao **Tel** (010) 6404 2944 **Fax** (010) 6403 3926 **Rooms** 100   **Map** 2 C3

Budget Chinese-managed hotel in a small *hutong* close to the main shopping street of Wangfujing. Service can be frosty and staff speak little English, but rooms are light and airy with clean bathrooms, and those on upper floors offer pleasant *hutong* views.

Far East International Youth Hostel (Yuan Dong Qingnian Lüshe)
90 Tieshuxie Jie **Tel** (010) 5195 8561 **Fax** (010) 6301 8233 **Rooms** 24   **Map** 4 B3

The city's most charming YHA hostel, with dorms (110 beds in total) and private rooms available both in a pleasantly decorated conventional hotel building and a courtyard house across the street. The surrounding area was an Imperial-era red-light district and maintains its lively atmosphere. **www.hihostels.com**

Feiying Binguan
10 Xuanwu Men Xi Dajie **Tel** (010) 6317 1116 **Fax** (010) 6315 1165 **Rooms** 46   **Map** 4 A2

Among the cheapest of the Youth Hostelling International hotels in Beijing, and the most convenient for transportation. Private twins and dorm rooms are pristine, and management are fairly helpful. Facilities include a recently opened bar and restaurant. **www.hihostels.com**

Hade Men Fandian
2A Chongwen Men Wai Dajie **Tel** (010) 6711 2244 **Fax** (010) 6711 6865 **Rooms** 229   **Map** 5 E2

Among the older hotels in Beijing, but renovated to a standard above other Chinese-run options in this price range. Service, unfortunately, has not kept pace with the facilities. Rooms are comfortable, if a bit gaudy, with nice views from the upper floors. **www.hademenhotel.com**

Red House Hotel (Ruixiu Binguan)
10 Chunxiu Lu **Tel** (010) 6416 7810 **Fax** (010) 6416 7600 **Rooms** 40   **Map** 3 E2

Dorms, hotel rooms, and apartments with kitchen and laundry facilities for short- or long-term rent. Rooms feature dark wooden floors, faux-antique furnishings, and multi-jet capsule showers. There's a popular football bar on the ground floor, and it's just a few minutes' walk to the entertainment district of Sanlitun. **www.redhouse.com.cn**

Key to Symbols *see back cover flap*

Xindadu Youth Hostel (Xindadu Guoji Qingnian Lüshe)

21 Chegongzhuang Dajie **Tel** *(010) 6831 9988 ext. 180* **Fax** *(010) 8837 3701* **Rooms** *38*

One of the newest of the YHA hostels taking over Beijing budget accommodations. Dorm beds (200 in total) are the only option, but rooms are pristine and rates are some of the lowest in the city. Convenient access to Beijing West Railway Station.

Zhaolong International Youth Hostel (Zhaolong Qingnian Lüshe)

2 Gongren Tiyuchang Bei Lu **Tel** *(010) 6597 2299 ext. 6111* **Fax** *(010) 6597 2288* **Rooms** *24*   **Map** *3 D3*

A quiet option despite the proximity to Sanlitun bar district. Dorms are decently tidy and guests have access to a self-catering dining room, games room, reading room, and bike rentals. Staff keep strict order, locking doors at 1am even on weekends.

Bamboo Garden Hotel (Zhuyuan Binguan)

24 Xiao Shi Qiao Hutong **Tel** *(010) 5852 0088* **Fax** *(010) 5852 0066* **Rooms** *40*   **Map** *2 A1*

Close to the lakes, this is the oldest of Beijing's traditional hotels, with the largest and most elaborate courtyards, although rooms are mostly located in two buildings that lack the intimacy and charm of other smaller competitors. Rockeries and covered pathways make for pleasant lounging surrounds. **www.bbgh.com.cn**

City Hotel Beijing (Chengshi Binguan)

4 Gongren Tiyuchang Dong Lu **Tel** *(010) 6500 7787* **Fax** *(010) 6500 7668* **Rooms** *200*   **Map** *3 E3*

Sound budget option within walking distance of Sanlitun's numerous bars, restaurants, and shops. Rooms are clean and comfortable enough, although décor is somewhat dated. Service is above usual three-star Chinese hotel standards with staff speaking some English. **www.cityhotel.com.cn**

Comfort Inn & Suites

6 Gongren Tiyuchang Bei Lu **Tel** *(010) 8523 5522* **Fax** *(010) 8523 5158* **Rooms** *96*   **Map** *3 D3*

Rooms are tastefully decorated, with large desks, comfortable sofas, and plush duvets. Catering more for business people on lengthy stays, service can be found wanting. The location nevertheless provides access to Sanlitun's many bars, restaurants, and shops. **www.choicehotels.com**

Cuimingzhuang Binguan

1 Nan Heyan Dajie **Tel** *(010) 6513 6622* **Fax** *(010) 6526 1516* **Rooms** *134*   **Map** *2 B5*

Recently renovated, conveniently located, and affordable. Rooms are simple but clean, and are surprisingly large compared to other hotels in the area. The service staff are more pleasant than normally found in a Chinese hotel; quiet, unobtrusive, and unusually fastidious. **www.cuimingzhuanghotel.com.cn**

Haoyuan Binguan

Dengshi Dong Kou, 53 Shijia Hutong **Tel** *(010) 6512 5557* **Fax** *(010) 6525 3179* **Rooms** *19*   **Map** *2 C4*

Smallest, most obscure, and possibly most pleasant courtyard hotel in Beijing. Rooms in the front courtyard are unremarkable, but larger units in the tree-shaded rear courtyard are exquisite, with Ming-style furniture. Walking distance to Wangfujing shopping and subway. **www.haoyuanhotel.com**

Hejing Fu Binguan

7 Zhangzi Zhong Lu, Ping'an Dadao **Tel** *(010) 6401 7744* **Fax** *(010) 8401 3570* **Rooms** *140*   **Map** *2 B3*

One of the largest courtyard hotels in town, Hejing Fu occupies three courtyards in total, each dotted with intricately carved statuary. Suites are luxuriously appointed with traditional trappings that reflect the house's imperial pedigree. Close to the imperial lakes and Forbidden City.

Lu Song Yuan Binguan

22 Banchang Hutong **Tel** *(010) 6404 0436* **Fax** *(010) 6403 0418* **Rooms** *50*   **Map** *2 B3*

The details are similar to those in other courtyard hotels, but here they somehow add up to a more comfortable atmosphere. A good variety of accommodations from cheap youth hostel-style facilities right up to suites as well as a charming teahouse and well-stocked bookshelves. **www.the-silk-road.com**

Novotel Peace Hotel

3 Jinyu Hutong **Tel** *(010) 6512 8833* **Fax** *(010) 6512 6863* **Rooms** *337*   **Map** *2 C5*

Run by French hotel group Accor, this is the most affordable of the foreign-managed hotels in Wangfujing, although the service could be a little more enthusiastic. Executive rooms are good value, and the house restaurants cover a variety of cuisines. **www.accorhotels-asia.com**

Qomolangma Hotel

149 Gulou Xi Dajie **Tel** *(010) 6401 8822* **Fax** *(010) 6401 1130* **Rooms** *100*   **Map** *2 A2*

A few minutes' walk from the Drum and Bell Towers, some attractive *hutongs*, and the imperial lakes, and located in a former Buddhist temple, this courtyard hotel is full of character. Simple, cosy rooms have Ming-style furniture, some offering courtyard views.

Scitech Hotel

Jianguo Men Wai Dajie 22 **Tel** *(010) 6512 3388* **Fax** *(010) 6512 3542* **Rooms** *294*   **Map** *3 F5*

A good-value option for shoppers and hedonists, four-star Scitech abuts a large department store and popular nightclub Banana. Standard rooms decorated in earthy tones are small, but are otherwise comfortable and well-appointed. **www.scitechgroup.com**

Beijing Hilton

1 Dong Fang Lu, Dong San Huan Bei Lu **Tel** *(010) 5865 5000* **Fax** *(010) 6465 3051* **Rooms** *375* **Map** *3 F1*

A recent refurbishment has transformed the formerly tired Hilton into a stylish hotel with large rooms sporting designer flourishes and huge bathrooms. Good value option close to the embassies, shopping, and nightlife centers of Nuren Jie and Sanlitun. **www.beijing.hilton.com**

Beijing International Hotel (Beijing Guoji Fandian)

9 Jianguo Men Nei Dajie **Tel** *(010) 6512 6688* **Fax** *(010) 6512 9972* **Rooms** *916* **Map** *5 F1*

Austere lobby and uninspiring dining options lack five-star panache, but spacious, dignified rooms represent good value, with complimentary broadband access. Staff are reasonably efficient but not particularly friendly, however, the location close to Wangfujing, the Forbidden City, and Central Business District cannot be faulted. **www.bih.com.cn**

Crowne Plaza

48 Wangfujing Dajie **Tel** *(010) 6513 3388* **Fax** *(010) 6513 2513* **Rooms** *360* **Map** *2 B4*

The Crowne Plaza recently underwent a much-needed overhaul. Comfortable rooms with tasteful decoration give onto a nine-story atrium. Reasonable value, and within walking distance of Wangfujing subway and the Forbidden City. **www.crowneplaza.beijing.ichotelsgroup.com**

Gloria Plaza

2 Jianguo Men Nan Dajie **Tel** *(010) 6515 8855* **Fax** *(010) 6515 8533* **Rooms** *420* **Map** *5 F1*

Tired rooms with dated décor, but a good central location opposite the Ancient Observatory and convenient for Jianguo Men subway, tourist sights, and the CBD. Also features Sampan, one of Beijing's best Cantonese restaurants, and a huge sports bar. **www.gphbeijing.com**

Holiday Inn Lido

6 Jiangtai Lu, Jichang Lu **Tel** *(010) 6437 6688* **Fax** *(010) 6437 6237* **Rooms** *340*

Close to both the airport and the International Exhibition Center but awkwardly far from tourist sights, the expat-oriented Lido is surrounded by shopping, dining, and recreational facilities. Rooms are large with simple, tasteful décor, and very big beds. **beijing-lido.holiday-inn.com**

Howard Johnson Paragon

18A Jianguo Men Nei Dajie **Tel** *(010) 6526 6688* **Fax** *(010) 6527 4060* **Rooms** *288* **Map** *5 F1*

Comfortable and close to both Beijing Station and its subway stop, and just a short taxi ride to Wangfujing and Tian'an Men Square. Rooms, although not large, are recently renovated, and international standards ensure a quality of service not found in most other nearby hotels. **www.hojochina.com**

InterContinental Financial Street Beijing

11 Jinrong Jie (Fucheng Men Nan Dajie) **Tel** *(010) 5852 5888* **Fax** *(010) 5852 5999* **Rooms** *330* **Map** *1 D5*

Newly established, luxury boutique hotel located in "Financial Street", Beijing's rapidly growing western business district, features tasteful, modern décor throughout. Although far from tourist sights, spacious rooms are good value with large plasma TVs and impressive bathrooms. **www.ichotelsgroup.com**

Jinglun Hotel

3 Jianguo Men Wai Dajie **Tel** *(010) 6500 2266* **Fax** *(010) 6500 2022* **Rooms** *600* **Map** *3 F5*

Recently renovated business district hotel with simple, elegant rooms equipped with broadband internet and other modern amenities. Minutes' walk from Guomao subway, China World Mall, the Silk Market, and numerous restaurants, the Jinglun is excellent value for the location. **www.jinglunhotel.com**

Marco Polo

6 Xuanwu Men Nei Dajie **Tel** *(010) 6603 6688* **Fax** *(010) 6603 1488* **Rooms** *294* **Map** *4 A1*

Boutique-style luxury and a quiet but convenient location make this one of the city's best-value hotels. Still relatively new it offers palatial, nicely decorated rooms at rates much lower than competitors around the Xidan and Xuanwumen shopping districts. **www.marcopolohotels.com**

Novotel Xin Qiao

2 Dong Jiao Min Xiang **Tel** *(010) 6513 3366* **Fax** *(010) 6512 5126* **Rooms** *700* **Map** *5 E2*

Big discounts and a central location near Tian'an Men Square, Chongwen Men subway station, and shopping centers compensate for bland rooms and poor service. Still, rooms are cable internet-equipped and restaurants are varied and reasonably priced. **www.novotel.com**

Park Plaza Hotel

97 Jin Bao Jie **Tel** *(010) 8522 1999* **Fax** *(010) 8522 1290* **Rooms** *216* **Map** *2 C5*

Set back from the street, the stylish new Park Plaza is a peaceful oasis in a fast developing precinct. Rooms are modish in decoration, with bathrooms featuring designer touches including mosaic tiles. Convenient for the Forbidden City and a short walk from Wangfujing. **www.parkplaza.com/beijingcn**

Renaissance Hotel

36 Xiaoyun Lu **Tel** *(010) 6468 9999* **Fax** *(010) 6468 9939* **Rooms** *212* **Map** *3 F1*

Four-star no-frills business hotel close to the International Exhibition Center, also providing access to myriad dining and shopping options on Xiaoyun Lu and the adjacent Nuren Jie. Rooms are relatively few in number, but large in size, luxurious but subtle. **www.marriott.com**

Key to Price Guide *see p178* **Key to Symbols** *see back cover flap*

Traders Hotel Beijing
1 Jianguo Men Wai Dajie **Tel** *(010) 6505 2277* **Fax** *(010) 6504 3144* **Rooms** *570* **Map 3 F5**

In the heart of the business district, thoroughly wired, and offering every possible business facility, but also comforts such as a very popular Southeast Asian buffet that spills onto a terrace in summer. Next to the China World Shopping Mall and its subway station. **www.shangri-la.com**

Xinhai Jinjiang Da Jiudian
61 Jinbao Jie **Tel** *(010) 5816 3388* **Fax** *(010) 5816 3288* **Rooms** *231* **Map 2 C5**

A new addition to the Wangfujing area, the Xinhai is free of the gaudiness of other Chinese-managed hotels. Rooms are tasteful, albeit small, but have huge showers. Service is efficient and hotel entertainment includes a small bowling alley with bar.

The Ascott Beijing
108B Jianguo Men Wai Dajie **Tel** *(010) 6567 8100* **Fax** *(010) 6567 8122* **Rooms** *272* **Map 3 F5**

Acclaimed top-end living for international executives in the heart of the Central Business District, also providing 1–3 bedroom apartments for overnight stays. Walking distance from China World Mall and Guomao subway, service is exceptional and apartments are elegantly furnished and fully equipped. **www.theascottbeijing.com**

Beijing Marriott West
98 Xi San Huan Bei Lu **Tel** *(010) 6872 6699* **Fax** *(010) 6872 7302* **Rooms** *155*

Good value due to its somewhat inconvenient location in the western section of Beijing. Décor is lavish, heavy on the gold and feathers, and would be suffocating were it not for the larger-than-average room size. Six apartments with cooking facilities are also available. **www.marriott.com**

China World Hotel
1 Jianguo Men Wai Dajie **Tel** *(010) 6505 2266* **Fax** *(010) 6505 3165* **Rooms** *716* **Map 3 F5**

The most comprehensively luxurious hotel in Beijing, and often the choice of visiting heads of state. Located in the heart of the main business district, with connections to the subway and a swish shopping mall, it houses some of the best restaurants in town. **www.shangri-la.com**

Grand Hyatt Beijing
1 Dong Chang'an Jie **Tel** *(010) 8518 1234* **Fax** *(010) 8518 0000* **Rooms** *825* **Map 2 B5**

In the glittering Oriental Plaza shopping complex on Wangfujing, no other Beijing luxury hotel is better located, and few are as well equipped. Cantonese, Beijing, and Japanese restaurants here are among the city's finest, and fitness and spa facilities are among the best. **www.beijing.grand.hyatt.com**

Great Wall Sheraton
10 Dong San Huan Bei Lu **Tel** *(010) 6590 5566* **Fax** *(010) 6590 5398* **Rooms** *850* **Map 3 F2**

Although one of the biggest hotels in Beijing, rooms are surprisingly small with tired décor. Still, service is pleasant, and the Cantonese restaurant on the 21st floor gets good reviews, providing fine views of the neighboring Sanlitun diplomatic area. **www.starwoodhotels.com**

Hotel New Otani Chang Fu Gong
26 Jianguo Men Wai Dajie **Tel** *(010) 5877 5555* **Fax** *(010) 6513 9236* **Rooms** *500* **Map 3 D5**

Targeted at high-end business travelers, this Japanese-run hotel is convenient to the CBD and Jianguo Men subway, and offers several worthwhile restaurants and bars. Rooms are a bit small, but feature complimentary broadband and tasteful decoration. **www.newotani.co.jp**

Kempinski Hotel
50 Liangma Qiao Lu **Tel** *(010) 6465 3388* **Fax** *(010) 6462 2204* **Rooms** *526* **Map 3 F1**

Near the new embassy district, the Kempinski offers excellent service. The real selling point is its access to Western conveniences in the attached Lufthansa Center, including airline offices, medical facilities, restaurants and bars, and high-end shopping. **www.kempinski-beijing.com**

Kerry Center Hotel
1 Guanghua Lu **Tel** *(010) 6561 8833* **Fax** *(010) 6561 2626* **Rooms** *487* **Map 3 F5**

The youngest of Shangri-La's Beijing stable combines the group's high service standards with bright, modern room design. Part luxury shopping complex, the Kerry is also home to one of Beijing's best Cantonese restaurants, the city's hottest cocktail bar (Centro), and extensive health facilities. **www.shangri-la.com.cn**

La Suite Interdite
2 Bei Chizi Er Tiao **Tel** *N/A* **Rooms** *2* **Map 2 B4**

Exclusive, privately owned courtyard residence that includes two rustic but charming self-contained units (not for separate hire) offering a slice of imperial living five minutes' walk from the Forbidden City. Rates include breakfast; other meals can be arranged on request. **suite_interdite@yahoo.com**

Lee Garden Serviced Apartments (Liyuan Gongyu)
18 Jinyu Hutong **Tel** *(010) 6525 8855* **Fax** *(010) 6525 7999* **Rooms** *199* **Map 2 B5**

Primarily catering to long-stay guests, the Lee Garden also offers short-term and overnight accommodations. Large 1–3 bedroom apartments include kitchen and laundry facilities, with shared spa, sauna, and children's playroom. Close to the Forbidden City and a short stroll from Wangfujing. **www.lgapartment.com**

Peninsula Palace Hotel

8 Jinyu Hutong **Tel** *(010) 8516 2888* **Fax** *(010) 6510 6311* **Rooms** *530*   **Map** *2 C5*

Luxurious and recently renovated rooms have large plasma TVs; marble bathrooms have another small screen. Several outstanding restaurants, a luxury mall with names like Prada and Gucci, excellent service, and a central Wangfujing location, make this one of the city's best choices. **www.peninsula.com**

Prime Hotel

2 Wangfujing Dajie **Tel** *(010) 5816 6999* **Fax** *(010) 5816 9988* **Rooms** *402*   **Map** *2 B4*

Don't be put off by the ostentatious lobby with fountain and grand piano playing itself. Rooms and beds are huge, and represent good value for such a central location. In addition to Chinese and Western, there are Japanese and French restaurants on site. **www.primehotel.cn**

Shangri-La Beijing

29 Zizhuyuan Lu **Tel** *(010) 6841 2211* **Fax** *(010) 6481 8002/3* **Rooms** *528*

Peacefully located in gardens to the west of the city, not far from the Summer Palace. Recently renovated to a high standard, and with the addition of a brand new tower and excellent restaurants and bars, not to mention Shangri-La's usual five-star service. **www.shangri-la.com**

St. Regis Beijing

21 Jianguo Men Wai Dajie **Tel** *(010) 6460 6688* **Fax** *(010) 6460 3299* **Rooms** *273*   **Map** *3 F5*

Close to the main embassy area and business district, the St. Regis has small but beautifully decorated rooms with free access to an on-call butler. There are excellent Italian and steak restaurants, as well as an exclusive health club and outdoor putting green. **www.starwoodhotels.com**

Swissôtel Beijing

2 Chaoyang Men Bei Dajie **Tel** *(010) 6553 2288* **Fax** *(010) 6501 2501* **Rooms** *430*   **Map** *3 D3*

Convenient for Dong Si Shi Tiao subway, the restaurants and bars of Sanlitun, and some cultural sites. Rooms are tired and small, and don't offer great value for money, but service is helpful as would be expected at a Raffles-owned hotel. **www.beijing.swissotel.com**

Wangfujing Grand

57 Wangfujing Dajie **Tel** *(010) 6522 1188* **Fax** *(010) 6522 3849* **Rooms** *405*   **Map** *2 B4*

Good value in one of Beijing's priciest and most central hotel districts, with views of the Forbidden City from the west-facing rooms. There's adequate service thanks to Hong Kong management and all new fixtures thanks to a recent renovation. **www.wangfujinghotel.com**

SHANGHAI

Captain Hostel

37 Fuzhou Lu **Tel** *(021) 6323 5053* **Fax** *(021) 6321 9331* **Rooms** *21*   **Map** *2 C3*

The best cheap option in Shanghai. A stone's throw from the Bund, with river views from the recently refurbished roof-top bar. Dorm beds (132 in total) and rooms are clean and comfortable. All typical hostel extras (day trips, internet, bicycle hire) are available. **www.captainhostel.com.cn**

Astor House Hotel (Pujiang Fandian)

15 Huangpu Lu **Tel** *(021) 6324 6388* **Fax** *(021) 6324 3179* **Rooms** *116*   **Map** *3 D2*

This historic building was, a century ago, Shanghai's most luxurious hotel. Recent refurbishments suggest it aspires to former glories, yet the Astor remains primarily a budget option. Still, spacious rooms with wood-paneled floors are available, some with fantastic Bund views. **www.pujianghotel.com**

Meteorological Hotel (Qixiang Binguan)

166 Puxi Lu **Tel** *(021) 6439 3510* **Rooms** *88*

Despite its drabness and absence of English, this budget hotel is in a wonderfully historic pocket of Shanghai, next to the St. Ignatius Cathedral and a short walk from Guangqi Park and other Jesuit sights, not to mention Xujiahui's mega-malls and subway stop.

Motel 168

1119 Yan'an Xi Lu **Tel** *(021) 5117 7777* **Rooms** *510*

Leading the charge of new budget hotels across China's main cities, Motel 168 offers no-frills accommodations with clean, compact rooms, and features walls in bright colors. The Yan'an Lu branch, near Jing'an Temple, has the best location of the ten in Shanghai. **www.motel168.com**

YMCA Hotel

123 Xizang Nan Lu **Tel** *(021) 6326 1040* **Fax** *(021) 6320 1957* **Rooms** *150*   **Map** *2 B4*

Built in 1929 right in the heart of town, and one of Shanghai's better budget hotels, although the rooms, dorms, and shared bathrooms are dowdy, and the hot water thermoses seem like a throwback to Chinese hotels of old. Little English is spoken. **www.ymcahotel.com**

Key to Price Guide *see p178* **Key to Symbols** *see back cover flap*

Broadway Mansions

20 Beisuzhou Lu **Tel** *(021) 6324 6260* **Fax** *(021) 6918 1904* **Rooms** *234*   **Map** *2 C1*

Replete with 20th-century history, this distinctive brick building constructed in 1934 on Suzhou Creek, just minutes north of the Bund, offers eight room types, many boasting recent refurbishments, with wildly varying prices and views. Staff are friendly; breakfast, less so. **www.broadwaymansions.com**

The Bund Hotel

525 Guangdong Lu **Tel** *(021) 6352 2000* **Fax** *(021) 6352 2777* **Rooms** *189*   **Map** *2 B3*

You'd be forgiven for thinking "What Bund?" upon discovering that People's Square is closer to this hotel than Shanghai's famed waterfront. The location is still handy, though, and neither rooms nor service will disappoint. Fresh *phở* at the Vietnamese restaurant is a dining highlight. **www.thebundhotel.com**

City Hotel

5–7 Shaanxi Nan Lu **Tel** *(021) 6255 1133* **Fax** *(021) 6255 0211* **Rooms** *274*   **Map** *1 E3*

On the northern fringe of the French Concession, this is a decent, central four-star option with a business bent. The basic rooms won't win design awards, but do have broadband and satellite TV. Skip the Shanghainese restaurant for the excellent eateries nearby. **www.cityhotelshanghai.com**

Green Garden Hotel

328 Weifang Lu **Tel** *(021) 5081 2222* **Fax** *(021) 5058 0117* **Rooms** *151*   **Map** *3 F5*

New environmentally friendly four-star hotel aimed at business travelers, particularly Japanese, offering *tatami* suites, Inax bidets, and a Japanese restaurant. Well located in the Lujiazui Financial District but less convenient for Shanghai's main tourist spots. **www.greengardenhotel.com**

Hengshan Binguan

534 Hengshan Lu **Tel** *(021) 6437 7050* **Fax** *(021) 6433 5732* **Rooms** *233*

Well located on one of the city's prettiest streets, and opposite Xujiahui Park, the Heng Shan Binguan is a perfect starting point for French Concession walks. Choose a room with care, however, as they vary in size and quality, from smart and spacious to smoky and poky. **www.hotelhengshan.com**

Hengshan Moller Villa

30 Shaanxi Nan Lu **Tel** *(021) 6247 8881* **Fax** *(021) 6289 1020* **Rooms** *45*   **Map** *1 E3*

Built by a 1930s shipping magnate with a castle fetish, this bizarrely bricked and turreted edifice is less impressive inside than out, with unexceptional, frumpy rooms and a particularly dreary modern annexe. A novelty, but not a bargain. **www.mollervilla.com**

Holiday Inn Vista

700 Changshou Lu **Tel** *(021) 6276 8888* **Fax** *(021) 6266 1888* **Rooms** *290*

Away from Shanghai's clusters of international hotels, this Holiday Inn is close to the Jade Buddha Temple and Mogan Shan Lu art district. A roof-top swimming pool and golf simulator provide further quirkiness. Rooms, while modern and well-equipped, are less distinctive. **www.shanghai-vista.holiday-inn.com**

Metropole Hotel

180 Jiangxi Zhong Lu **Tel** *(021) 6321 3030* **Fax** *(021) 6329 8622* **Rooms** *141*   **Map** *2 C3*

The fabulous Art Deco exterior and a location close to the Bund recall 1930s Shanghai. Unfortunately so does the hotel's lighting: entertainment areas and rooms are gloomy, and the restaurant lacks charm. Staff are approachable and, for the most part, affable. **www.metropolehotel-sh.com**

Okura Garden Hotel Shanghai

58 Maoming Nan Lu 58 **Tel** *(021) 6415 1111* **Fax** *(021) 6415 8866* **Rooms** *492*   **Map** *1 E4*

This Japanese-managed luxury hotel has an almost unsurpassed location, close to the subway, the French Concession, and vibrant Maoming Lu. Lush gardens, potable tap water in the marble bathrooms and staff members with excellent language ability complete the plush picture. **www.gardenhotelshanghai.com**

Old House Inn (Lao Shiguang)

No.16, Lane 351, Huashan Lu **Tel** *(021) 6249 6118* **Fax** *(021) 6249 6869* **Rooms** *12*

Perhaps the best of Shanghai's handful of boutique hotels, the Old House Inn is central yet peaceful: the creaking of wooden floors is all you'll hear. Delightful old furniture highlights the dozen unique rooms; shuttered windows open onto a courtyard. There's an innovative Western restaurant downstairs. **www.oldhouse.cn**

Pacific Hotel

108 Nanjing Xi Lu **Tel** *(021) 6327 6226* **Fax** *(021) 6372 3634* **Rooms** *181*   **Map** *2 A2*

Wedged between Shanghai's famous Art Deco Park Hotel and a brand new Radisson, the Pacific Hotel still exudes grandness, thanks to its Bund-matching façade and elegant clock tower, sadly unmatched by some tired interior areas. Rooms facing People's Park are easily the best.

Rendezvous Merry Hotel

396 Yan'an Xi Lu **Tel** *(021) 6249 5588* **Fax** *(021) 6249 5315* **Rooms** *342*   **Map** *1 D3*

A short stroll from Jing'an Temple and Shanghai's glitziest shopping, this four-star hotel comprises newly renovated and modern rooms with dark timber finishing. Surrounding office blocks feel a fraction too close, so aim for a high floor. Efficient business and fitness services available. **www.rendezvoushotels.com.au**

Seagull Hotel
⊕⊕⊕

60 Huangpu Lu **Tel** *(021) 6325 1500* **Fax** *(021) 6324 1263* **Rooms** *128*   **Map** *3 D2*

With its hard-to-beat waterfront location where Suzhou Creek meets the Huangpu River, the Seagull's refurbished rooms are only adequate but there's the compensation of views of the Bund and Lujiazui. Enjoyable roof-top dining under the glow of the neon Epson advertisement which crowns the hotel. **www.seagull-hotel.com**

Tai Yuan Villa
⊕⊕⊕

160 Taiyuan Lu, near Yongjia Lu **Tel** *(021) 6471 6688* **Fax** *(021) 6471 2618* **Rooms** *19*   **Map** *1 D5*

Perfect for history buffs, this 1920s mansion has housed Ho Chi Minh and Kim Il Sung, and was home to Jiang Qing (Mao's last wife). Inside, polished wood and curios abound; outside is a delightful garden. Business-minded gym junkies might prefer the Grand Hyatt.

Yangtze Hotel
⊕⊕⊕

740 Hankou Lu **Tel** *(021) 6351 7880* **Fax** *(021) 6351 6974* **Rooms** *183*   **Map** *2 B2*

Recent renovations have added sparkle (and broadband) to the so-so rooms of this Art Deco building, the Far East's third largest hotel in 1934. Near People's Square and the Nanjing Lu pedestrian mall, the Yangtze boasts a large Chinese clientele. Phrasebooks recommended. **www.e-yangtze.com**

Cypress Hotel
⊕⊕⊕⊕

2419 Hong Qiao Lu **Tel** *(021) 6268 8868* **Fax** *(021) 6268 1878* **Rooms** *149*

This four-star retreat boasts a forest, flowing streams, and even a fishing pond. Sounds remote, yet Hongqiao domestic airport is within a half mile (a kilometer), and the expressway conveys a taxi to downtown in under 30 minutes. Rooms and restaurants are adequate, recreational facilities excellent. **www.cypresshotel.com**

Donghu Hotel
⊕⊕⊕⊕

70 Donghu Lu **Tel** *(021) 6415 8158* **Fax** *(021) 6415 7759* **Rooms** *280*   **Map** *1 E4*

A stone's throw from bustling Huaihai Lu, this lush garden hotel is encircled with high walls that make it a haven and help emphasize its long history. Newer sections lack character so aim for Building 1, with its traditional Chinese furniture. **www.donghuhotel.com**

Hotel Equatorial Shanghai
⊕⊕⊕⊕

65 Yan'an Xi Lu **Tel** *(021) 6248 1688* **Fax** *(021) 6248 1773* **Rooms** *509*   **Map** *1 D3*

Possibly the best value four-star option in town, perfectly located opposite quaint Jing'an Park and a five-minute walk to Jing'an Temple and the adjoining subway station. Rooms are quiet, despite the expansive windows and proximity to the Yan'an overpass. **www.equatorial.com**

Jinjiang Hotel
⊕⊕⊕⊕

59 Maoming Nan Lu **Tel** *(021) 6258 2582* **Fax** *(021) 6472 5588* **Rooms** *515*   **Map** *1 E4*

Once known as the Cathay Mansions and the scene of some important political events, this famous garden hotel in the French Concession has restyled itself for the 21st century. Rooms are elegant, facilities numerous, and the surrounding area houses a number of superb restaurants.

Mayfair Hotel Shanghai
⊕⊕⊕⊕

1555 Dingxi Lu **Tel** *(021) 6240 8888* **Fax** *(021) 6210 5500* **Rooms** *860*

This enormous hotel is some way from the city center but conveniently above a subway station. Nearby Zhongshan Park is a pleasant retreat. Recent refurbishments have made public areas luxurious, but both rooms and service are more modest. Chez Lily serves delightful Yangzhou cuisine.

Novotel Atlantis
⊕⊕⊕⊕

728 Pudong Dadao **Tel** *(021) 5036 6666* **Fax** *(021) 5036 6677* **Rooms** *303*

The location is perfect for Pudong's shiny new museums and parks, although you're a long taxi ride from historic Shanghai. Rooms are clean and modern; one floor is reserved for female guests. A revolving restaurant provides superb views back to the city center. **www.novotel.com**

Park Hotel
⊕⊕⊕⊕

170 Nanjing Xi Lu **Tel** *(021) 6327 5225* **Fax** *(021) 6327 6958* **Rooms** *252*   **Map** *2 A2*

The tallest building in Asia when it was completed in the 1934, the 22-story Park Hotel is now dwarfed by nearby offices. Still, the Art Deco feel and convenient Nanjing Lu and People's Square location make for a quirky stay. Service is inconsistent.

Peace Hotel
⊕⊕⊕⊕

20 Nanjing Dong Lu **Tel** *(021) 6321 6888* **Fax** *(021) 6329 0300* **Rooms** *380*   **Map** *2 C2*

Period charm rather than service or plumbing attract guests to this Art Deco leftover on the Bund, which needs an upgrade in both furnishings and service. But its wood paneling and stained glass certainly capture Shanghai's "Paris of the East" period. **www.shanghaipeacehotel.com**

Pudong Shangri-La Shanghai
⊕⊕⊕⊕

33 Fucheng Lu **Tel** *(021) 6882 8888* **Fax** *(021) 6882 6688* **Rooms** *957*   **Map** *3 D3*

A stately tower with an elegant lobby and a brand new modern counterpart with superbly designed rooms place this among the largest hotels in Shanghai. Shangri-La is justly famed for its service standards, and many rooms have fine views across the river to the the Bund. **www.shangri-la.com.cn**

Key to Price Guide *see p178* **Key to Symbols** *see back cover flap*

Purple Mountain Hotel

778 Dongfang Lu **Tel** *(021) 6886 8888* **Fax** *(021) 6886 8800* **Rooms** *400*

An excellent business choice and close to Shanghai's newest exposition and convention facilities, this spotless five-star offers sizeable, stylish rooms, great views of Pudong, and a delightful outdoor pool popular for weekend parties in summer. It's a half-hour taxi to the French Concession though. **www.pmhotel.com.cn**

Radisson Hotel Shanghai New World

88 Nanjing Xi Lu **Tel** *(021) 6359 9999* **Fax** *(021) 6358 9705* **Rooms** *520*   *Map 2 A2*

Newly opened five-star with a distinctive saucer-shaped top (housing a revolving restaurant and excellent bar), opposite People's Park and the Nanjing Lu pedestrian mall. A vast golden lobby belies the more simply adorned yet utterly comfortable and fully equipped rooms. **www.radisson.com**

Radisson Plaza Xing Guo Hotel

78 Xingguo Lu **Tel** *(021) 6212 9998* **Fax** *(021) 6212 9996* **Rooms** *190*

An historic hotel with perhaps the best gardens of any accommodations in Shanghai – Chairman Mao was once a frequent guest. With serene, spacious rooms, the Radisson's only drawback is its distance from the Bund, although the attractions of the French Concession are just a short walk away. **www.radisson.com**

Ramada Plaza

719 Nanjing Dong Lu **Tel** *(021) 6350 0000* **Fax** *(021) 6350 6666* **Rooms** *387*   *Map 2 B2*

Approaching its 10th birthday, this chunky four-star hotel is superbly located right next to People's Square and minutes from the Shanghai Museum, yet remains unexceptional save for a large and kitsch lobby where fake palms compete for attention with Doric columns. **www.ramadahotels.com**

Regal International East Asia Hotel

516 Hengshan Lu **Tel** *(021) 6415 5588* **Fax** *(021) 6445 8899* **Rooms** *350*

Located on tree-lined Hengshan Lu in a consular district of the French Concession, the Regal has bright rooms with plenty of space and pleasant views. Sports buffs will enjoy the squash court, bowling alley, and Shanghai International Tennis Center. **www.regal-eastasia.com**

Ruijin Guesthouse

2 Ruijin Er Lu **Tel** *(021) 6472 5222* **Fax** *(021) 6473 2277* **Rooms** *62*   *Map 1 F5*

The 1917 mock-Tudor home of a British industrialist, now with a slightly shabby elegance but with large, modern, recently refitted bathrooms, is now the central building of a collection of villas standing in 17 acres (7 hectares) of gardens, recalling Shanghai's heyday.

Sofitel Hyland Hotel

505 Nanjing Dong Lu **Tel** *(021) 6351 5888* **Fax** *(021) 6351 4088* **Rooms** *389*   *Map 2 B2*

Excellent downtown location – the check-in counter is only a few yards from Shanghai's most bustling streets – with great views from higher floors of the 30-story tower. The rooms are adequate, though slightly poky. A German restaurant contributes to the hotel's European feel. **www.accorhotels.com**

88 Xin Tiandi

380 Huangpi Nan Lu **Tel** *(021) 5383 8833* **Fax** *(021) 5383 8877* **Rooms** *53*   *Map 2 A4*

Impressive boutique hotel set within the Xin Tiandi entertainment district, comprising chic apartment-style rooms with comprehensive business facilities and kitchenettes (including microwave and refrigerator). Yet with Xin Tiandi's legion of new restaurants at the doorstep, you'll hardly need to cook. **www.88xintiandi.com**

Crowne Plaza Shanghai

400 Panyu Lu **Tel** *(021) 6280 8888* **Fax** *(021) 6280 3353* **Rooms** *496*

Slightly out of the way, the Crowne Plaza is nevertheless luxurious and well-appointed. Rooms are spacious with high ceilings and marble bathrooms. Star spotters converge for one week each year during the Shanghai International Film Festival, held at the adjoining cinema center. **www.shanghai.crowneplaza.com**

Four Seasons Hotel Shanghai

500 Weihai Lu **Tel** *(021) 6256 8888* **Fax** *(021) 6256 5678* **Rooms** *443*   *Map 1 F3*

One of the more up-market establishments on the Puxi side, the Four Seasons is held in high regard by regular visitors to Shanghai for its butler service, large marble bathrooms, and luxurious health club. The location is unprepossessing but it's a short walk to People's Square and the French Concession. **www.fourseasons.com**

Grand Hyatt Shanghai

Jinmao Tower, 88 Shiji Dadao **Tel** *(021) 5049 1234* **Fax** *(021) 5049 8382* **Rooms** *555*   *Map 3 E3*

This spectacular hotel begins at the 53rd of 88 storys in China's (for now) tallest building. Large, ultra-modern rooms with spacious bathrooms and separate shower cubicles have bird's-eye views over the Bund and Pudong, as do an assortment of excellent restaurants. **shanghai.grand.hyatt.com**

Hilton Hotel

250 Huashan Lu **Tel** *(021) 6248 0000* **Fax** *(021) 6248 3848* **Rooms** *772*

A favorite with business travelers since it opened in 1987, the Hilton's status seems to be under threat as newer hotels emerge. Still, service is first rate, the spa is superb, and the top-floor bar commands enviable views of the French Concession. **www.hilton.com**

Holiday Inn Pudong Shanghai

899 Dong Fang Lu **Tel** *(021) 5830 6666* **Fax** *(021) 5830 5555* **Rooms** *389*

Dull rooms and tiny bathrooms, but the Holiday Inn boasts full supporting facilities including an Irish pub, and at lower prices than the other familiar brand names on the Pudong side of the river. A business rather than a leisure choice, perhaps. **www.ichotelsgroup.com**

Hong Qiao State Guest House

1591 Hong Qiao Lu **Tel** *(021) 6219 8855* **Fax** *(021) 6275 3903* **Rooms** *176*

Travelers who've tired of international high-rise hotels will enjoy the Hongqiao State Guest House whose vast, grassy grounds are dotted with villas. Refurbished rooms are clean and airy. Aside from a nearby street of shops in Gubei district, you'll need taxis to reach the sights. **www.hqstateguesthotel.com**

Howard Johnson Plaza

595 Jiujiang Lu **Tel** *(021) 3313 4888* **Fax** *(021) 3313 4880* **Rooms** *360*   **Map** *2 B2*

Nanjing Lu's pedestrian mall looks shabbier every day, yet fresh luxury hotels continue to rise in its vicinity. The only-just-five-star Howard Johnson Plaza arrived in 2003, and its comfortable rooms, trendy wine bar and responsive staff make for an agreeable stay. **www.hojochina.com**

JW Marriott Hotel Tomorrow Square

399 Nanjing Xi Lu **Tel** *(021) 5359 4969* **Fax** *(021) 6375 5988* **Rooms** *342*   **Map** *2 A3*

Wood-paneled doors, exceptional service and remarkable 360 degree views of People's Square and central Shanghai are just some of the attractions. Checking in on the 38th floor with its floor-to-wall windows is an exhilarating experience in itself. Among Shanghai's best hotels. **www.marriott.com**

Portman Ritz-Carlton

1376 Nanjing Xi Lu **Tel** *(021) 6279 8888* **Fax** *(021) 6279 8800* **Rooms** *590*   **Map** *1 E3*

The most thoughtful and attentive service in China: omnipresent when needed, invisible when not. The tower has its feet in an array of top-notch shopping, banking, ticket agencies, and more. Smart, newly refurbished rooms has every facility and expansive views across Puxi. **www.ritzcarlton.com**

Regent Shanghai

1116 Yan'an Xi Lu **Tel** *(021) 6115 9988* **Fax** *(021) 6115 9977* **Rooms** *511*

Spacious rooms in one of the city's newest luxury hotel are equipped with wide-screen plasma TVs, broadband Internet, and designer baths, and all have stunning views of central Shanghai. Chic design, a luxurious swimming pool and spa, open-kitchen restaurants, and a cigar lounge complete the plush picture. **www.regenthotels.com**

Renaissance Shanghai Pudong Hotel

100 Changliu Lu **Tel** *(021) 3871 4888* **Fax** *(021) 6854 0888* **Rooms** *369*

Conveniently located for conference delegates or business travelers, this stylish Pudong hotel has an attention to aesthetic detail often lacking in five-star properties. Rooms and public areas follow an East-meets-West theme, with antique cabinets, mosaics, and calligraphy-etched glass. Staff also impress. **www.renaissancehotels.com**

Renaissance Yangtze Hotel Shanghai

2099 Yan'an Xi Lu **Tel** *(021) 6275 0000* **Fax** *(021) 6275 0750* **Rooms** *544*

Conveniently close to Hong Qiao airport and the expressway to the city center, this newly upgraded five-star hotel has immaculate rooms, smiling service and excellent dining. The Cru bar, with cigar humidors and lazy jazz, is one of the classier nightspots in Shanghai. **www.renaissancehotels.com**

Shanghai Marriott Hotel Hongqiao

2270 Hong Qiao Lu **Tel** *(021) 6237 6000* **Fax** *(021) 6237 6275* **Rooms** *316*

Recently upgraded to five-star status, the Marriott boasts spacious, well-appointed rooms, impeccable service, and advanced business facilities, with wireless broadband available throughout the hotel. There are excellent steaks at the Manhattan Steak House. Close to the domestic airport and zoo. **www.marriott.com**

Sheraton Grand Tai Ping Yang

5 Zunyi Nan Lu **Tel** *(021) 6275 8888* **Fax** *(021) 6275 5420* **Rooms** *496*

Recently revitalized with ornate rooms and a stunning new lobby featuring imported Italian marble, the Sheraton is conveniently close to the domestic airport, though hardly central. The Bauernstube farmhouse-style delicatessen has some of the best imported meats and cheeses in China. **www.sheratongrand-shanghai.com**

Sofitel Jin Jiang Oriental Pudong Shanghai

889 Yanggao Nan Lu **Tel** *(021) 5050 4888* **Fax** *(021) 5050 4895* **Rooms** *446*

In a peaceful area a little out of the center, the Jin Jiang Sofitel has good-sized, well-appointed, proper shower cubicles, and baths next to picture windows with views towards the river. There's French, Shanghainese, Cantonese, and Japanese fine dining and easy access to the airport. **www.sofitel.com**

St. Regis Shanghai

889 Dong Fang Lu **Tel** *(021) 5050 4567* **Fax** *(021) 6875 6789* **Rooms** *318*

Modern, stylish, and beautifully furnished rooms with large bathrooms and proper shower cubicles, plus 24-hour butler service at the push of a button. Free cocktails daily and other executive floor-style services available to all guests. Not surprisingly, this hotel is very popular. **www.stregis.com**

Key to Price Guide *see p178* **Key to Symbols** *see back cover flap*

The Westin Shanghai

88 Henan Zhong Lu **Tel** *(021) 6335 1888* **Fax** *(021) 6335 2888* **Rooms** *301*　　　　　　**Map** 2 C3

The colorful style of the lobby, with its internally lit glass staircase, extends to the stylish modernity of the rooms. Bathrooms have torrential overhead showers in proper shower cubicles, and more extensive pampering is available at a branch of the famous Banyan Tree Spa. **www.westin.com/shanghai**

SHANGHAI FARTHER AFIELD

HANGZHOU Fuchun Resort

Fuyang Section, Hangfu Yanjiang Lu **Tel** *(0571) 6346 1111* **Fax** *(0571) 6346 1222* **Rooms** *84*

Probably the Yangzi Delta's best resort. With traditional architecture and advanced facilities, the hotel is impressive enough, although Fuchun's five fully serviced villas are its crowning glory, each with a dramatic indoor swimming pavilion and sweeping views of tea-laden terraces. **www.fuchunresort.com**

HANGZHOU Hyatt Regency Hangzhou

28 Hu Bin Lu **Tel** *(0571) 8779 1234* **Fax** *(0571) 8779 1818* **Rooms** *390*

Hyatt's brand new China property is a smarter-than-average horseshoe-shaped mansion, with a vast lobby incorporating indoor/outdoor café and extensive shopping. Many rooms have lake views, and others have private terraces with miniature gardens. **hangzhou.regency.hyatt.com**

HANGZHOU Radisson Plaza Hotel Hangzhou

333 Tiyuchang Lu **Tel** *(0571) 8515 8888* **Fax** *(0571) 8515 7777* **Rooms** *283*

Slickly managed city center shiny tower, close to West Lake, fully equipped with entertainment, fitness, and dining options. Well-furnished rooms are large enough to hold a full-sized sofa and the bathrooms have proper shower cubicles as well as baths. **www.radisson.com**

HANGZHOU Shangri-La Hotel Hangzhou

78 Bei Shan Lu **Tel** *(0571) 8797 7951* **Fax** *(0571) 8707 3545* **Rooms** *387*

Two hotels originally reserved for top officials now fused into one, built in the 40-acre (16-hectare) grounds of a now-vanished temple. Many of the amply-sized high-ceilinged rooms overlook West Lake. Quite simply one of the most pleasant hotels in China. **www.shangri-la.com**

HANGZHOU Sofitel Westlake Hangzhou

333 Xi Hu Dadao **Tel** *(0571) 8707 5858* **Fax** *(0571) 8702 8466* **Rooms** *200*

Smart, colorful interior decor, sharp service, and relatively small scale make this hotel a deservedly popular choice, along with its central, lake-side position, handy for the burgeoning Xi Hu Tiandi bar and restaurant area. Roof-top bar with splendid lake views. **www.sofitel.com**

SUZHOU Suzhou New Century Hotel

23 Guangji Lu **Tel** *(0512) 6533 8888* **Fax** *(0512) 6533 6798* **Rooms** *188*

Although the standard of service varies wildly from selfless to surly, the hotel's clean, light rooms make this a reasonable three-star choice. The famous Liu Yuan ("The Garden for Lingering In") is just a pleasant ten-minute stroll away. **www.sz-newcenturyhotel.cn**

SUZHOU Bamboo Grove Hotel

168 Zhuhui Lu **Tel** *(0512) 6520 5601* **Fax** *(0512) 6520 8778* **Rooms** *356*

Stark, concrete bus bay and garish lobby aside, the Bamboo Grove is modeled on traditional Suzhou architecture, including a sizeable pond with zigzag bridge and pointed pavilion. Rooms are comfortable, although the whole establishment is showing signs of wear and tear. **www.bg-hotel.com**

SUZHOU Gloria Plaza Hotel

535 Ganjiang Donglu **Tel** *(0512) 6521 8855* **Fax** *(0512) 6521 8833* **Rooms** *294*

The main lobby is perhaps a little sombre in tone but all eight categories of rooms are uniformly bright and spacious and the staff are generally sprightly and helpful. A canal running north of the hotel leads to some of Suzhou's best scenery. **www.gphsuzhou.com**

SUZHOU New World Aster Hotel

488 Sanxiang Lu **Tel** *(0512) 6829 1888* **Fax** *(0512) 6829 1838* **Rooms** *400*

This hotel is ten minutes west of the city center, at the junction of the old town and the burgeoning economic district. Views from the sightseeing elevators and top-floor restaurant are superb. Rooms are well furnished and recreational facilities abound.**www.aster.com.cn**

SUZHOU Sheraton Suzhou Hotel and Towers

259 Xinshi Lu **Tel** *(0512) 6510 3388* **Fax** *(0512) 6510 0888* **Rooms** *407*

The architecture of this impeccable hotel reflects the heritage of old Suzhou, with a central building modeled on the city's famous Panmen Gate. Canals wind through the quiet, elegant gardens, and the luxurious rooms feature spacious marble bathrooms. **www.sheraton.com**

WHERE TO EAT

Once you dine in Beijing or Shanghai, you may start to question your prior conceptions of Chinese food. The local restaurants in these two cities serve up cuisine of such variety and delight that it will quickly dissolve memories of the pale imitations of Chinese food experienced back home. Beijing's slender wheat noodles, *jiaozi* dumplings, and roast duck are vastly different from Shanghai's rope-like noodles, *shengjian* fried buns, and braised crabs. But both

Bamboo steamer of dim sum

cities also offer the best of China's regional cuisines, from well-known fiery Sichuanese, and subtle Cantonese (quite different from that served at home), to the lesser-known sweet and fruity tastes of sub-tropical Yunnan in the southwest, the vinegary noodles of Shanxi, and the hard-to-define but always excellent dishes of the Hakka (Kejia) minority of the southeast. Chinese consider the opportunity to sample different foods one of the main reasons to travel, and so should you.

Stylish dining at Laris, part of Shanghai's Three on the Bund complex

TYPES OF RESTAURANT

Whether you are looking to eat in the splendor of an imperial pavilion in Beijing or a chic Shanghai café, you will find a restaurant boom taking place in China. Freed from state control, entrepreneurs are thinking up tempting new ways to indulge in the country's favorite pastime. You never have to walk far to find restaurants in China and when you do, do not let first appearances put you off – many gourmet restaurants boast simple décor and harsh lighting. Look instead for happy crowds of diners and a different concept of "atmosphere:" in Chinese eyes, the more lively and noisy (*renao*) a restaurant is, the better.

OPEN ALL HOURS

You can breakfast on the street by 6am, but all hotels should serve breakfast until at least 9am and usually later. Lunch is typically from 11am until 2pm, after which some restaurants shut until the evening shift starts around 5pm. In the evening closing times can be very late, while some places never shut. At one time, booking was rare, except for the most popular and high-end establishments, but these days it's always wise to book in advance, particularly in Shanghai.

HOTEL FOOD

If you are tired and hungry, and staying at one of China's more expensive hotels, then room service can provide the usual international fare, and unchallenging made-for-foreigners Cantonese one-dish meals.

In Beijing and Shanghai many of the best restaurants, both Chinese and foreign, are located in hotels. The English menus are convenient, but prices can be inflated. The more intrepid diner who makes a few forays outside the comfort of four- or five-star hotels will reap handsome dividends.

STREET FOOD

As China smartens up for the Olympics, the World Expo, and other global events, street-food vendors must sometimes play hide-and-seek with the authorities. Yet their portable stalls form a vital part of the everyday life of China, selling cheap and popular foods such as breakfasts of dough sticks (*youtiao*) and beancurd (*doujiang*), or snacks like scallion pancakes (*jian bing*), sweet potatoes (*shanyu*) roasted in old oil drums, deep-fried beancurd cubes (*zha doufu*), and local fruits. A reliable way to locate delicious street food is to

Scorpion kebabs – cooking renders the sting ineffective

Steaming food on the street – simple, fast, and efficient

stroll through a night market (*ye shi*), a culinary and visual feast where clouds of vapour escape from bamboo steamers, and the sky glows red from the flames of oil-drum stoves. The sizzle of cooking and clamor of vendors shouting for business should stir your appetite, and if deep-fried scorpions or cicadas on skewers prove too exotic, be assured that plenty of other foods will take your fancy. If the food is hot and freshly cooked, hygiene problems are rare. The market off Wangfujing Street (*see p72*) in Beijing is the most famous of the night markets.

LITTLE EATS

Cheap and nourishing snacks such as those found at night markets are known collectively as *xiao chi*, or "little eats." Restaurants that specialize in them are called *xiao chi dian*; they sell different types of noodles or dumplings, stuffed buns, or pancakes. Open early for breakfast, they may serve simple stir-fried dishes too, and shut only when the last guest leaves. The setting is usually basic, but the food is hearty, tasty, and very reasonably priced. The very visible success of Western fast-food restaurants (McDonald's and KFC are everywhere) has led to local restaurant chains adopting the same style to serve native Chinese fast-food dishes and snacks. These are generally far tastier and healthier than their Western counterparts.

THE OTHER CHINA

Beijing and Shanghai showcase not only regional cuisine from all over Han China, but also a whole range of ethnic specialties belonging to the many minority nationalities, from the Korean border to the Tibetan plateau. Minorities' restaurants are an "exotic" attraction for Chinese as well as foreign tourists. In some Dai restaurants, offering the Thai-like cuisine of southern Yunnan, guests are greeted with scented water, given a lucky charm, and may later be invited to join in the singing and dancing. In more upmarket Uighur restaurants, serving lamb-heavy dishes

Rice and chopsticks

from the Muslim northwest, belly dancing is sometimes included as part of the entertainment.

VEGETARIAN SURPRISE

The Chinese understanding of a good life is inextricably associated with meat. They find it hard to understand why someone who could afford to eat meat would choose not to. Nevertheless, you will find a few vegetarian restaurants in Beijing and Shanghai. Some use soya protein to imitate meat with extraordinary authenticity. Others simply use Chinese cooking methods to bring out the best in pulses and vegetables. Ordinary restaurants can lay on good vegetarian meals too, as long as you can repeat, "Wo shi chi su de. Wo bu chi rou," ("I'm vegetarian. I don't eat meat"), and don't mind the odd bit of meat or chicken stock.

INTERNATIONAL FOOD

Almost all kinds of foreign food, from Brazilian to Indian can be found in Beijing and Shanghai. Italian is probably the most popular of Western cuisines, ravioli and spaghetti being easy concepts for the dumpling- and noodle-loving Chinese to appreciate. Some have justifiably earned wide acclaim, such as Aria in Beijing, and M on the Bund in Shanghai. Other Asian cuisines, namely Korean, Japanese, and Thai, are also well represented, and more readily accepted by the chopstick-wielding Chinese.

Eating together, an important aspect of Chinese social life

Dining Etiquette

The Chinese are quite informal at meal times. Confucius may have been renowned for his silence while eating, but these days a busy Chinese restaurant can be a deafening place as waiters crash plates about and diners shout orders at the waiters. It may seem daunting but just join in and expect praise for your chopstick skills – even if you struggle, your willingness to try will be appreciated.

Dinner in a private room, a popular Chinese way of doing business

EARNING SOME FACE

The Chinese do not expect visitors to be fully versed in proper banquet etiquette, but awareness of a few essentials can earn "face" both for yourself and your host, whatever the occasion. The other guests will appreciate that you have some respect for Chinese culture and traditions.

When attending, or hosting, a formal meal, note that the guest of honor is usually placed on the seat in the middle, facing the door. The host, traditionally positioned opposite the guest, now more often sits to his or her left.

If you come as a guest, be punctual and do not sit down until you are given your seat – seating arrangements can be very formal and based on rank. Once seated, do not start on the food or drink before your host gives the signal. Some of the delicacies on offer may test your courage but it is an insult if the food is untouched. Leave some food on the plates: empty bowls imply that the host is too poor or mean to lay on a good spread.

In addition to the above, there are further rules that should be kept in mind. If you are applauded as you come into the room, don't feel shy about applauding back. Reply to any welcome toast with your own (short) speech and toast. In your speech and any subsequent conversation avoid broaching sensitive subjects, in particular Chinese politics.

Show respect to your elders and superiors by ensuring that the rim of your glass is lower than theirs when clinking glasses, and drain your drink in one swift movement.

THE ART OF ORDERING

If you are someone's guest, you may be asked to order something, or state some sort of preference – if you do not do so, a ten-course banquet could soon appear. Feel free to name your favorite dish, or point at the object of your desire, possibly something swimming in a fish tank at the entrance to the restaurant. Freshness is all-important in Chinese cuisine.

A meal might begin with cold starters such as pickled vegetables, 1,000-year old eggs, seasoned jellyfish, or cold roasted meats. Main courses should be selected for harmony and balance. A typical order would be a variety of different meats and vegetables, cooked in different and complementary ways. The last dish, or *cai*, is usually soup. Then comes *fan*, a grain staple such as rice, noodles, or bread (*mantou*), without which a Chinese diner may feel they have not eaten. At informal meals you can have rice at the start of the meal – although you may want to remind the waiting staff of this – but not at a banquet, or your host will assume his dishes are inadequate.

English-language menus are becoming more common. An increasing number of restaurants actively encourage visitors to get out of their chairs and choose ingredients from tanks, cages, and supermarket-type shelves. Your Chinese friends (and waiters and onlookers) will likely be

A variety of dim sum dishes – no need to finish them all

delighted by any interest you show in the whole experience. In the end, when language or phrase book fail, simply look around and point at whatever appeals on other tables, or even head into the kitchen to find what you want.

INVITED TO DINNER

A formal meal often takes place in a private room and usually begins with a toast. The host serves his guest with the choicest morsels, and then everyone is permitted to help themselves. Simply watch others for guidelines on when to use serving utensils, and when, more informally, your own chopsticks will do.

Only in restaurants regularly frequented by lots of foreigners, or which also have Western dishes on the menu will knives and forks be available.

Seafood – abundant in Beijing and Shanghai

The host almost always orders more dishes than is necessary. While it is, as stated earlier, polite to try everything, it is far from necessary to finish it all.

DOS AND DON'TS

The Chinese are fairly relaxed about table manners. Slurping shows appreciation, enables better appreciation of flavor, and sucks in air to prevent burning the mouth. Holding your bowl up to your mouth, to shovel rice in, is another practical solution. You may happily reach across your neighbors, but do not spear food with your chopsticks, and do not stand them upright in a bowl of rice either, as it looks like an offering to the dead. If you have finished with the chopsticks lay them flat on the table or on a rest. You shouldn't suck greasy fingers, or use them to pick bones out of your mouth – spit bones or shell onto the table, into the saucer that was under your bowl, or more delicately into

a napkin. Toothpicks are ubiquitous, but do cover the action with your free hand.

And generally don't be shy about shouting for attention as enthusiasm for food is much appreciated. Eating alone is alien to the Chinese way of thinking. They believe that eating in a group – sharing both the dishes and the experience – significantly increases the enjoyment.

THE END OF THE MEAL

A platter of fresh fruit and steaming hot towels signal the end of the meal is coming. In more formal meals, just as you should await the start of a meal, do not stand up before your host, who will rise and indicate that the dinner has ended and ask if you've had enough. The correct answer is "yes." The person who invited you

Dining outdoors in Shanghai, possible for much of the year

usually shoulders the full weight of the bill, so accept graciously. Offering to pay is fine, even polite; insisting too hard suggests that you doubt the host's ability to pay.

Prices are fixed and written down in most restaurants, and on bills. Tipping is not necessary and the only places that include a service charge are the upmarket restaurants within hotels. These are also the only places likely to take international credit cards.

PARTY FOOD

In a culture obsessed with both symbolism and eating, many foods that have earned special meaning and must be consumed on set occasions. Round mooncakes, dotted with moon-like duck egg yolks, are a must at Mid-Autumn Festival. At Spring Festival, the whole family cooks *tangyuan*, round sweet dumplings made of glutinous rice flour, because *yuan* can also mean "reunion." Fish is auspicious, because the character for fish (*yu*) sounds like the one for "abundance" and offers the hope of good fortune in the year ahead. Meat dumplings (*jiaozi*) are another New Year favorite as their shape is said to resemble the symbol for prosperity. Birthdays are often celebrated with noodles, a symbol of longevity, while red beans are a metaphor of longing and love. To celebrate new arrivals, parents hand out eggs painted red for luck – an even number for a boy, an odd number for a girl.

What to Eat in Beijing

Communities developed beside the Yellow River before 6000 BC, but it is not until about 1500 BC, when written records started, that a picture of the dietary habits of the ancient Chinese becomes clear. They kept pigs and grew millet, wheat, barley, and rice and even fermented their grain to make alcoholic beverages. Later (around 1100 BC), soybeans were added to the Chinese diet, then by-products such as soy sauce and beancurd (tofu). Late-founded Beijing had no distinctive cuisine of its own, but as the center of a mighty empire it imported elements and influences from a variety of sources.

Chinese leaf, also known as Tianjin cabbage

ingredients – shark's fin, bird's nest soup, and abalone, all imported from the south – feature as well as artistic presentation and poetic names. Beijing cuisine can be summed up as the distillation of the creations of generations of Imperial Palace chefs over almost a millennium.

Candied apples, a common Beijing street food

THE PALACE KITCHEN

Kublai Khan made Beijing the capital in 1271 and brought simple Mongolian influences to the imperial kitchens – lamb, roasting, and the hotpot. These were foods that didn't require a lot of equipment, ideal for pastoral nomads and armies on the move. Elaborate preparation and expensive

MONGOLIAN AND MUSLIM CUISINE

One highly successful alien invader is the Mongolian hotpot, a simple one-pot dish. Although Buddhists, the Mongol minority within China are not vegetarians – their traditional nomadic lifestyle made vegetable

Marinated, roast duck

Steamed pancakes

Scallions

Sliced cucumber

Special duck sauce

A whole Peking duck with traditional accompaniments

REGIONAL DISHES AND SPECIALTIES

Peking duck – an Imperial meal – must be the best known dish in north Chinese cuisine. The duck, a local Beijing variety, is carefully dried, and then brushed with a sweet marinade before being roasted over fragrant wood chips. When ready it is carved by the chef and eaten wrapped in pancakes with a special duck sauce, and slivered scallions and cucumbers. To accompany the duck, diners might also be served duck liver pâté, and duck soup to finish. Beijing is also known for a wide variety of cold dishes that start a meal, for stuffed breads and pastries, and for *jiaozi* (dumplings). Look out for *zha jiang mian* (Clanging Dish Noodles), in which ingredients are added at the table to a central bowl of noodles, the bowls loudly clanged together as each ingredient goes in.

Duck pears – like a duck's head

Mu xu pork: *stir-fried tiger lily buds, scrambled egg, black fungus, and shredded pork – eaten with pancakes.*

growing impractical), and the hotpot is served with a choice of finely shaved lamb or beef, or sometimes more exotic meats. Modern Beijing has a great many dedicated hotpot restaurants, and it is one of the cheapest ways of group eating.

Chinese Muslims are treated as a separate ethnic minority in China, known as the Hui, with enclaves in every major city. Beijing also has small pockets of Turkic Uighur people from the Xinjiang region of the Northwest, also Muslim, so none eat pork. Xinjiang men, originally from the far northwest of China, can often be found hunched over troughs of coals at the

The art of pouring tea, exhibited in a Beijing restaurant

streetside, selling *kao rou chuan*, or lamb kabobs dusted with cumin. Another Uighur specialty are thick *lao mian* or "pulled noodles" made by endlessly doubling, twisting, and stretching a rope of dough, and widely available in Beijing.

Some of the wide variety of foods on display at a night food market

SHANDONG

Shandong is the birthplace of Confucius, and its cuisine is generally regarded as the oldest and best in China. Shandong has produced the largest number of famous master chefs, and it is said that the iron wok originated here. Most of the Chinese influences in Beijing cooking come from this province. As one of the most important agricultural areas of China, Shandong supplies Beijing with most of its ingredients – its main crops are wheat, barley, sorghum, millet, and corn. Additionally, fisheries are widely developed along the Yellow River and the north China coast, particularly the Shandong peninsula where the specialties are all kinds of fish, shrimp, shellfish, abalones, sea slugs, and sea urchins.

ON THE MENU

Drunken empress chicken
Supposedly named after Yang Guifei, an imperial concubine overly fond of her alcohol.

Stir-fried kidney-flowers
These are actually pork kidneys criss-cross cut into "flowers" and stir-fried with bamboo shoots, water chestnuts, and black fungus.

Fish slices with wine sauce
Deep-fried fish fillet braised in a wine sauce.

Phoenix-tail prawns King prawn tails coated in batter and bread crumbs, then deep fried.

Lamb in sweet bean sauce
Tender fillet of lamb sliced and cooked in sweet bean paste with vinegar to give it that classic sweet and sour taste.

Hot candied apples
A popular Chinese dessert.

Lamb and scallions: *sliced lamb rapidly stir-fried with garlic, leeks or scallions, and sweet bean paste.*

Mongolian hotpot: *thinly sliced lamb, vegetables, and noodles dipped in boiling water and an array of sauces.*

Sweet and sour carp: *the quintessential Shandong dish traditionally made with Yellow River carp.*

What to Eat in Shanghai

Shanghai draws its population from neighboring provinces, and these people have brought with them their regional tastes and preferences. The surrounding provinces are traditionally referred to as the "Lands of Fish and Rice," and indeed Central China is one of the country's leading agricultural regions with some of the most fertile land. Both wheat and rice are grown here as well as barley, corn, sweet potatoes, peanuts, and soybeans. Freshwater fisheries abound in the network of lakes and rivers, while deep-sea fishing has long been established on the coast.

Garlic chives and bok choi

Market stall displaying the wide variety of dried goods available

SHANGHAI

The characteristics of Shanghai cuisine are summarized as "exquisite in appearance, rich in flavor, and sweet in taste." A favorite ingredient is the hairy crab from the Yangzi estuary (although overfishing means they actually come from elsewhere nowadays) and the eel. The sweetness and oiliness of many Shanghai dishes is balanced by lighter elements from

neighboring older schools of cuisine – Huaiyang and Suzhe. Among the dishes Shanghai is famous for are its thick fried noodles, its *shengjian mantou*, which are bread dough balls stuffed with meat and "steamed in oil," and *xiaolong mantou*, little pasta sacks filled with

pork, crab meat, and scalding soup. Calling both of these *mantou* rather than *bao* as elsewhere in China marks you out as a local. The distinctive pungent smell of *chou doufu*, or "stinky" tofu, invented not far away in Shaoxing is also found gusting around Shanghai streets.

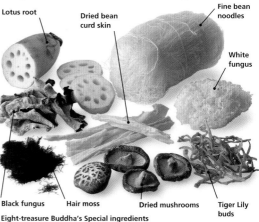

Lotus root

Dried bean curd skin

Fine bean noodles

White fungus

Black fungus   **Hair moss**   **Dried mushrooms**   **Tiger Lily buds**

Eight-treasure Buddha's Special ingredients

REGIONAL DISHES AND SPECIALTIES

Two of the area's great cities, Nanjing and Hangzhou, were at different times capitals in central China. Whenever there was a change of capital, the vast imperial kitchens changed location bringing the staff with them resulting in a cross-fertilization of recipes and methods from one region to another. One favorite imperial dish despite its lowly name is Beggar's Chicken – a whole chicken is stuffed with vegetables and herbs, wrapped in lotus leaves, and encased in clay before being baked. The clay container is then broken at the table releasing the beautifully concentrated aromas. (For hygiene reasons, top hotels find clayless solutions to the same delicious result.) Another specialty is *Dongpo rou*, a soya pork dish named for the Song poet exiled to Hangzhou. Freshwater crabs are best during the months of October and November.

Fermented bean curd

Lions' heads: *pork meatballs braised with Chinese leaf – meant to look like lions' heads and manes.*

HUAIYANG AND SUZHE

Based specifically around the deltas of the Huai and Yangzi Rivers, Huaiyang cuisine is most famous for its excellent fish and shellfish – the freshwater crabs from the waters of Tai Hu are superb. Suzhe cuisine, however, covers a wider area – the provinces of Jiangsu and Zhejiang – and includes culinary centers such as Nanjing and Hangzhou that both served as capital cities. Along with stews flavored with a light stock, the region is famous for its "red cooking" – food braised in soy sauce, sugar, ginger, and rice wine. "Chinkiang Vinegar" is black rice vinegar from Zhenjiang, Jiangsu, and is acknowledged to be the best rice vinegar in China. The province of Zhejiang, of course, produces China's best rice wines from Shaoxing and top quality hams from Jinhua. It is also worth trying the Long Jing (Dragon Well) green tea grown around West Lake in Hangzhou.

Park cafés – popular places to snack on some filled dumplings

ANHUI

Shanghai is also influenced by the little known Anhui cuisine, from farther inland.

Hairy crabs, a Shanghai delicacy

Despite being landlocked, Anhui still enjoys a lot of fish thanks to its extensive network of lakes and rivers. The province is also another of the key agricultural regions in China, and it produces a great number and variety of crops and vegetables. One of Anhui's most famed ingredients are its tender white bamboo shoots. These crisp shoots feature large in the vegetarian cuisine prepared in the Buddhist mountain retreats and are often combined with a variety of exotic woodland mushrooms. Finally the world-famous Keemun red tea comes from the hills of Yimeng in south Anhui.

ON THE MENU

Beggars chicken A whole chicken stuffed with flavorings and cooked in a clay pot.

Fried prawns in shells Prawns still in their shells are rapidly fried and then braised in a soy and tomato sauce.

Three-layer shreds Steamed shredded ham, chicken, and pork with bamboo shoots and black mushroom – should be called five-layer shreds.

Freshwater crabs Simply steamed with scallions, ginger, soy, sugar, and vinegar.

Steamed belly pork with ground rice Also known as Double-braised Pork, this long-cooked dish literally melts in your mouth.

Eight-treasure Buddha's Special A generic name for a delicious vegetarian dish which can actually contain any number of different ingredients.

Tofu casserole: *tofu with sea cucumbers, ham, prawns, mushrooms, bamboo shoots, and bok choi in a stew pot.*

Squirrel fish: *a bream is filleted, coated with batter, deep-fried, and served with a sweet-and-sour sauce.*

Sweet and sour spare ribs: *deep-fried bite-size pork spare ribs braised in soy, sugar, and vinegar.*

What to Drink

Tea of course is the most popular drink in China. There are countless arguments for drinking the infusion of the bush *Camellia sinensis,* and just as many legends about its origin. But if tea

Fresh tea leaves

is the most popular drink, there is a wide range of others for the visitor. Beer is popular with meals and wine is available in many upscale restaurants. Chinese spirits can range from the extremely pleasant to the almost dangerous. Likewise approach the "health tonics," like snake wine, with caution – as if the reptilian "sediment" in the bottle isn't enough, they can be fiercely alcoholic.

Tea may be served both during and after a meal

TYPES OF TEA

Green is the most common tea, baked immediately after picking. Flower tea is a mixture of green tea with flower petals. Black tea colors during the fermentation process and the reddish brew that results explains its Chinese name – red tea. The most highly prized is oolong, a lightly fermented tea. Brick tea is black or green, pressed into blocks. Eight Treasure tea *babaocha* has many ingredients including dates, dried longan, and wolfberry, and Tibetans enjoy yak butter tea.

Gaiwan or three-piece tea cup

Lid keeps leaves in the cup, not the mouth

Saucer to prevent fingers burning

Black: hongcha, *actually called "red tea" in Chinese.*

Green: lucha, *uses leaves dried without fermentation.*

Pu'er: *from Yunnan, is compressed into "bricks."*

Flower: huacha *a mix of petals – jasmine, rose, and chrysanthemum.*

The famous "Hairy Peak" green tea

Coffee: *as café culture enters China, coffee drinking is fashionable among the middle classes. Starbucks may have an outlet inside the Forbidden City, but freshly-ground coffee is rare outside major hotels.*

Tea and coffee drink: *those who want a fashionable coffee drink, but cannot do without their daily shot of tea, can try this blend of tea and coffee.*

SOFT DRINKS

Even as a cold drink, tea is dominant. Iced tea is very popular, especially with the young. Besides the usual array of fruit juices, there is hawthorn juice in Beijing, pomegranate juice from Xinjiang, and lychee and sugar cane juice from down south. As well as the global drink brands, local challengers include Tianfu Cola, and the energy drink Jianlibao, made with honey. As China overcomes its dairy aversion, milk and yoghurt drinks multiply, as well as soya-bean (*doujiang*) and coconut milk.

Bamboo cane juice

Iced green tea

Coconut milk drink

BEER

Europeans first introduced beer to China in the early 20th century; in the 21st, China has taken over as the world's biggest brewer, so you are never far from a very acceptable light lager. Both Beijing and Shanghai have their own local breweries.

Tsingtao beer   **Yanjing beer**

WINE

Although grape seeds traveled the Silk Roads, China has historically preferred grain alcohol. The quality is rapidly improving, but red wine is still a safer order than white – considered good for the heart, and a lucky color too.

Great Wall   **Dragon Seal**

SPIRITS

For millennia the Chinese have been distilling grains into *baijiu* or "white spirits" ranging from strong to deadly. Classified into three types: the *qingxiang*, or light bouquet, group includes Fenjiu from Shaanxi; Guizhou's famous Maotai is a classic *jiangxiang*, soy bouquet; *nongxiang*, strong bouquet, is championed by Sichuan giant Wuliangye.

RICE WINE

Despite being called "wine," some care is required as this can vary in strength from a mild 15–16 % alcohol, to the double- or triple-fermented wines at up to 38 % ABV. Good rice wine is best drunk warm and goes well with cold starters.

Maotai *"eight times fermented and seven times distilled" is favored for toasts at banquets. At the other end of the scale* erguotou *is cheap and effective – the people's drink.*

Maotai   **Erguotou**

Shaoxing rice wine

Shaoxing: *This is among the best of the* huangjiu *(yellow spirits), noted for its moderate alcohol content (about 16%) and mellow fragrance.*

Strong rice wine

DRINKING CULTURE

Chinese youth drinking in a local modern teahouse

Teahouses are enjoying something of a revival in China, as appreciation of traditional tea culture recovers after years of proletarian austerity. While *cha* (tea) stimulates quiet contemplation, *jiu* (alcohol) lubricates noisy celebrations. Despite reveling in the drunkenness of their poets such as Li Bai (*see p20*), the Chinese have not been as badly affected by alcoholism as many other societies. Public drunkenness is frowned upon – except maybe in the ever more popular karaoke bars. Traditionally only soup was drunk with meals, but this is changing, especially when eating with foreigners. "Gan bei!" or "dry the cup" is the repeated clarion call to toasting bouts and drinking games. Beware the legendary drinking capacity of the northeast Chinese, and don't drink alone or on an empty stomach.

Choosing a Restaurant

Chosen for their excellent food, good value, and
convenient or interesting location, the restaurants in this
guide cover a wide price range. They are listed by town
or city in the same order as the chapters appear in this
book. Where a restaurant has both an English and a
Chinese name, the English name is given first.

PRICE CATEGORIES
The following price ranges are the
equivalent of a meal for two made up
of a range of dishes, served with tea,
and including any service charges.

Ⓨ under ¥100
ⓎⓎ ¥100–¥250
ⓎⓎⓎ ¥250–¥500
ⓎⓎⓎⓎ over ¥500

BEIJING

Beijing Roast Duck Restaurant (Beijing Dadong Kaoyadian)   Ⓨ
Building 3, Tuanjiehu Beikou, Dong San Huan Bei Lu **Tel** *(010) 6582 2892*   **Map** *3 F4*

There's no finer Beijing duck than that served here – full-flavored and with just the right balance between tender
meat and crispy skin. Far less famous than the Quanjude establishments that dot Beijing, it nevertheless surpasses its
rival on every level, including price.

Bite A Pitta   🗐 🍴   Ⓨ
30A Tianze Lu (near entrance to Super Bar Street) **Tel** *(010) 6467 2961*   **Map** *3 F1*

Despite the unmistakable laminex and brightly colored décor of a fast food establishment, Biteapitta does Beijing's
best Mediterranean snacks, including falafel, chicken shwarma, and a number of feta cheese and vegetable filo
wraps. Tasty and very reasonable prices.

Elephant   🗐 🍴   Ⓨ
50 m north up lane opposite Yatai Dasha on Yabao Lu **Tel** *(010) 8561 4073*   **Map** *2 C3*

Popular restaurant in Beijing's Russian district serving cheap, hearty Russian and Ukrainian staples such as borscht,
stroganoff, and dumplings, along with several nightly dance performances from scantily-attired Russian girls. Kitsch
decorations and a colorful Russian and Mongolian crowd make for an unusual cultural experience.

Fu Jia Lou   🗐   Ⓨ
23 Dong Si Shi Tiao **Tel** *(010) 8403 7831*   **Map** *3 D3*

One of the best survivors from now-passed craze for old-style Beijing restaurants, Fu Jia Lou recreates the pre-1949
dining experience: general bustle, shouting waiters, and pungent, sour Beijing dishes that will redefine your idea of
Chinese food.

Lao Beijing Zhajiang Mian Da Wang   🗐   Ⓨ
29 Chongwen Men Wai Dajie **Tel** *(010) 6705 6705*   **Map** *5 E3*

This bustling institution near the Temple of Heaven is decorated with Ming-style ornaments and serves traditional
Beijing snacks like *mifen rou* (steamed pork belly with rice powder) and *zhajiang mian* (bean sauce noodles). Kitsch
and a bit touristy, but cheap and very tasty fare.

Noodle Loft   🗐   Ⓨ
20 Xidawang Lu **Tel** *(010) 6774 9950*

A surprisingly sleek, modern restaurant dishing up regional Shanxi dishes with tidy presentation and a modern twist.
Excellent snacks and cold starters such as the salty mashed pumpkin and fungus and caraway salad complement
fresh noodle dishes and main courses. Excellent value.

Pamer   🗐   Ⓨ
3 Lianhua Chi Dong Lu **Tel** *(010) 6326 3635*

Cheap, gaudy, and a bit run-down, this is nevertheless the city's best producer of Uighur cuisine. Specialty items join
a wide variety of thick, supremely satisfying noodles in spicy tomato sauce, served with unleavened bread for a meal
that's just plain good.

Three Guizhou Men   🗐   Ⓨ
6 Guanghua Xili **Tel** *(010) 6502 1733*   **Map** *3 F5*

Authentic Guizhou cuisine, uncompromisingly spicy and sour, is generally too coarse for foreign tastes, but the
interpretation here, blended with conventional Chinese flavors, is genuinely enjoyable. The atmosphere is stylish, in
keeping with the local hipster fondness for minority cuisines.

Yuxiang Renjia   Ⓨ
20 Chaoyang Dajie, 5th floor of Lianhe Dasha **Tel** *(010) 6588 3841*   **Map** *3 D4*

One of a chain of swish but economical Sichuan restaurants scattered all over the city, Yuxiang Renjia is at least as
good, and far cheaper, than its many more famous competitors. This is real Sichuanese: oily, intensely spicy, and
totally addictive.

Key to Symbols *see back cover flap*

Afunti (Afanti)

2A Houguaibang Hutong, Chaoyang Men Nei Dajie **Tel** *(010) 6527 2288* **Map** *2 C4*

The most famous and popular Uighur establishment in Beijing, this child-friendly restaurant is best known for its after-dinner table-top dancing, done to live Muslim (and sometimes Latin) folk music. Dishes are nicely executed, but prices reflect the frills.

Alameda

Nali Market, off Sanlitun Bei Lu (Bar Street) **Tel** *(010) 6417 8084* **Map** *3 F3*

Trendy, intimate restaurant serving Brazilian-inspired contemporary cuisine. Succinct but well balanced menu includes a handful of excellent value set meals that change weekly with the availability of fresh ingredients, with consistently good steaks. The small wine list is carefully chosen but expensive. Service is attentive.

Bellagio (Lu Gang Zhen)

6 Gongren Tiyucheng Xi Lu (south of west gate of Workers' Stadium) **Tel** *(010) 6551 3533* **Map** *3 E3*

Packed around the clock with hip, young Beijingers, this Taiwanese chain serves quality Hakka dishes from China's south such as "three cup chicken," as well as fruit smoothies and red-bean ice desserts in a bustling, modern dining room with floor-to-ceiling windows.

Cafe Sambal

43 Doufuchi Hutong **Tel** *(010) 6400 4875* **Map** *2 A2*

A stylish Malaysian restaurant that's a big favorite with expatriates in want of an alternative to Chinese fare. The exquisite dishes are prepared by a genuine Malay chef. The attractive courtyard setting makes for a great place to relax over a drink or meal in summer.

Da Zhai Men

20 Shouti Nan Lu **Tel** *(010) 8835 6687*

Specializing in palace cuisine but also serving Cantonese, Sichuan, and Beijing snacks, this cavernous new restaurant is dressed up like an imperial court. Locals praise the food's authenticity; foreigners enjoy the floorshow, which includes acrobats, magicians, kung fu, and clowns.

Han Cang

Ping'an Da Dao, opposite north gate of Beihai Park **Tel** *(010) 6404 2259* **Map** *1 C3*

This bustling two-story establishment with a huge outdoor dining area facing the Qian Hai (lake) is always packed with locals and foreigners enjoying simple, tasty Hakka dishes. An army of waiters briskly delivers house specialties, including foil-wrapped fish and salt-baked shrimp.

Hatsune

8A Guanghua Dong Lu, 2nd floor Heqiao Dasha C **Tel** *(010) 6581 3939* **Map** *3 F5*

Charmingly creative rolls at surprisingly affordable prices make this one of the city's best Japanese options. Stylish surroundings, attentive service, and fresh fish flown in regularly from Japan suggest a much more expensive experience. A place to indulge yourself.

Huang Cheng Lao Ma

39 Nanqingfengzha Houjie (in Dabeiyao) **Tel** *(010) 6779 8801*

Beijing's most upscale hotpot restaurant is ideal for foreign visitors nervous at the questionable hygiene of local establishments but who still want the experience of do-it-yourself Chinese dining. Broths range from mild to impossibly spicy, and ingredients are all extremely fresh.

Jazz-Ya

Nali Market, off Sanlitun Bei Lu (Bar Street) **Tel** *(010) 6415 1227* **Map** *3 F3*

A rare flash of class and style off Sanlitun's notorious Bar Street, Jazz-Ya is like a trendy Tokyo club, dishing up pricey sushi, salads and Japanese grills as a complement to the cool jazz, smooth décor, and slick wait-staff. Very much a place to see and be seen.

Kong Yiji

Desheng Men Nei Dajie, on the Hou Hai shore **Tel** *(010) 6618 4917/4915* **Map** *1 C2*

Perpetually packed with local epicures, this is simply among the best two or three Chinese restaurants of any style in the city. There's an enormous range of delicate dishes from the Yangzi River delta and the atmosphere is pure Chinese-style culinary joy.

Le Cafe Igosso

Dong San Huan Nan Lu (400 m south of Dabeiyao Bridge on east side) **Tel** *(010) 8771 7013*

Obscurely located but a worthy find, Igosso serves inexpensive, quality Italian and rich desserts in a narrow loft space. Wooden floors and rich, dark-wood paneling lend the place an exclusive club-like ambience. Jazz ensembles perform by the bar on weekends.

Lemon Leaf

15 Xiaoyun Lu **Tel** *(010) 6462 5505* **Map** *3 F1*

Opened by a Taiwanese pop star, Lemon Leaf is renowned for excellent hotpot in a swish dining room with soft lighting and velour booths. Try the yin-yang hotpot with Thai-style sweet-and-sour broth and coconut curry. Perfect for groups of two to four.

Liqun Kaoyadian

11 Beixiangfeng Hutong (enter from Zhengyi Lu, off Qian Men Dong Dajie) **Tel** *(010) 6705 5578*   **Map 5 D2**

Peking duck at this chaotic, little courtyard restaurant tucked away in a *hutong* east of Qian Men, can be sublime or disappointing. Generally worth trying your luck, though, if only for the rough-and-ready ambience. Very popular, so book ahead.

Lotus in Moonlight

12 Liufang Nanli **Tel** *(010) 6465 3299*   **Map 3 E2**

With its bright, pastel interior, Lotus practically glows with health and is popular for its range of vegetarian options, including traditional "fake meat" dishes and innovative modern vegetable combinations, as well as an extensive tea selection. Like meat, alcohol is prohibited here.

Makye Ame

2nd floor, A11 Xiushui Nan Jie, Jianguo Men Wai Dajie **Tel** *(010) 6506 9616*   **Map 3 F5**

This branch of a popular Lhasa restaurant is pricey but, like its Uighur counterpart Afunti *(see p199)*, offers ethnic atmosphere and live folk entertainment that more than justifes the expense. Dishes use Tibetan ingredients but are slightly more fanciful than authentic Tibetan fare.

Matsuko

22 Dong San Huan Bei Lu, south of Changhong Qiao **Tel** *(010) 6582 5208*   **Map 3 F3**

This no-frills Japanese restaurant serving standard sushi, sashimi, tempura, and noodle dishes rarely has a free table. Cheap buffet lunch specials include unlimited Asahi beer. Décor is kitsch Japanese with *tatami* rooms, soothing green walls, and fake bamboo.

Otto's

14 Di'an Men Xi Dajie **Tel** *(010) 6405 8205*   **Map 1 E3**

Cheap and cheerful, light-filled establishment opposite the Qian Hai (lake) serves simple Cantonese dishes and hot-pot in a bustling setting. Perennially packed, locals flock here for the *bifengtang* claypot dishes – the local answer to paella. Pick from specials plastered on the walls or dine "à la carte."

Pure Lotus

3rd floor, Holiday Inn Lido, 6 Jiangtai Lu **Tel** *(010) 8703 6668*

The dining room of this branch of a holier-than-thou vegetarian restaurant chain features striking Eastern-inspired artworks and fittings to match similarly presentable "meat inspired" food. It serves tofu dressed as mutton, beans cooked to look and taste like pork, and vegetarian Peking duck.

Raj

38 Mao'er Hutong, Di'an Men Wai Dajie **Tel** *(010) 6401 1675*   **Map 2 A2**

In a *hutong* district near Hou Hai (Back Lake), Raj serves cheap and authentic southern Indian cuisine. The various lassi drinks and naan breads are particularly good. Although the décor inside is a little kitsch, the pleasant outdoor patio is simple and quaint.

Sorabol

Lufthansa Center basement, 50 Liangma Qiao Lu **Tel** *(010) 6465 3388 x5712*   **Map 3 A1**

Quality Korean BBQ restaurant serving plates of fresh meat, seafood, and vegetables for you to cook on individual table skillets. Simple menu also includes huge Korean dumplings and the usual array of pickled treats. Waitresses in elaborate *hanbok* contrast with the basic décor.

Souk

Chaoyang Park west gate (Chaoyang Gongyuan Xi Men) (behind Annie's restaurant) **Tel** *(010) 6506 7309*

This hugely popular restaurant-cum-bar dishes up Middle Eastern and North African staples, including dips, salads and kabobs. Recline on beds with cushions and satin shrouds, while enjoying the very good house sangria, an apple tobacco hookah pipe, and regular DJs.

South Silk Road

19A Shichahai Qian Hai Xiyan **Tel** *(010) 6615 5515*   **Map 1 F3**

Serves authentic but stylish Yunnanese food. Diners can sample all manner of flowers, insects and mysterious animal parts, as well as more conventional dishes such as bacon and herb rolls. Classy private rooms upstairs with gorgeous lake views.

Tai Bo Tian Fu Shan Zhen

9 Erqi Juchang Lu, behind Chang'an Dasha **Tel** *(010) 6801 9641*   **Map 3 F3**

Southwestern China produces many varieties of the world's most precious wild mushrooms, over 30 types of which are stewed with a whole black-skinned chicken to form the basic hotpot broth here. Choose from a long list of other ingredients to add yourself.

The Tree

Hutong west of Sanlitun Bei Lu (Bar Street), opposite Sanlitun Hospital. **Tel** *(010) 6415 1954*   **Map 3 F2**

An amiable, ex-pat frequented pub hidden in a Sanlitun *hutong* serving good wood-fired pizzas with Belgian beers on tap. Enjoy soothing acoustic tunes from Filipino cover bands and gaze at abstract nude portraits on the walls. Regulars swear by the Flemish-style bitterballen pizza.

Key to Price Guide *see p198* **Key to Symbols** *see back cover flap*

Vincent Café 🍴❤️🌐 ¥¥

798 Art District, 2 Jiuxian Qiao Bei Lu, Da Shan Zi **Tel** *(010) 8456 4823*

A quirky slice of Brittany located in northeast Beijing's avant-garde art precinct, Vincent serves sweet crêpes, savory galettes and Breton cider in a cheery loft space with a pleasant outdoor terrace. It's the perfect place to lunch if you're doing a tour of the galleries.

Din Tai Fung (Ding Tai Feng) 🌐 ¥¥¥

22 Hujiayuan Yibei Building, off Dong Zhi Men Wai Xiao Jie **Tel** *(010) 6462 4502* **Map** *3 E2*

Internationally acclaimed Taiwanese chain restaurant serving pricey Shanghainese cuisine and specializing in delicious *xiao long bao* (soup-filled dumplings). Slick décor across two storys, numerous private rooms and an open kitchen/steamer room to entertain diners. Service is as attentive as the price warrants.

Huang Ting 🌐 ¥¥¥

8 Jinyu Hutong (inside Peninsula Palace Hotel) **Tel** *(010) 8516 2888 Ext. 6707* **Map** *2 C5*

Old Beijing recreated with thousands of bricks from demolished *hutong*, along with wooden screens, carved stone friezes, and door guardian stones. Dishes such as deep-fried shrimps with wasabi-mayonnaise show a Hong Kong influence, but you can also get classic Beijing roast duck.

Made in China 🌐 ¥¥¥

1 Dong Chang'an Jie (inside Grand Hyatt Hotel) **Tel** *(010) 8518 1234, ext 3608* **Map** *2 B5*

Brick walls hung with cooking implements give the impression of eating with the family. The kitchen is open allowing diners to view ducks roasting and nimble fingers speedily making disks of dough and spooning in fragrant fillings to make the little parcels known as *jiaozi*, a Beijing speciality. Superb.

Morel's 🍴❤️🌐 ¥¥¥

Gongren Tiyuchang Bei Lu (opposite north gate of Workers' Gymnasium) **Tel** *(010) 6416 8802* **Map** *3 E3*

One of the longest-standing Western restaurants in town, this homely spot serves simple, high-quality Belgian fare, which has come to define comfort food in the minds of many expats. As an accompaniment to the food, the list of Belgian beers is second to none.

My Humble House 🍴❤️🌐 ¥¥¥

W3/1st floor, Oriental Plaza West Tower, 1 Dong Chang'an Jie **Tel** *(010) 8518 8811* **Map** *2 B5*

Service is inconsistent, but this smart, new branch of the Singapore chain serves intriguing fusion cuisine in a chic, modern setting. Beautiful presentation throughout from the decorative pond in the light-filled atrium to the lines of poetry woven into the descriptions of dishes.

Noble Court ¥¥¥

1 Dong Chang'an Jie (inside Grand Hyatt Hotel) **Tel** *(010) 8518 1234 ext. 3821* **Map** *2 B5*

Among Beijing's finest Cantonese restaurants, elegantly decorated and beautifully run, Noble Court also serves a nice range of finely crafted dim sum and Beijing-style snacks, plus excellent seafood, and customary excesses such as shark's fin and bird's nest.

The Source (Du Jiang Yuan) 🌐 ¥¥¥

14 Banchang Hutong, Kuanjie **Tel** *(010) 6400 3736* **Map** *2 B3*

Another hidden gem in the *hutong*, this Sichuan restaurant's menu is limited to a handful of delectable set meals, but the food is authentic and immaculately presented. Set in a romantic courtyard property on two floors containing several intimate private rooms.

Taj Pavilion 🍴❤️ ¥¥¥

1 Jianguo Men Wai Dajie, China World Mall **Tel** *(010) 6505 5866* **Map** *3 E5*

This is the city's classiest and most consistent Indian dining option, with none of the gaudy Shiva posters or ear-splitting live entertainment common in other outlets in Beijing. Just flavorsome, filling, slightly pricey curries and other northern Indian standards.

Aria 🍴❤️🌐🈂️ ¥¥¥¥

1 Jianguo Men Wai Dajie, (2nd floor, China World Hotel) **Tel** *(010) 6505 2266 ext. 36* **Map** *3 E5*

Up a spiral staircase lined with bottles from a vast cellar, Aria offers possibly the most satisfying dining experience in Beijing, from amuse-bouche to dessert. A multi-course "miniatures menu" with wine pairings provides a tour of an inventive but never pretentious Asian-French fusion menu that's pure pleasure.

CourtYard 🍴❤️🌐 ¥¥¥¥

95 Donghua Men Dajie **Tel** *(010) 6526 8883* **Map** *2 B5*

Beijing's most famous fusion restaurant isn't quite the revelation it's made out to be, but is nevertheless excellent. The menu emphasizes execution over innovation, and the wine list is unrivaled. But the biggest draw is definitely the view across the moat to the Forbidden City.

Crab Apple House 🌐 ¥¥¥¥

32 Xi Heyan, Xuanwu Men Dajie **Tel** *(010) 8315 8663* **Map** *4 B2*

A handful of charming, intimate private rooms of varying size set around a courtyard garden. Dishes are inscribed in Chinese on quaint carved wooden menus and consist almost exclusively of the Huaiyang variety; light, fragrant, and beautifully presented creations.

Danieli's
        ¶◗❚ ▣   ¥¥¥¥

21 Jianguo Men Wai Dajie, (in the St. Regis Hotel) **Tel** *(010) 6460 6688 ext. 2441*   **Map** *3 E5*

One of the best and most credible of Beijing's Italian fine dining establishments. Entrées are nicely executed, service is extremely thorough, and the wine list is superb, all which combines to give a sense of being temporarily transported out of China.

Green T. House
        ▣   ¥¥¥¥

6 Gongti Tiyuchang Xi Lu **Tel** *(010) 6552-8310/8311*   **Map** *3 E3*

It takes an inventive menu to distract from Beijing's most jaw-dropping, China-meets-Alice-in-Wonderland design, but from nuggets of roasted lamb nestling among woolong tea and fennel, to green tea wasabi shrimp, everything is inventive, all is superb, and all contains tea.

Jing
        ¶◗❚ ▣   ¥¥¥¥

8 Jinyu Hutong, Wangfujing (in Peninsula Palace Hotel) **Tel** *(010) 6559 2888 ext. 6714*   **Map** *2 C5*

Few restaurants in China can even dream of being as stylish as Jing, with its gleaming open kitchens, video art, and Asian-influenced fusion menu with everything from seared goose liver with caramelized apples to tandoori lamb with cumined lentils, and large wine list. Nearly perfect.

RBL
        ¶◗❚ ▣   ¥¥¥¥

53 Dong'an Men Dajie **Tel** *(010) 6522 1389*   **Map** *2 B5*

A classy, modern sushi bar serving dainty seafood nibbles in a long, narrow dining room with open kitchen and contemporary art on the walls. Attached bar, Icehouse, is less effective as a blues club, but intriguing for its setting in a former imperial icehouse.

Tiandi Yijia
        ▣   ¥¥¥¥

140 Nan Chizi Dajie **Tel** *(010) 8511 5556*   **Map** *2 B5*

Upscale restaurant serving expensive imperial food in a light-filled courtyard residence. Decorations artistically blend Eastern symbols with Western irony. Dishes such as *lapi* (mung bean noodles) and crispy beef, can be exquisite or unforgivably bland, but ambience and service will not disappoint.

SHANGHAI

Bi Feng Tang
        ¥

175 Changle Lu **Tel** *(021) 6467 0628*   **Map** *1 D4*

There is better Cantonese food in Shanghai, but not around the clock. Choose the Changle Lu branch of this bursting-at-the-seams restaurant chain and enjoy comforting pork buns, spring rolls, and other dim sum options, all served 24 hours a day.

Mediterranean Sandwich and Coffee Bar
        ▤ ¶◗❚   ¥

415 Dagu Lu **Tel** *(021) 6327 0897*

Formerly in Hong Qiao, this delightful café serves authentic Mediterranean fare featuring hummus, kabobs and crisp salads. For taste and value, the felafel wrap in laffa bread is among the city's best options for a non-Chinese lunch. Try baklava and Turkish coffee for dessert.

Nan Xiang Steamed Bun Restaurant
        ▤   ¥

85 Yu Yuan Lu **Tel** *(021) 6355 4206*   **Map** *2 C4*

One of those rare long-standing institutions (originally founded 1900) which actually lives up to its reputation, and where the pork and crab dumplings are well worth waiting for. Walk up the stairs to a higher, more pricey dining room with a much shorter wait.

Old Station
        ▤   ¥

201 Caoxi Bei Lu **Tel** *(021) 6427 2233*

Well-executed Shanghai classics at budget prices in a choice of highly unusual settings: the high-ceilinged halls of a former French monastery, or two connected luxury railway carriages, one formerly used by the Dowager Empress Cixi, and the other by Song Qingling, wife of Sun Yat Sen.

Pamirs Xinjiang Restaurant
        ▤   ¥

166 Fumin Lu **Tel** *(021) 5403 3237*   **Map** *1 D4*

Downstairs from the street-side barbeque stacked with lamb kabobs is a gloomy dining room brightened by some of the city's best Xinjiang food, from ground beef in piping hot flatbreads to chunky eggplant stews and hearty noodle dishes. Traditional Uighur minority dress abounds.

1221
        ▣   ¥¥

1221 Yan'an Xi Lu **Tel** *(021) 6213 6585*

1221 serves a Canton-influenced and less oily version of Shanghainese dishes including a refreshing pork and papaya soup, a garlicky string beans, and a spicy boiled beef with warm sesame loaf. Away from the center of town but worth the short taxi ride.

Key to Price Guide *see p198* **Key to Symbols** *see back cover flap*

1931

112 Maoming Nan Lu **Tel** *(021) 6472 5264* **Map** *1 E4*

Eating at this cozy little restaurant is like being in a 1930s private house, the walls hung with advertising and photographs from the period. Few of the dishes are obviously Shanghainese, although all are light and pleasant, and excellent value for money.

239

239 Shimen Yi Lu **Tel** *(021) 6253 2837* **Map** *1 E3*

Drab, office-like exterior, but inside is a stylish red and black space dotted with risqué photo art. Highlights of an extensive continental menu include an earthy mushroom risotto, olive-crusted organic salmon, and a sublime chocolate pudding. Close to the Four Seasons Hotel.

A Future Perfect

Lane 351, House 16, Huashan Lu **Tel** *(021) 6248 8020*

Delightfully located along a quiet lane, this striking restaurant features futuristic décor and imaginative, well-executed global cuisine: try the seafood chowder, full of salmon chunks and served in a hollowed-out cob loaf. Wines are fairly priced and cocktails are made with premium ingredients.

Anadolu

4–7 Hengshan Lu **Tel** *(021) 5465 0977*

Perfectly located on beery Hengshan Lu, this is Shanghai's best late-night kabob house. Forget the functional dining room at the back: order a tender lamb döner wrapped in fluffy bread and smothered in sauce and eat it at the counter too.

Azul Tapas Lounge

18 Dong Ping Lu **Tel** *(021) 6433 1172* **Map** *1 D5*

Shanghainese like tapas, and most agree that Azul is among the best places to sample these snack-size Spanish delights. The friendly Peruvian-born restaurateur oversees a blue-tiled bar and alcoves full of sequined pillows, and also serves heartier mains, such as an osso buco with saffron risotto.

Bali Laguna

189 Huashan Lu **Tel** *(021) 6248 6970* **Map** *1 D3*

A slice of the tropics in Shanghai, this is a wooden villa with Balinese décor, perched on the side of a lotus-filled lake in a leafy park across from Jing'an Temple. An all-Indonesian menu includes common satays and *nasi goreng* but executed with a fine touch.

Bao Luo

271 Fumin Lu **Tel** *(021) 6279 2827* **Map** *1 D4*

Blink and you'll miss the entrance – but once inside it opens out into a cavernous space with lots more rooms upstairs. A favorite of local gourmets (plus renowned chef Jean-Georges Vongerichten), Bao Luo is justifiably acclaimed for cheap and classic Shanghainese dishes, like divinely sweet stir-fried eggplant in pancakes.

Coconut Paradise Thai Cuisine

38 Fumin Lu **Tel** *(021) 6248 1998* **Map** *1 D4*

Rivals the better known Simply Thai as the best of its kind in Shanghai. The setting is a stunning Thai-style house overlooking a verdant garden. Inside, flickering candles illuminate wooden statues while softly spoken waiters deliver tangy salads, bowls of steaming soup, and nutty phad Thai noodles.

Crystal Jade

South Block Xin Tiandi, Lane 123, Xingye Lu **Tel** *(021) 6385 8752* **Map** *2 A4*

Exceptional Cantonese, Shanghainese, and other Chinese favorites in the upscale Xin Tiandi complex. Highlights include the spicy, nutty *dan dan mian* (made from one long, fresh noodle), superb *xiaolongbao* (Shanghainese dumplings), and many varieties of steamed buns. Bookings are essential at weekends.

Dong Bei Ren

1 Shaanxi Nan Lu **Tel** *(021) 5228 9898* **Map** *1 E4*

Colorfully decorated cheap-eats hall serving wholesome northeast dishes, including simply prepared *jiaozi* and surprisingly flavorful tofu. Bottles of *baijiu* are a popular accompaniment, so tables can get rowdy. Oh, and no need to sing for your food as warbling waiters will take care of that.

Element Fresh

Shanghai Center, 1376 Nanjing Xi Lu **Tel** *(021) 6279 8682* **Map** *1 E3*

When oodles of street noodles have lost their shine, Element Fresh provides the perfect tonic of salads and sandwiches: try a gigantic, crunchy Niçoise washed down with freshly squeezed carrot-and-apple juice. Now in three stylish locations around town.

Fai Go Hotpot

795 Julu Lu **Tel** *(021) 5403 8811* **Map** *1 E3*

This Hong Kong chain is the Rolls Royce of hotpot restaurants. Choose from a cosmopolitan collection of base soups such as abalone or Thai green curry, perfect for dunking the imported meats, myriad mushrooms, and wilt-free greens. Who said hotpot couldn't be elegant?

Gran Bodega   ﹖⊙ 🔖   ¥¥
789 Wuyi Lu (in the Royalton Hotel) **Tel** *(021) 5206 0719*

Gran Bodega is an authentic Mediterranean restaurant with a chef from Catalan Spain. Meat dishes reign supreme – try the delicate *cochinillo asado* (roasted baby pig) or *jamón ibérica* (cured boar ham) served on crusty bread. Accompany with one of the many interesting wines stocked by this attractive cellar-style restaurant.

Gu Yi   🔖   ¥¥
87 Fumin Lu **Tel** *(021) 6249 5628*   **Map** *1 D3*

The unassuming corner of Julu and Fumin Lu now boasts exceptional eateries galore, among them Gu Yi. Bland palates beware! Everything in this outstanding Hunanese restaurant comes with chillies, from pork ribs to cold pressed chicken, even a side dish of cucumbers.

House of Flour   ﹖⊙   ¥¥
Room 105, Shanghai Legend, 635 Bibo Lu **Tel** *(021) 5080 6230*

European-style café in an almost rural setting in Pudong. The owner, an expert pastry chef, bakes delightful breads which he fills with salads, roasted vegetables, cold cuts, and curries. These and the espresso are worth the 20-minute metro ride from downtown.

Iiiit!   ﹖⊙ 🔖   ¥¥
Building No. 4, The Summit Clubhouse, 99 Wulumuqi Zhong Lu **Tel** *(021) 5404 2837*

This cozy kiosk wedged into the corner of a plush apartment complex made a quiet entry onto Shanghai's salad-and-sandwich scene but became hugely popular in no time. Home-style paninis, rustic pizzas, healthy smoothies and juices, and plenty of leafy greens.

Pasti   📋﹖⊙ 🔖   ¥¥
1228 Beijing Xi Lu **Tel** *(021) 6279 4726*   **Map** *2 A4*

This quaint trattoria with only nine small tables not only serves the best bruschetta in town, but the pastas are generous and unpretentious. The space is a little small, though, so be prepared to make friends with diners on neighboring tables.

People 7   🔖   ¥¥
805 Julu Lu **Tel** *(021) 5404 0707*   **Map** *1 D4*

People 7 is minimalist and clever, from the "trick" bathrooms to the asymmetrical glassware and chunky stone bowls that the modern Chinese food arrives in. Even the breadsticks are cutting edge. These embellishments don't overshadow the cuisine, which is generally first-rate.

Quanjude   🔖   ¥¥
4th floor, 786 Huaihai Zhong Lu **Tel** *(021) 5404 5799*   **Map** *1 E4*

There's no need to travel to Beijing to find top quality Beijing duck. This immense hall, four floors above bustling Huaihai Lu, is stuffed with eager eaters watching white-gloved waiters transform whole birds into soups and slices of tender meat for rolling up with pancakes.

Rendezvous   ﹖⊙ 🔖   ¥¥
Building B, 1486 Nanjing Xi Lu **Tel** *(021) 6247 2307*   **Map** *1 D3*

Rendezvous' long-haired American-Chinese proprietor might look vegan but his menu certainly isn't. This bright and cheesy American diner on Nanjing Lu (and three other locations) makes the best burgers in town, as well as a fine pancake breakfast. It's cheap, too.

Shen Yue Xuan   🔖   ¥¥
849 Huashan Lu **Tel** *(021) 6251 1166*

Big Cantonese restaurants are rarely peaceful, yet Shen Yue Xuan's garden setting renders it almost an oasis. Perfect for a weekend dim sum brunch, when a table-load of pork buns, shrimp dumplings, and egg tarts will satisfy everyone's appetite for minimal cost.

Shudi Lazi Yu Guan   📋 🔖   ¥¥
187 Anfu Lu **Tel** *(021) 5403 7684*   **Map** *1 D4*

A little grubby, yet this simple Sichuan eatery does a roaring trade. The signature spicy fish soup is laden with chunks of silken seafood bobbing in a fiery broth of chillies and peppercorns. Basketfuls of live frogs peer fretfully at more ambitious eaters.

Simply Thai   ﹖⊙ 🔖   ¥¥
5C Dong Ping Lu **Tel** *(021) 6445 9551*   *1 D5*

This extremely popular Thai restaurant is efficient, relaxed, and inexpensive. The soups and salads benefit from the freshness of the ingredients and all the curries are well-spiced and hearty. If the weather's right, take a table on the deck outside. There's also a branch in Xin Tiandi.

SOAHC Restaurant and Tea Garden   🔖   ¥¥
Xingye Lu, South Block, Xin Tiandi **Tel** *(021) 6385 7777*   **Map** *2 A4*

Clunky name aside ('chaos' spelt backwards), this is one of the more visually appealing restaurants in Shanghai, with ponds, polished wood and innovative lighting. The classically presented Yangzhou cuisine, from pumpkin croquettes with sesame to eel fillet with peppercorns, is similarly impressive.

Key to Price Guide *see p198* **Key to Symbols** *see back cover flap*

Tapas Bar

207-4 Maoming Nan Lu **Tel** *(021) 6415 9567*

Map 1 E5

Impeccable interior, smiling management and staff, a chalkboard menu filled with authentic Spanish tapas options, ceramic jugs of fruity sangria, and excellent lunch specials make this restaurant-bar in now-quiet Maoming Lu a relaxing and rewarding option for anyone seeking salpicao or chorizo.

Vegetarian Lifestyle

258 Fengxian Lu **Tel** *(021) 6215 7566*

Map 1 B2

Zao Zi Shu boasts no eggs, meat, fish, fowl, or MSG. Fake meat dishes are prominent, most of them created with tofu, and many of the patrons are monks in flowing robes. After eating, you can browse the restaurant's new-age bookstore.

Yin

Jinjiang Hotel Gourmet Street, 59 Maoming Nan Lu **Tel** *(021) 5466 5070*

Map 1 E4

Chef Dan presides over an inventive and satisfying menu that includes his signature Guizhou-style fish in zesty sauce and sliced lamb with ten spices. Stylish décor in this 1929 hotel includes antique furniture and elegant table settings, complemented by mellow yet effective service.

Yuan Yuan

1st & 2nd floor K. Wah Center, 108 Xiangyang Bei Lu **Tel** *(021) 5108 3377*

Map 1 E4

Recommended by several high-profile Shanghai chefs, Yuan Yuan is an expanding chain of no-frills Shanghainese restaurants specializing in seafood, prepared in the sticky, sweet, and boozy sauces that are so cherished by locals. Sautéed yellow croaker is a favorite.

Casanova

Building 3–4, 913 Julu Lu **Tel** *(021) 5403 4528*

Map 1 D4

Italian expatriates flock to this quaint old house, and with good reason. Despite an unremarkable décor and a dowdy downstairs bar, Casanova comes up trumps with soft-shell crab linguine and other perfect pastas, plus complimentary biscotti and limoncello to finish.

Cucina

Jinmao Tower, 88 Shiji Da Dao (inside Grand Hyatt) **Tel** *(021) 5049 1234*

Map 3 E3

One of a collection of restaurants ringing the 56th floor of the Grand Hyatt, this trattoria's busy show kitchen has to work hard to distract from the spectacular views (on clear days, at least), but the home-made pizzas and pastas, and excellent seafood will do it.

Mesa

748 Julu Lu **Tel** *(021) 6289 9108*

Map 1 D3

Mesa's modern Australian décor and cuisine has been consistently popular since its opening. A typical three-course meal might comprise carpaccio, lamb rump, and tangy lemon-curd tartlet. The spacious upstairs deck is popular for weekend brunches.

Moon's the Great Steakhouse

Xin Tiandi Plaza, Lane 123, Xingye Lu **Tel** *(021) 6336 5683*

Map 2 A4

Imported prime ribs aged three weeks and cooked on a custom-made slanted grill, served with sides of mash or salad. An equally beefy wine list fittingly includes plenty of big Australian reds. The dimly lit décor brings an element of refinement to proceedings.

New Heights

7th floor, Three on the Bund, 3 Zhongshan Dong Yi Lu **Tel** *(021) 6321 0909*

Map 2 C3

The other restaurant operated by acclaimed international chef David Laris (*see p206*) takes the top floor of the Three on the Bund complex and entices diners with a globe-trotting menu that ranges from a souped up croque monsieur to Vietnamese duck and fish and chips, all at very reasonable prices. A great lunch option.

Palladio

1376 Nanjing Xi Lu (inside Portman Ritz-Carlton) **Tel** *(021) 6279 8888*

Map 1 E3

Sumptuous menu of extravagant Italian dishes with hints of Napoli, suggesting meals should be taken at a gentle pace over an extended period of time, although briskly served business set lunches are excellent value for money, too. Highly recommended.

Prego

88 Henan Zhong Lu (inside The Westin Shanghai) **Tel** *(021) 6335 1786*

Map 2 C3

Irresistibly light and refreshing dishes are beautifully presented, and made with the finest imported ingredients. An ebullient Italian in charge in the kitchen ensures that all is well at your table. Despite stiff competition, Prego stakes a strong claim to being the best Italian restaurant in Shanghai.

Sens & Bund

6th floor, 18 Zhongshan Dong Yi Lu **Tel** *(021) 6323 9898*

Map 2 C2

Jacques and Laurent Pourcel, French twins with a constellation of Michelin stars, present exquisite dishes with a Spanish/Italian slant and a Bund view. Terrines, risottos, and purées abound, many featuring seafood, and all emphasizing color and texture. Upstairs is one of Shanghai's hippest nightspots, Bar Rouge.

Shintori Null II
803 Julu Lu **Tel** *(021) 5404 5252*   **Map** *1 D4*

Rustic paths wind through bamboo to a sliding metal door. Inside is a chic industrial space and possibly Shanghai's best Japanese food. Enjoy the beefsteak in Pu-leaf – a winning variation on Beijing duck – but leave room for the green tea tiramisu.

South Beauty
881 Yan'an Zhong Lu **Tel** *(021) 6247 5878*   **Map** *1 E3*

South Beauty's setting, an ornately decorated mansion with roof terrace and vast gardens, threatens to overwhelm the Sichuan/Cantonese menu and so-so service. On the other hand, some of the hot and spicy items, particularly seafood, are innovative in presentation with remarkable flavors.

T8
181 Taicang Lu, No. 8 North Block, Xin Tiandi **Tel** *(021) 6355 8999*   **Map** *2 A4*

An army of chefs work their magic in an open kitchen on intelligent combinations of Chinese and Italian ideas, such as Chinese duck pizza, seared salmon with char siu pork, and mushroom soup with truffle oil, in the theatrically lit and ultra-modern interior of a revamped traditional house.

Vedas
550 Jianguo Xi Lu **Tel** *(021) 6445 8100*

Clean and comfortable Indian restaurant which has quickly established itself as Shanghai's leader in biryanis. Superb management, stylish presentation, and flavorful samosas, curries and breads. And a worthwhile Sunday brunch alternative to bacon and eggs from a hotel buffet.

Whampoa Club
5th floor, Three on the Bund, 3 Zhongshan Dong Yi Lu **Tel** *(021) 6321 3737*   **Map** *2 C3*

A completely comprehensive menu of traditional Shanghainese favorites in luxurious surroundings, some given a surprising modern twist (such as almond and cocoa fried spare ribs) or simply re-invented to accentuate the flavors. A tea sommelier offers 50 different fine teas from around China.

Club Jinmao
Jinmao Tower, 88 Shiji Da Dao (inside Grand Hyatt) **Tel** *(021) 5049 1234*   **Map** *3 E3*

Eat Shanghainese with the whole of Shanghai set out below you at this elegant restaurant, discreetly tucked away near the top of the tower's 88 storys, and reached by a private elevator. This is Shanghainese food at its most subtle, and service at its most attentive.

Fook Lam Moon
2nd floor, 33 Fucheng Lu (inside Pudong Shangri-La Hotel) **Tel** *(021) 5877 3786*   **Map** *3 D3*

The latest and most luxurious branch of this legendary Hong Kong restaurant. Cold Shanghai-style appetizers keep the local clientele happy, but shark's fin and crabmeat soup, roasted suckling pig, and a wide range of southern Chinese favorites justify the unequalled reputation.

Jade on 36
33 Fucheng Lu (inside Pudong Shangri-La Hotel) **Tel** *(021) 6882 3636*   **Map** *3 C3*

High on the Shangri-La's new tower, Jade offers a stimulating menu of "cuisine de voyage" that combines ingredients from everywhere in stunningly inventive ways that look odd in the menu, too beautiful to eat when they arrive, but leave the palate eager for more.

Jean Georges
4th floor, Three on the Bund, 3 Zhongshan Yi Lu **Tel** *(021) 6321 7733*   **Map** *2 C3*

The Shanghai branch of Jean-Georges Vongerichten's garlanded New York restaurant offers French with hints of Asia (lemon grass, coconut), each dish small but perfect in every way. Try the seasonal set menu which makes the best of available ingredients, and something from the 5000-bottle wine cellar.

Kissho Japanese Restaurant
42nd floor, 889 Yanggao Nan Lu (inside Sofitel Jinjiang Oriental Hotel) **Tel** *(021) 5050 4888*

Imported Osaka beef, extensive sake collection, freshly scraped wasabi, the finest tuna belly, and modern elements such as foie gras on toast. Popular with Japanese residents and visitors alike, and arguably the next best thing to a trip to Japan.

Laris
6th floor, Three on the Bund, 3 Zhongshan Dong Yi Lu **Tel** *(021) 6321 9922*   **Map** *2 C3*

Australian David Laris's white-on-white dining room is the perfect setting for his menu of "global cuisine" – subtle, intelligent, but never pretentious dishes which may just make this the very best foreign restaurant in Shanghai. An evening with one of the tasting menus will be long remembered.

M on The Bund
7th floor, 20 Guangdong Lu **Tel** *(021) 6350 9988*   **Map** *2 C3*

Atop a 1920s bank building overlooking the river, the pioneer of posh Bund dining continues to excel with a menu of celebrity restaurateuse Michelle Garnaut's favorites, including signature soft-as-butter salted lamb and light-as-air Pavlova. An essential Shanghai experience.

Key to Price Guide *see p198* **Key to Symbols** *see back cover flap*

Nadaman

*33 Fucheng Lu (inside Pudong Shangri-La Hotel) **Tel** (021) 6882 8888 ext. 7220*   **Map** *3 D3*

Five varieties of the Japanese aristocratic *kaiseki ryori* multi-course set meals, with an endless stream of small but exquisite dishes. The Nadaman is the Shanghai branch of a restaurant with 175 years of tradition, but not shy of modern invention, and a favorite with Japanese visitors.

The Yongfoo Elite

*200 Yongfu Lu 200 **Tel** (021) 5466 2727*

The abalone-heavy Shanghai and Cantonese menu is a little pricey, but served in an ancient former British Consulate building, the Yongfoo Elite reputedly took two years to furnish. The results are extraordinary, from the verandah shaded by an ancient magnolia to the ornate candelabra.

SHANGHAI FARTHER AFIELD

HANGZHOU Zhangshengji

*77 Shuangling Lu **Tel** (0571) 8602 6666*

A partially pictorial menu makes ordering the light and delicate local cuisine very easy. The palatial multi-story restaurant is always busy with local people, and unlike the restaurants favored by tour guides, prices are low and the quality high.

HANGZHOU Crystal Garden

*12 Dongpo Lu **Tel** (0571) 8706 7777*

Smart, brightly lit three-story interior atrium with traditional square tables and wooden stools serving Hangzhou, Shanghai, and Huaiyang cuisine. A picture menu with English makes ordering steamed mince pork and roe balls and chicken in rice wine very easy.

HANGZHOU Shang Palace

*78 Bei Shan Lu (inside Shangri-La Hotel) **Tel** (0571) 8797 7951*

The best-known examples of local Huaiyang cuisince such as "beggar's chicken" and Dongpo pork prepared alongside the lightest and most delicate of Cantonese specialities, all perfectly executed and served in recently refurbished and opulent surroundings by the most attentive of staff.

HANGZHOU Va Bene

*Building No. 8, 147 Nan Shan Lu, Xi Hu Tiandi **Tel** (0571) 8702 6333*

An Italian is in charge of the large open kitchen of this latest incarnation of the Hong-Kong-based Italian chain, set among lake-edge groves of maple and bamboo in Hangzhou's answer to Shanghai's trendy Xin Tiandi area. Try beef carpaccio or salmon with horseradish, or reasonably priced pizzas or a set menu.

SUZHOU Sarawak House

*516 Shiquan Jie **Tel** (0512) 6518 4406*

Run by a friendly Australian-Malaysian known as Big Al, this restaurant offers cheap, wholesome curries and signature satays with spicy peanut sauce. The décor may be bland, yet tables by the windows have the best canal view of almost any Suzhou restaurant.

SUZHOU Chuanfulou Dajiudian

*1 Guanqian Jie Bifeng Fang **Tel** (0512) 6522 8877*

Sichuan and Suzhou dishes presented in a variety of stone pots and porcelain plates in a spotless yet charming setting. Highlights of the comprehensive menu include Chuan Fu roast beef (sizzling and invigorating) and stir-fried local mushrooms (simple yet stunning).

SUZHOU Deyue Lou

*8 and 43 Guanqian Jie Taijian Long **Tel** (0512) 6523 8940*

This renowned 400-year-old restaurant has twice appeared on Chinese cinema screens. It's probably the best place to sample squirrel-shaped mandarin fish and other Suzhou specialities. Presentation is outstanding – particularly the dumplings, some of which come shaped like hedgehogs or geese.

SUZHOU Wang Si Wineshop

*35 Guanqian Jie Taijian Long **Tel** (0512) 6522 7277*

Despite its tired interior, the Wang Si Wineshop serves memorable local cuisine, with an emphasis on the ingredients' medicinal properties. Try one of the wild vegetable dishes or the succulent "beggar's chicken," wrapped in lotus leaves and baked in mud.

SUZHOU Celestial Court

*259 Xinshi Lu (inside Wugong Xilaideng Dajiudian) **Tel** (0512) 6510 3388*

In a peaceful, elegant setting in Suzhou's best hotel, the Celestial Court presents such gastronomic delicacies as shark's fin soup, abalone, and bird's nest. Humbler dishes including wonton soup with crabmeat are also presented with superb attention to detail.

SURVIVAL
GUIDE

PRACTICAL INFORMATION

Chthe explosion in both international and domestic tourism, and most accessible sights get very crowded, especially during the summer season. Due to the absence of any non-profit network of tourist information centers, visitors often have to rely on hotels for guidance, which is often far from reliable. China International Travel Service branches, listed below, exist to sell over-priced services, not to provide impartial

Symbol of the China Tourist Board

advice, and local competitors may anyway be better. A thorough reading of this and other books before departure is recommended. In Beijing and Shanghai the tourist infrastructure, including transportation, hotels, and restaurants, is mostly on a par with international standards. However, communication still poses difficulties, as English is not spoken widely and its usage is generally restricted to tour groups, four- and five-star hotels, and restaurants catering to tourists.

WHEN TO GO

Although there are great climatic disparities within China, spring and fall are generally the best months to travel, and the time when Chinese also take to the road in far vaster numbers than those of foreign visitors. The peak foreign tourist season, however, is during summer (June to September), best avoided if you don't like the heat – it is baking hot in Beijing, and steamy in Shanghai. Winter is fiercely cold in Beijing, and rather dank and penetrating in Shanghai. Climate and rainfall charts are found on pages 35–7. Planning your trip to coincide with one of the major holiday and festival periods (see pp34–7) can lead to a fun and colorful trip, experiencing China at its

liveliest. However, tickets for air, train, and bus transportation can be very difficult to acquire, while tourist sights will be swamped with local sightseers, and most hotels and guesthouses will have raised their rates.

WHAT TO TAKE

In Beijing from November until March, you will require a good, warm jacket, gloves, sweater, warm socks, thermal leggings, sturdy footwear, and lip balm. During the same period in Shanghai, you still need a sweater and warm clothes. In summer, across most of China, you only need loose-fitting shirts or T-shirts, and thin trousers. Shorts will also do. Bring a first-aid kit (see p216), raincoat, sun hat, deodorant, phrase book, and reading material in English.

Beijing in winter – bring a warm jacket and waterproof footwear

ADVANCE BOOKING

In Beijing, advance booking of hotel rooms is only really necessary during the peak holiday periods around May 1 and October 1, and perhaps during the Chinese New Year. However, in Shanghai, you should always book in advance. Train tickets can only be bought a few days in advance, and should never be puchased on-line through agents, as mark-ups are horrendous. Use local agents in Beijing and Shanghai to make the booking for you for a fee of typically ¥20 to ¥30 per ticket. Bus tickets need not be booked in advance, and although there's no need to book air tickets in advance, booking a few days before may increase the amount of discount. No agency within an airline terminal should charge a fee, but those inside hotels or expat business areas cannot be relied upon to offer the full discount available. Always shop around. Airplane and bus tickets also become scarcer and more expensive during major holiday periods.

VISAS & PASSPORTS

A passport, valid for at least six months, and a visa are necessary to enter the People's Republic of China. However, most foreign nationals don't require a visa for entering Hong Kong and Macau where mainland visas

Shopping for Communist mementos in a Shanghai market

can be purchased more easily than anywhere else. Chinese embassies and consulates around the world issue a standard single-entry, 30-day visa, although multiple-entry 60-day visas, and 90-day visas can sometimes also be obtained. Long-duration multiple-entry visas are easily obtainable in Hong Kong. When completing the visa application form, you must specify what parts of China you plan to visit. Avoid mentioning Tibet, or Xinjiang, even if you plan to visit these regions, as you may be questioned about your occupation and intent of visit. Any list you provide is not binding. Always carry your passport, as it is an essential document for checking into hotels, and the Public Security Bureau *(see p216)* may insist on seeing it. Photocopying the visa page and the personal information page

A symbol of former European influence in Shanghai

will speed up replacement if your passport is lost or stolen. Visa extensions are sometimes granted for 30 days by the foreign affairs branch of local PSBs (police). Note that heavy fines are levied if you over-stay your permitted period in China.

PERMITS

Travelers will find that most of China is accessible, and no special permits are required for any areas in or around Beijing and Shanghai.

EMBASSIES & CONSULATES

Most countries have an embassy in Beijing and many also have a consulate in Shanghai. Consular offices can re-issue passports and assist in case of emergencies, such as theft, imprisonment, and hospitalization. If needed, your hotel can help to put you in touch with your embassy or consulate.

CUSTOMS INFORMATION

When entering China, visitors are entitled to a duty-free allowance of 70 fluid ounces (2 liters) of wine or spirits, 400 cigarettes, and a certain amount of gold and silver. Foreign currency exceeding US$5,000, or its equivalent, must be declared. Items that are prohibited include fresh fruit, rare animals and plants, and arms and ammunition. Chinese law specifies limits on the export of certain items, such as particular herbal medicines. Also, objects

predating 1795 cannot be taken out of China, while antiques made after that date will need to have an official seal affixed. Although foreign visitors are largely left alone, it is not advisable to take in politically controversial literature, especially if it's written in Chinese.

IMMUNIZATION

Ensure that all of your routine vaccinations are up to date, such as tetanus, polio, and diphtheria. It is advisable to also get vaccinated against hepatitis A and B, typhoid, meningococcal meningitis, and cholera. Visitors traveling from countries where yellow fever is endemic must provide proof of vaccination against the disease. Malaria medication is essential for those visiting rural areas, as is a Japanese encephalitis vaccination, but neither are necessary for visits to Beijing and Shanghai, or most other major cities. For up-to-date travel-health information and more advice on immunization try *www.mdtravelhealth.com.*

INSURANCE

It is advisable to take out an insurance policy for medical emergencies, preferably including provision for an air ambulance home, and for trip cancellation, loss of baggage by airlines, and travel delay. Policies covering theft of valuables need to be carefully examined as exclusions and deductibles often make these worthless, and common sense and caution are often both more effective and cheaper. Remember to make sure that any adventure activity or sport that you may undertake during your trip is covered by your policy.

Hotel receptions – a useful source
of tourist information

TOURIST INFORMATION

China has yet to recognize the
value of professional tourist
information centers, either at
home or abroad. Those that
exist in Beijing and Shanghai
are under-funded and poorly
staffed, although they are
useful for obtaining free
maps. The state-approved
China International Travel
Service (CITS) (*see p211*),
originally set up to cater to
the needs of foreign visitors,
today functions as any other
local operator, offering
nothing more than tours,
tickets, and rented cars. A
limited choice of government-
run travel agencies abroad
promote China tourism.
However, they fail to offer
professional and unbiased
advice, instead steering
customers toward group tours
and standard hotels.

ADMISSION CHARGES

Most temples, parks, palaces,
museums, and historical
monuments can only be
entered after paying a fee.
Temples charge anything from
¥5 to ¥40. Star sights, such as
Beijing's Forbidden City, can
charge up to ¥60 in summer,
plus an assortment of extra
charges for certain areas and
special exhibitions. Shanghai's
Oriental Pearl Television
Tower costs ¥100 if all its
various platforms and
exhibitions are visited. It is
often hard to see where the
money goes as many of
China's temples and

monuments appear severely
neglected. At some sights,
particularly parks, you may
have a choice of a *men piao*
which merely allows access
to the grounds, and a *tao piao*
or *tong piao*, which includes
access to buildings in the
price. Occasionally there are
further fees for storing bags.
The sale of tickets usually
ceases half an hour or so
before the sight closes for the
day, but staff may choose also
to begin ushering visitors out
at that point, so as to get
home in good time. Guides
swarm around entrances to
major sights but
should mostly
be avoided, as
even when
their English is
acceptable their
knowledge often
amounts to no
more than the
Party-approved information
on signs, and is no less
opaque and inaccurate.

HOLIDAYS & OPENING HOURS

The main holiday periods are
Chinese New Year (Spring
Festival), and around May 1
(Labor Day) and October 1
(National Day). The period of
disruption lasts for around 14
days at Chinese New Year,
and for a week around the
May and October holidays.
Accommodation prices rise
as domestic tourism peaks.
Tourist sights, restaurants,
and shops, however, mostly
remain open except some-
times around Chinese New
Year itself.

Road sign in both Pinyin
and Chinese characters

LANGUAGE

The official language of
China is Putonghua (literally
"common speech"), known
outside China as Mandarin.
Putonghua is the native
language of the north, but it
is used across the country for
communication between
speakers of several other
Chinese languages, and can
be used throughout China.
English is largely useless
for communication outside
of hotels. The tonal nature of
Putonghua makes it difficult
for English speakers
to become
accustomed to
the language
without a little
serious study
with a teacher.
Pinyin, which
is a written
romanization
system, helps in the recog-
nition of sounds but the
diacritical marks to indicate
tone are all too often omitted,
and without tone there is no
meaning. A few basic phrases
in Putonghua are listed on
pages 238–40.

FACILITIES FOR THE DISABLED

If you are a wheelchair user,
China will definitely be hard
going. Even relatively modern
and progressive Beijing and
Shanghai offer only very basic
facilities for the disabled,
both in public transportation
and accommodations, if any
at all. Public buildings and
places of interest are rarely
fitted with ramps or rails.

Admission fees to most sights are little more than a nominal sum

Chinese children enjoying time in a Shanghai park

Many of the sidewalks in urban areas are littered with obstacles and occasional potholes, and typically have high curbs, making wheel-chair access troublesome. The scarcity of safe crossing points on urban roads drives pedestrians onto overhead walkways; otherwise they have to join the crowds surging through the traffic. Rooms with services for disabled visitors are only available at the better hotels and even then they are mostly not well thought out. Elevators are common in most hotels over three storys high.

FACILITIES FOR CHILDREN

The Chinese love childen, and they are usually welcome everywhere in China. Even though baby-changing rooms are extremely rare, and very few restaurants have child seats, traveling with very young children can have its advantages as people will generally go out of their way to accommodate you in most places and situations. Super-markets are well supplied with diapers, baby wipes, creams, medicine, clothing, infant milk formula, and baby food. However, the baby food is of a sweeter variety and nearly always processed. Chinese rarely give pacifiers to their children, but you can find them in department stores. Bring a set of plastic cutlery for your child, or children, as most restaurants only have chopsticks.

PHOTOGRAPHY

In both Beijing and Shanghai specialty stores can provide any kind of film imaginable, although the Chinese have already embraced digital photography. Photographing people in China is generally not a problem, but it is courtesy to first ask for their permission. Photography is rarely allowed inside temple halls and museums, or at archeological sites. There are usually signs to indicate where photography is not permitted, including airports, harbors, and railroads.

Plugs with two and three prongs

ELECTRICITY

The electrical current in China is 220 volts. The most common plug arrangement is two flat prongs, as in North America. Sockets will not take plugs with a third earthing pin, or those with one flat blade larger than the other. Most are also designed to take European-style two round pins, and many plates also have space for Australian-style two flat pins, generally used for devices such as in-room fridges drawing higher current. The British three square-pin arrangement is rare outside smart hotels. A power-surge cable will protect laptops against voltage fluctuations, which are common in China. It is best to avoid cheap Chinese batteries, as they are very shortlived and may leak.

However, often the Western-brand batteries you will see around will be fakes.

TIME & CALENDAR

Despite its vast size, China occupies only one time zone, and there is no daylight saving time. So, China is seven or eight hours ahead of Greenwich Mean Time (GMT), two or three hours behind Australian Eastern Standard Time, 15 or 16 hours ahead of US Pacific Standard Time, and 12 or 13 hours ahead of US Eastern Standard Time. The Western Gregorian calendar is used for all official work, although the dates for traditional festivals follow a lunar calendar.

CONVERSION CHART

The metric system is used in all parts of China.

Imperial to metric
1 inch = 2.5 centimeters
1 foot = 30 centimeters
1 mile = 1.6 kilometers
1 ounce = 28 grams
1 pound = 454 grams
1 pint (US) = 0.473 liters
1 gallon (US) = 3.785 liters

Metric to imperial
1 centimeter = 0.4 inches
1 meter = 3 feet 3 inches
1 kilometer = 0.6 miles
100 gram = 3.53 ounces
1 kilogram = 2.2 pounds
1 liter = 2.11 pints (US)

Midday in Shanghai – so midday in Beijing too

General Etiquette

Despite rapid modernization, China remains a traditional society governed by strong family values. Beijing and Shanghai give the outward impression of Western modernity, but older generations retain a deep-seated and family-oriented conservatism. Confucian values promote respect for elders and those in positions of authority. Religious observance is not widespread, and is largely separate from mainstream social behavior. The Chinese are, above all, welcoming and generous, and visitors are often amazed at their hospitality. If invited to someone's home, a gift of chocolates, French wine, or some other imported treat will be greatly appreciated.

Worshipers praying at a shrine at one of Beijing's many temples

GREETING PEOPLE

Shaking hands is common-place in big cities, and certainly considered the norm with foreign visitors. Although the Chinese are not particularly tactile in their greetings, bodily contact is quite common between friends, even of the same sex. It is quite common to see young men walking arm in arm, or with their arm around another's shoulder. The usual Chinese greeting is "Ni hao" (How are you?) or "Nimen hao" in its plural form, to which you reply "Ni hao" or "Nimen hao" – the polite form is "Nin hao".

Chinese people will not blanch at asking you how much you earn, how old you are, or whether you are married. Such questions are seen as nothing more than taking a friendly interest in a new acquaintance. When proffering business cards, the Chinese do so using the fingertips of both hands, and receive cards in the same manner. For businessmen, cards are essential, preferably with Chinese on one side and English on the other.

DRESS

Once they reach the age of 30 or 40, the Chinese tend to dress conservatively, favoring dark and inconspicuous colors such as brown and black. In cities, people wear jeans, T-shirts, and skirts, and many youngsters dress provocatively and dye their hair. Don't worry too much about what you wear, but try to avoid looking scruffy. It is also acceptable for both sexes to wear shorts in hot weather.

FACE

Reserved in manner and expression, the Chinese also harbor strong feelings of personal pride and respect. The maintenance of pride and the avoidance of shame is known as "face." Loss of face creates great discomfort and major embarrassment for Chinese, so although you may often be frustrated by bureaucratic red tape and delays, or the incompetence of hotel staff, try not to embarrass anybody in public. Be firm but polite, and use confrontation only as a very last resort.

CHINESE HOSPITALITY

If invited out for dinner, expect to see the diners competing to pay the entire bill, rather than dividing it up between them. It is a good idea to join in the scramble for the bill, or at least make an attempt – your gesture will be appreciated, though almost certainly declined. For more on dining etiquette, see pages 190–91.

PLACES OF WORSHIP

Although there are no dress codes for Buddhist, Daoist, or Confucian temples, visitors to mosques should dress respectfully – avoid wearing shorts or short skirts – and cover your upper arms. Buddhist, Daoist, and Confucian temples are relaxed about visitors wandering about, but do be considerate toward worshipers. Also, check whether you can take photographs within temple halls, as this is often not permitted. Taking photos in courtyards, however, is usually not a problem. Some Buddhist and Daoist temples are active, such as Beijing's Lama Temple, and you should show respect towards the resident monks.

Advice for burning incense

ANNOYANCES

The Chinese habit of staring, especially in smaller towns and rural areas, can be a little annoying. It can also still be encountered in Beijing and Shanghai, since these cities attract a lot of migrant workers and peasant tourists. However, the intent is rarely hostile. Another annoyance that visitors face are constant calls of "Hellooo!" or "Laowai!" (foreigner). It is best either to ignore them or smile, as replying often results in bursts of laughter. In

A busy shopping street, stalking ground for "art student" scamsters

Beijing and Shanghai, people sometimes strike up conversation to practice their English, but caution is necessary as increasingly these approaches are lead-ins to scams. Around Beijing's Wangfujing shopping street, Liulichang, Tian'an Men Square and the Forbidden City, and on Shanghai's main shopping streets, decline to accompany "art students" who in the guise of fund-raising will pressure you to buy hugely overpriced art. Similarly be wary of "language students" who suggest entering a nearby café or bar and who will leave you with a bill for thousands of *renminbi*. Also watch for "accidental" encounters with seemingly friendly and helpful English speakers who eventually suggest partaking in a tea ceremony.

Although more orderly queues are beginning to replace the usual mêlée at ticket offices, you still need to be prepared for a lot of pushing and shoving. Spitting is still widespread, although there is always a crack-down in the run-up to major international events, such as the 2008 Olympics. Despite the best attempts of public educators, spitting remains common on buses and trains, and it is not considered rude to spit in mid-conversation, so do not take offense.

SMOKING & ALCOHOL

As the world's largest producer and consumer of cigarettes *(xiangyan)*, China is a smoker's paradise. Despite the appearance of no-smoking zones and rudimentary anti-smoking campaigns, Beijing and Shanghai remain shrouded in a haze of nicotine clouds. Smoking is now banned on domestic flights, on trains (except in connecting passages between carriages), and on buses, but unless the latter are air-conditioned, and sometimes even then, the rule is ignored. Smoking during meals is acceptable, especially if there are other smokers present. The Chinese are very generous when it comes to offering cigarettes, so remember to be equally generous in return. They also enjoy drinking alcohol, and there is no taboo against moderate intoxication. The usual accompaniment during a meal is beer *(pijiu)*, or spirits *(baijiu)*. People rarely drink wine *(putaojiu)*, although it is readily available at restaurants serving Western cuisine (and China makes its own wines). If someone raises a toast to you ("Ganbei!"), it is good form to return the toast later.

A popular white spirit, or *baijiu*

BARGAINING

As a foreign national in China, it is essential to bargain *(taojia huanjia)*. You may often be overcharged – sometimes by large amounts – in markets and anywhere else where prices are not indicated. Some restaurants charge higher prices on the English menu than on the Chinese one. You should bargain to reduce your hotel room-rate: no one pays rack rate and substantial discounts are almost always available, especially at Chinese-run hotels. Always ask for a discount on airfares, too. Always bargain pleasantly and with a smile. At markets let the vendor speak first, and don't be afraid to counter offer with ten percent or less. First prices to foreigners are often as much as 15 times higher than what will eventually be accepted. Your next offer should only be fractionally higher than your first. The prices in large shops and government emporia *(guoying shangdian)* may appear to be fixed, but Chinese will routinely ask for discounts, and frequently get them, too. Asking is normal practice, so never be afraid.

TIPPING

There is no tipping in China, so do not tip guides, bell boys, taxi drivers, or anyone else. In China the price you agree for the service is the one you pay, although some restaurants in larger hotels now routinely add a service charge. Away from hotels and tourist areas waitresses will pursue you down the street to return the change they think you've forgotten.

BEGGING

China's imbalanced economic progress and huge population of rural poor have resulted in large numbers of beggars, especially in Beijing and Shanghai. Foreign visitors naturally attract attention, and groups of children are often sent by their parents to extract money. The best strategy is to ignore them and walk away.

Bargaining for your purchases is absolutely essential

Personal Security & Health

The police in China, or *jingcha*, are more commonly known to foreigners as the Public Security Bureau (PSB) or *gong'an ju*. But most visitors to Beijing and Shanghai are unlikely to encounter the PSB, unless extending their visas, or reporting loss or theft. Only the largest police stations (*jingcha ju*) have English-speaking staff, so contact your embassy or consulate first for guidance. Protect your valuables and important documents at all times, stay and eat in clean places, and drink only mineral water. Hotel receptions will swiftly arrange initial medical attention, but for more serious problems head for a private foreign-run clinic.

Crowds at a Beijing bus station, favored targets for petty theft

GENERAL PRECAUTIONS

Traveling in China is generally safe, and foreign visitors are unlikely to be the victims of crime, apart from petty theft, and occasional scams. Sadly, anyone who approaches looking to speak English with you should be treated with caution: friendly Chinese who suggest a chat over tea, or pretty girls who want to practice English over a drink, may in both cases be in cahoots with a bar or café and looking to leave you with an artificially pumped-up bill for thousands of *renminbi*. Refuse to pay, make plenty of noise, and insist on calling the police. On buses and trains guard your camera and valuables, wear a money belt at all times, and secure your luggage to the rack on overnight train journeys.

SECURITY

Always carry your passport with you for identification. At some sights, you will be asked to deposit your bag before making a visit. Hotels in China are reliably secure, but management will not accept responsibility should anything vanish. If you are staying in a hostel dormitory then be very cautious.

Be discreet when taking out your wallet. It is best to pocket only as much cash as you need for the day and keep the rest in a money belt under your clothes, along with your passport and other valuable documents. Take particular care at bus and railway stations, at airports, and at crowded tourist sites.

It is always a good idea to carry photo-copies of the personal information and China visa pages of your passport, as well as any other important documents, such as insurance. These should be stored separately from the originals in case of theft or loss.

WOMEN TRAVELERS

China is regarded as a very safe destination for women, and sexual harassment of visitors is extremely rare.

GAY & LESBIAN TRAVELERS

The gay and lesbian scene is growing, but still relatively underground. China is still a highly conventional society, and homosexuality is largely disapproved of and misunderstood – although its classification as a mental disease was removed in 2001. Both Beijing and Shanghai have several gay bars and clubs, however they are prone to being raided by the police and closed down.

HOSPITALS & MEDICAL FACILITIES

Take out comprehensive medical insurance before you travel. Beijing and Shanghai have private hospitals, where there are exclusive clinics with English-speaking staff (avoid state-run institutions), but such places can be very expensive. Whether you carry insurance documents or not, you will not be allowed to depart before the bill is settled, usually in cash.

Pharmacies (*yaodian*), identified by green crosses, are plentiful and easily found. They stock both Western and Chinese medicine, and can treat you for minor injuries or ailments. There are also branches of Western drugstores such as Watson's. Even so, it is advisable to take adequate supplies of any prescription drugs you require.

PUBLIC BATHROOMS

Public bathrooms are traditionally of the squat variety. In Beijing and Shanghai they are generally very well looked after and quite clean. However, there

Beijing PSB
officer

is little privacy and toilet paper is a rarity, so carry your own supply. You usually have to pay around ¥0.30. If you are unused to squat toilets they can be uncomfortable, so the visitor should take full advantage of hotel and fast-food restaurant bathrooms.

Distinctive green cross of a pharmacy

HEAT, HUMIDITY, & POLLUTION

If you're traveling in summer then drink plenty of fluids to guard against dehydration. Wear loose-fitting cotton clothing and sandals, a sun-hat and sunglasses, and use plenty of sunscreen. Many of China's cities, including Beijing and Shanghai, experience chronic levels of pollution. This aggravates chest infections, and asthmatic travelers should always carry their medication.

FIRST-AID KIT

Organize a basic first-aid kit, which should contain your usual choices of cold relief remedies, motion sickness, and anti-diarrhea tablets, insect repellent, and oral rehydration solutions. These are all available in Beijing and Shanghai, but not necessarily in your favourite brands.

STOMACH UPSETS & DIARRHEA

If you are adversely affected by a change of diet, stick to Western food and simple

Street food – only eat it when it is cooked in front of you

boiled food, such as plain rice, until any diarrhea subsides. Most importantly, drink lots of fluids, as diarrhea quickly leads to dehydration, and use oral rehydration solution (ORS). Do not eat raw salads, cut fruit, or cold dishes, or drink fresh juice except in top-notch foreign-run hotels. Never drink tap water or brush your teeth with it – use bottled mineral water. Only eat street food that is freshly cooked in front of you.

SEXUALLY TRANSMITTED & OTHER INFECTIOUS DISEASES

Experts are predicting 10 million AIDS cases in China by the year 2010. Hepatitis B, also transmitted through contact with infected blood, is spread through sexual contact, unsterilized needles, tattoos, and shaves from roadside barbers, but unlike AIDS it can be prevented with a vaccine. When visiting a clinic, ensure that the doctor opens a new syringe in front of you, or bring your own disposable syringe for the doctor to use. Avoid any other procedure using needles, such as tattooing, ear-piercing, or acupuncture.

WATER-BORNE DISEASES

Visitors should be on their guard against dysentery. Bacillary dysentery is accompanied by severe stomach pains, vomiting and fever. Amoebic dysentery has similar symptoms but takes longer to manifest. Pre-travel vaccination against hepatitis A, cholera, and typhoid is advisable.

INSECT-BORNE DISEASES

Those planning visits solely to Beijing and Shanghai (and Hangzhou and Suzhou) do not need to take malarial prophylaxis. For trips to rural areas consult a tropical medicine specialist.

DIRECTORY

IN AN EMERGENCY

Police
Tel 110

Fire
Tel 119

Ambulance
Tel 120

HOSPITALS & MEDICAL FACILITIES

Beijing
Hong Kong International Medical Clinic, 9th floor, Swissotel, Chaoyang Men Bei Dajie 2. **Tel** (010) 6501 4260.
International SOS, BITIC Ying Yi Building, Xingfu Sancun Bei Jie 1. **Tel** (010) 6462 9112/9100 (24-hr).

Shanghai
New Pioneer International Medical Center, 2nd floor, Geru Building, Hengshan Lu 910. **Tel** (021) 6469 3898.

EMBASSIES & CONSULATES

Australia
Dongzhi Men Wai Dajie 21, Beijing. **Tel** (010) 6532 2331. CITIC Square, 1168 Nanjing Xi Lu, Shanghai. **Tel** (021) 5292 5500.

Canada
Dongzhi Men Wai Dajie 19, Beijing. **Tel** (010) 6532 3536. Room 64, Shanghai Center, 1376 Nanjing Xi Lu, Shanghai. **Tel** (021) 6279 8400.

Ireland
Ritan Dong Lu 3, Beijing. **Tel** (010) 6532 2691.

United Kingdom
Guanghua Lu 11, Beijing. **Tel** (010) 6532 1961. Room 301, Shanghai Center, 1376 Nanjing Xi Lu, Shanghai. **Tel** (021) 6279 7650.

USA
Xiushui Bei Jie 3, Beijing. **Tel** (010) 6532 3831. 1469 Huai Hai Zhong Lu, Shanghai. **Tel** (021) 6433 6880.

TRAVEL HEALTH

Medical Advisory Services for Travelers Abroad
Tel (0113) 238 7575.
www.masta.org

MD Travel Health
www.mdtravelhealth.com

Banking & Local Currency

24-hr banking sign

Most foreign exchange transactions take place at major branches of the Bank of China, at counters run by the bank at airports and in major stores, or they are performed by hotels for their residents only. In Beijing and Shanghai there are plenty of ATMs that accept foreign cards, including at both international airports, and these are generally the most convenient way of acquiring Chinese currency. You cannot pay for goods or services with foreign cash or traveler's checks. Only larger hotels and the most upscale restaurants accept foreign credit cards.

BANKS & BANKING HOURS

The Bank of China has the most extensive network in the country, although several other major banks also operate nationwide. Some banks are only open 9am–noon and 2pm–4:30pm or 5pm Monday to Friday, but others are open all day, and some on Saturdays. All banks remain closed for at least the first three days of the Chinese New Year, and for three days at each of the October and May holidays.

AUTOMATED TELLERS

The Automated Teller Machines (ATMs) that accept foreign cards are principally those belonging to the Bank of China. Occasionally (at Beijing Capital Airport for instance) other Chinese bank ATMs work too, but the presence of familiar logos on the screen does not guarantee that foreign cards will work. There are many usable ATMs in banks, shopping malls, and

Hong Kong & Shanghai Banking Corporation (HSBC) ATMs

hotels around the centers of Beijing and Shanghai. Those machines that do accept foreign cards are part of the Maestro, Cirrus, JCB and Aeon networks. Check the back of your card for logos, and then visit your card issuer's website for locations of ATMs. Both Beijing and Shanghai have branches of the HSBC and Citibank, whose machines will take almost any card ever invented. Bank of China machines typically limit each withdrawal to ¥2,500, but usually allow second and third uses of your card.

CHANGING MONEY

Chinese currency is non-convertible; it is not widely available internationally, and if you do find it, it will be offered at a poorer rate of exchange than can be found in China. The currency is useless outside China. Within China, you can exchange currency at major banks and international airports. Most decent hotels will change money for guests. Exchange rates are decided centrally and distributed nationally on a daily basis. The occasional variant rate from a non-Bank of China bank is only fractionally better, so don't worry about where you exchange. Convert any left-over *renminbi* back before you leave, although usually only exchange counters at airports and ports will do this. You must present recent exchange or ATM receipts for double the amount you want to re-exchange. The "black market" for foreign currency offers only marginally better rates than the banks. Dealing with the shady characters involved is not worth the risk, and you may end up with counterfeit *renminbi*.

CREDIT CARDS

Credit cards are widely accepted in upscale restaurants and hotels, and in large tourist shops, but always check before attempting to make a purchase that your foreign card is accepted. The commonly accepted cards are MasterCard, Visa, JCB, Diners Club, and American Express.

DIRECTORY

BANK OF CHINA	HSBC	CITIBANK	AMERICAN EXPRESS
Beijing Asia Pacific Building, 8 Yabao Lu. **ATMs** *Oriental Plaza, 1 Dongchang'an Jie.*	**Beijing** Block A, COFCO Plaza 8, Jianguo Men Nei Dajie. **ATMs** *Oriental Plaza, 1 Dongchang'an Jie.*	**Beijing** 1st floor, Tower 1, Bright China Chang'an Building, 7 Jian Guo Men Nei Dajie.	**Beijing** Room 2313, China World Trade Center, 1 Jianguo Men Wai Dajie.
Shanghai Bank of China Tower, 200 Yin Cheng Lu, Pudong. **ATMs** *Zhongshan Dong Lu.*	**Shanghai** HSBC Tower, 101 Yin Cheng Lu, Pudong. **ATMs** *Shanghai Center, 1376 Nanjing Xi Lu.*	**Shanghai** Marine Tower, 1 Pudong Avenue, Pudong. **ATMs** *Adjacent to the Peace Hotel, Zhongshan Dong Lu.*	**Shanghai** Room 455, Shanghai Center, 1376 Nanjing Xi Lu.

Air tickets can be bought by credit card from some Civil Aviation Administration of China (CAAC) offices, but train tickets have to be paid for in cash. Cash advances can be made on credit cards at the Bank of China, but it's far cheaper to use the card in an ATM.

TRAVELERS' CHECKS

Some hotel foreign exchange counters will no longer exchange checks, and will send you to the Bank of China. All popular foreign brands are accepted, but occasionally cashiers nervous of responsibility will reject those that look unfamiliar. Keep the proof of purchase slips and a record of the serial numbers in case of loss or theft. Hold on to encashment slips, so you can reconvert spare *renminbi* before leaving the country.

CURRENCY

China's currency is called *yuan*, and also known as *renminbi*, literally People's Currency. One *yuan* divides into 10 *jiao*, which in turn divides into 10 almost worthless *fen*. In spoken Chinese, *jiao* are usually called *mao*, and *yuan* are *kuai*. Kuai means "piece of", and here is an abbrevation for "piece of money". The most common coins include 1 *yuan*, and 5 and 1 *jiao*. Bills in circulation are 1, 2, and 5 *jiao*, and 1, 2, 5, 10, 20, 50, and 100 *yuan*. There are also some *fen* coins and notes, but this tiny denomination is of no use unless used together in amounts of at least one *jiao*. Counterfeiting is widespread, and shopkeepers regularly scrutinize notes.

Bank Notes
The more recently printed bills have Mao Zedong on one side and a well-known heritage sight on the other. The older bills depict the traditional dress of various ethnic minorities.

1-*yuan* note

5-*yuan* note

10-*yuan* note

20-*yuan* note

50-*yuan* note

100-*yuan* note

Coins
Chinese coins are not widely circulated. There is a 1 yuan coin, some jiao denominations, as well as tiny and lightweight fen.

5 jiao

1 jiao

1 yuan

Communications

公用电话

Sign for a public
telephone

China has an efficient postal network with a variety of services, including registered post and express mail. Telecommunication systems are reasonably advanced and international telephone calls can be made from all but the cheapest hotels. The internet is hugely popular, and cafés with access are widespread. Broadband is increasingly available in all but the most modest of hotel rooms. The government, however, polices the net, and many websites are blocked, although sometimes not to those in the best foreign hotels. Foreign newspapers and magazines are sold in five-star hotel bookstores, but these may be censored as well.

A wheelchair-accessible phone
booth in Beijing

INTERNATIONAL & LOCAL TELEPHONE CALLS

International *(guo ji)* and long-distance *(guo nei)* phone calls can be made from most hotels and card telephones. It is not usually necessary to ask receptionists or operators to place the calls. In cheaper hotels you may be asked to first pay a deposit. Hotels are allowed to add only a small service charge to the cost of calls; local calls should be free. Most public phones require an IC (integrated circuit) card, sold in shops and kiosks wherever the letters "IC" are seen. These come in various values up to ¥100. International calls are best made using an IP (internet protocol) card; you dial a local access number and enter a code number hidden behind a scratch-off

panel on the card. Voice instructions are in both Chinese and English. IP cards typically come in ¥50 and ¥100 varieties, but these prices are always discounted. If you wish to use one with a payphone, you'll still need an IC card to enable you to dial the local access number.

MOBILE PHONES

Visitors with mobile phones from almost anywhere except North America and Japan can use the Chinese cellphone system (Americans can only use the Chinese system if they have an unlocked tri- or quad-band phone). Just buy a local pre-paid SIM card from any phone shop. Some cards work only in the town in which they were purchased, so if you wish to use the same number in Beijing and Shanghai, make sure you have the right kind of card. Even using a Beijing number

in Shanghai is vastly cheaper than using foreign companies' roaming options. If you do not have a phone compatible with the Chinese system, the cheapest option is to buy one, not rent. You can get cheap, though not always reliable, second-hand phones from electronics markets in both Beijing and Shanghai.

EMAIL & INTERNET FACILITIES

Personal computer ownership is still limited in China, so internet cafés *(wangba)* are found just about everywhere, although many are scruffy and basic. You can also get online at many China Telecom offices. Unless you need to get online urgently, avoid using hotel business centers or internet cafés aimed at tourists, as they are generally over-priced. Many foreign media sites are blocked by the government.

POSTAL SERVICES

The postal service in China is, for the most part, reliable, and the domestic service is reasonably fast. It takes less than a day for mail to reach local destinations, two or more days to inland destinations, while the international postal service takes as little as four days to send airmail and postcards overseas. Visitors can send mail by standard or registered post, while EMS (Express Mail Service) is a reliable way to send packages and documents abroad and within

Aztec, one of the largest cyber cafés in Shanghai

A choice of Chinese newspapers on display at a newsstand

the country. Most post offices are open all day seven days a week. Large hotels also usually have post desks. Take your mail to the post office, rather than dropping it in a mailbox. It will help postal staff sort your letter if you can write the country's name in Chinese characters. Aerograms and packaging materials are available at post offices.

COURIER SERVICES

Courier services are widely available in Beijing and Shanghai. While it is preferable to send large, bulky items by regular land, sea, or air cargo, important letters, documents, and smaller parcels are best sent through a courier agency, even though it may be significantly more expensive. International operatives United Parcel Service (UPS), Federal Express, and DHL are all present in China.

Mail box, Beijing

NEWSPAPERS & MAGAZINES

The dismal *China Daily* is China's official English-language newspaper. It is full of propanganda and little else. A limited selection of international newspapers and magazines can be found at many tourist hotel bookstores, although these are subject to occasional censoring. Beijing and Shanghai have a number of expat-written and edited entertainment and culture magazines, such as *that's*

Beijing and *that's Shanghai*, available free in cafés, bars, and hotel lobbies.

TELEVISION & RADIO

The state-run Chinese Central Television (CCTV) has CCTV9 as its flagship English station. It also broadcasts some English programs on CCTV4. Propaganda, bright-eyed promotion for China travel, and painfully slanted news with dull reports of interminable meetings of irrelevant committees are the norm. Because it is relatively new, CCTV9 can only rarely be found pre-tuned on hotel-room TVs. Cable and satellite television with BBC and CNN is only available in top-end hotels, although some Hong Kong channels with English programming appear lower down the scale. Chinese programs range from historical costume dramas (with political bias) and tepid soaps (intended to reinforce government social messages) to domestic travel (everything is perfect) and heavily biased news programs.

Many Beijing and Shanghai bars subscribe to satellite sport channels, so it is rarely a problem to get your fix of major international games and events.

The Chinese radio network, has only a few local English-language programs. You will need a shortwave radio to pick up the BBC World Service, Voice of America, and other international programs.

USEFUL DIALING CODES & NUMBERS

To call China from abroad, dial your international access code, China's country code 86, then 10 for Beijing or 21 for Shanghai, followed by the local number. When dialing long-distance from within China dial 010 and 021 respectively. Other city codes also have a leading zero. To make a local call, omit the area code.

To make an international call from China, dial 00, the country code, the area code omitting any initial 0, and the local number. Country codes include: UK 44; USA and Canada 1; Australia 61; New Zealand 64, and Ireland 353.

Dial 115 for international directory assistance or 114 for local directory enquiries, but both these services are in Chinese only.

Shanghai's iconic Oriental Pearl Tower, a TV transmitter

TRAVEL INFORMATION

Most visitors to China arrive by air, though overland routes exist with train links to neighboring Russia, Mongolia, Kazakhstan, and Vietnam, and bus links to Laos and Pakistan. It is also possible to arrive by sea; there are regular ferries from Japan and South Korea to China. Once you've arrived, flying internally is quite straightforward. Domestic air tickets are easy to buy, so wait until you arrive and then shop around

Arriving in China with luggage

for discounts. There are more than 30 flights daily between Beijing and Shanghai's Hong Qiao Airport, and nine on average between Beijing and Shanghai Pudong. China's rail network is efficient and comfortable, although buying tickets can seem daunting. Bus travel is improving with an increasing number of "luxury" and "no smoking" buses. Hiring a self-drive car is not possible, although hiring a car and driver is often the best way to take a trip out of town.

ARRIVING BY AIR

All major international airlines fly to China. China's own **Air China**, **China Southern**, and **China Eastern** between them cover most of the world's major airports. Services are basic but they are at least competitively priced. Hong Kong's **Cathay Pacific** has an extensive international network and service standards considerably higher than those of most other carriers of any nationality. China's three main international gateways are Hong Kong, Beijing, and Shanghai, and all three are superior in quality to most in Europe and North America.

AIR FARES

Ticket prices are most expensive between June and September. It can also be harder to find reasonably priced tickets during Chinese holidays: Spring Festival, the first week of May, and the first week of October. While flying indirectly to China via another country is cheaper than flying direct, traveling by a Chinese airline will often be cheapest.

ON ARRIVAL

Visitors are given up to three forms to complete: health, immigration, and customs, submitted one by one to officials between the plane and the arrivals hall, where there are foreign exchange

counters, ATMs, public telephones, left-luggage services, over-priced restaurants, very limited shops, and toilets. Airport tourist information counter staff speak poor English.

GETTING TO & FROM THE AIRPORT

In Beijing there are multiple bus routes into the city and there are also plans to extend the subway out to the airport. However, for the moment, taking a taxi remains the easiest option. Taxis wait for passengers at a marshaled rank outside the arrivals hall. Ignore the numerous touts. Insist on the driver using the meter. If you already have a hotel booked, check whether it offers a courtesy airport pick-up. In Shanghai there are bus services from both of the city's airports, although Hong Qiao, which is where

most domestic flights arrive and depart, is just 15 minutes away from the city center by taxi. Pudong, the international airport, is a considerably greater distance away, making a taxi journey an expensive proposition. However, it is connected to the subway system by the high-speed Maglev train, the world's fastest passenger service.

DEPARTURE

Check-in for international flights is officially two hours before departure. Most passengers are allowed 44 pounds (20 kg) of baggage. One additional item of hand luggage weighing up to 11 pounds (5 kg) is also usually permitted. Travelers to or from North America are generally allowed more luggage. The departure tax is included in the price of your ticket.

Buses dropping off travelers at the departures terminal, Beijing Airport

DOMESTIC AIRLINES

There are currently some 12 domestic carriers operating in China. You can book flights with some of these airlines from overseas, but rates are far better when booked in China. In-flight service and on-board food is universally poor, so fly prepared. Announcements are both in Chinese and English. Air China's international flying safety record is good, but the safety record of some of the other domestic airlines less so. Between Beijing, Shanghai, and other major cities the aircraft are usually brand new Airbus or Boeing planes. The baggage allowance is 44 pounds (20 kg) for economy class and 66 pounds (30 kg) for first and business class. You are also allowed up to 11 pounds (5 kg) of hand luggage, although airlines almost never weigh it. Excess baggage will be charged at one percent of the full fare per 2.2 pounds (1 kg). For domestic flights, the check-in time is an hour and a half before departure, although in practice very few passengers ever arrive that early. The airport tax for domestic flights is added to the price of the ticket at the time of purchase.

In-flight service on Sichuan Airlines, a domestic Chinese carrier

TICKETS, RESERVATIONS, & CANCELLATIONS

Tickets can be booked through ticket offices, travel agents, or the travel desks of some of the better hotels – you should not be charged a booking fee. Travel agents, especially those away from hotels and areas used by expats tend to offer the best prices. Not all ticket offices and travel agents accept credit cards and those that do may add a slight surcharge. It is often necessary to pay in cash. Visitors are required to show their passports when purchasing tickets.

There is generally no shortage of tickets unless you are looking to fly in the run up to or during one of the major holiday periods (see p37); at such times it is advisable to book well in advance.

Ticket prices are calculated according to a one-way fare, and a return-ticket is simply double that. Discounts on official fares are the norm, and whatever price you are first offered you should always ask for a discount. Children over the age of 12 are charged adult fares, but there are special cheaper fares for younger children.

If you need to change your flight ticket, you can usually get a refund as long as you cancel at least 24 hours before departure, and return your ticket to the same agent who sold it to you. However, discounted tickets may carry more restrictions.

AIR CHINA

Logo of China's national airline, Air China

Directory

AIRLINE OFFICES

Air China
Tel (010) 6601 7755, Beijing.
www.airchina.com.cn

British Airways
Tel (010) 8511 5599, Beijing.
www.britishairways.com

Cathay Pacific
Tel (0852) 2747 1888, Hong Kong.
www.cathaypacific.com

KLM
Tel (010) 6505 3505, Beijing.
www.klm.com

Northwest Airlines
Tel (010) 6505 3505, Beijing. (021) 6884 6884, Shanghai.
www.nwa.com

Qantas
Tel (010) 6467 4794, Beijing. (021) 6279 8660, Shanghai.
www.qantas.com.au

United Airlines
Tel (0852) 2810 8616, Hong Kong.
www.united.com

Virgin Atlantic
Tel (021) 5353 4600, Shanghai.
www.virgin-atlantic.com

CAAC OFFICES

Beijing
Tel (010) 6401 2233.

DOMESTIC AIRLINES

Air China
Tel (010) 6601 3336 (domestic), Beijing. (021) 5239 7227, Shanghai. (800) 820 1999 toll-free from outside Shanghai.
www.airchina.com.cn

China Eastern Airlines
Tel (010) 6468 1166, Beijing. (021) 5290 6688 (domestic), Shanghai. (0512) 6524 5035, Suzhou.
www.ce-air.com

China Southern Airlines
Tel (010) 6567 2203, Beijing. (0571) 8796 0000, Hangzhou. (021) 6211 3604, Shanghai.
www.cs-air.com

Shanghai Airlines
Tel (010) 6606 1260, Beijing. (021) 6255 8888, Shanghai. (800) 620 8888 toll-free from outside Shanghai.
www.shanghai-air.com

Traveling by Train, Bus & Ferry

The Chinese rail network is extensive, with tracks running over 32,300 miles (52,000 km) and still expanding rapidly. It is possible to reach every province of China by rail from Beijing and Shanghai, and there is a fast line between the two cities. But, while trains may be punctual, fast, safe, and reliable, bus tickets are much easier and cheaper to obtain. Along the east coast many bus services are perfectly efficient, comfortable and well-regulated, using luxury vehicles. Other areas vary. Driving is invariably rash, and road conditions can be bad, especially in the more remote areas. Only a very limited number of passenger ferries leaves Shanghai for Yangzi River destinations, and there are now few coastal services.

Train travel in China – generally a comfortable experience

TRAINS & TIMETABLES

Timetables are published in April and October each year, and are available at railway station ticket offices only. However, they are hard to read even if you know Chinese. There are very rarely English-speaking staff at stations, and telephoning enquiries is pointless unless you speak Chinese.

Trains are of several types: those with numbers prefixed by the letter "T" or "K" are express *(te kuai)* or fast *(kuai)* trains, and those whose numbers have no prefix are ordinary *(pu kuai)*, trains of varying speeds and unpredictable comfort. "Z" are new prestige services, including some running between Beijing and Shanghai. "Y" trains are tourist trains, although indistinguishable

from "T" or "K" services, and "L" services are additional trains laid on at holiday peak periods. Double-decker trains with soft-seat carriages run on a few short intercity routes such as Beijing–Tianjin or Shanghai–Hangzhou. All long-distance trains are equipped with sleeper carriages.

There is no smoking permitted except at carriage junctions, but enforcement is patchy. Most trains have dining cars but the food is poor and overpriced. Staff will continually push trolleys through the carriages selling instant noodles, snacks, mineral water, coffee, and newspapers. The noise level

in carriages is often very high, as announcements and music are regularly broadcast over the speakers, although soft sleeper compartments have a volume control.

CLASSES

Chinese trains have four main classes. The most luxurious is **Soft Sleeper** *(ruan wo)*, with four comfortable berths per compartment. It offers more privacy and security than less expensive classes, but in terms of price it is often little cheaper than flying. Still more expensive deluxe sleepers *(gaoji ruanwo)* with only two berths and sometimes with showers or private bathrooms are available on certain high-prestige routes, including Beijing to Shanghai.

Hard Sleeper *(ying wo)* can be an economical choice when traveling between cities overnight, especially as it also saves the cost of a night in a hotel. Carriages consist of doorless compartments, each with six bunks in two sets of three. The higher berths are slightly cheaper than the lower. Pillows, sheets, and blankets are provided, as are flasks of boiling water. Once aboard, the inspector will exchange your ticket for a token, and return the ticket at the end of the journey, which will be checked as you leave the station.

The cheapest class is **Hard Seat** *(ying zuo)*, with three people side-by-side on lightly cushioned seats. Carriages are usually crowded and dirty, the speakers blare endlessly, lights remain on at night, and compartments are filled with smoke. If you have no reserved seat you'll likely stand for the whole trip.

Available only on certain short daytime routes, **Soft Seat** *(ruan zuo)* carriages are

Long-distance bus, an economical way to travel between Beijing and Shanghai

Waiting at one of Beijing's 12 long-distance bus terminals

more comfortable and spacious than Hard Seat, and there is sometimes a choice of first and second class.

TRAIN TICKETS, FARES, & RESERVATIONS

On most routes, and certainly on those between Beijing and Shanghai, it is vital to buy tickets a few days before you travel. Train fares are calculated according to the class and the distance traveled. All tickets are one-way, so you will need to buy another ticket for the return journey. Joining the crowds at station ticket counters can be very trying, so unless the station has a separate ticket office for foreign visitors, which is the case at Beijing's main stations, ask your hotel or travel agent to arrange your bookings. They will usually charge a fee of ¥20–¥30 per ticket for this service. Tickets only go on sale 10–12 days in advance.

Note that getting hold of tickets during Spring Festival, and the May and October holiday periods can be very difficult, and it is inadvisable to travel at these times.

LONG-DISTANCE BUSES

Beijing and Shanghai both have several long-distance bus stations (*changtu qiche zhan*), so check carefully which station you want. Destinations are displayed in Chinese characters on the front of buses.

Long-distance buses vary enormously in quality, age, and comfort. You may find that several buses are running along the same route, so make sure you are sold a ticket for the fastest and most comfortable (*gaoji* or *haohua*) bus – or the cheapest (*zui pianyi*) bus, if you prefer.

Airport Bus halt sign

Ordinary buses such as those serving rural sights around Beijing, are the cheapest and have basic wooden, or lightly padded, seats. These buses stop often, so progress can be slow. They provide little space for baggage – there's no room under the seats and the luggage racks are minuscule. Backpacks are usually stacked next to the driver, for no additional charge.

Sleeper buses (*wopu che*) speed through the night, so reach their destination in good time. They usually have two tiers of bunks, or seats

that recline almost flat. The older models can be quite dirty, but others are so clean you are required to remove your shoes as you board.

Shorter routes are served by rattling minibuses (*xiao ba*), which depart only when every spare space has been filled by a paying passenger. Crammed to the roof, minibus trips can be uncomfortable.

Express buses (*kuai che*) are the best way to travel. Most have air conditioning, and enforce a no-smoking policy. Receipts are given for luggage stowed in the hold.

BUS TICKETS & FARES

Traveling by road is generally much cheaper than traveling by train. Tickets are sold at long-distance bus stations. Book the previous day if you want the front seat or absolutely must be on a particular bus, otherwise don't bother. Main bus stations invariably have computerized ticket offices with short queues, and tickets can also be purchased on board.

FERRIES & BOATS

An overnight ferry service for tourists runs along the Grand Canal between Suzhou and Hangzhou, and Shanghai also has services to Yangzi River ports including Nanjing and Wuhan. Note that ferry timetables change frequently and services may have been added or terminated. There are also international ferry services from Shanghai to Kobe and Osaka.

A ferry shuttles between Pudong and the Bund in Shanghai

City Transportation

Beijing and Shanghai both have subway systems that should be your first choice where possible. Both are in the process of being extensively expanded. City buses are slow and usually packed, but are very cheap. Taxis *(chuzu che)* are a necessity for most travelers, and, despite the language barrier and misunderstandings with drivers, they remain the most convenient way to get around. Bicycles once ruled the roads of China's cities and those who like to risk their lives can rent one and discover the hard way who are the rulers today.

Beijing traffic sign

Buses and taxis on a busy Beijing main road

BEIJING'S SUBWAY

The subway system in Beijing is undergoing major development in preparation for the 2008 Olympic Games. More lines are to be added to the four that currently exist, including a line to the airport.

The subway is a swift way to get around and to avoid the city's legendarily stationary traffic. The system is easy to use, although walks between lines at interchange stations can be long. There are three different fares: a ticket for ¥3 covers trips on Lines 1 and 2; ¥4 is for trips that include the eastern Batong extension to Line 1; ¥5 is for journeys on Line 13. Buy your ticket at the booth near the entrance. Tickets are undated, so, if you are in Beijing for a few days and you plan to keep using lines 1 and 2, it makes sense to buy a few. Show your ticket to the attendants at the

Sign for the Beijing subway

entrance to the platform. Line 13 has automated ticket gates, as will the lines that open up in the next few years.

SHANGHAI'S SUBWAY

The small, yet efficient, Shanghai subway system is clean and new, with the first line built in 1995. Lines 1 and 2 are most useful to tourists; the raised Line 3, or Pearl Line, travels the western outskirts of the city. Fares for Lines 1 and 2 range between ¥3 and ¥6, depending on the number of stops traveled. Check the map to determine your fare and then buy a ticket from the booth or machine. You can also buy ¥50 stored-value tickets. Put your ticket into the slot at the electronic barrier and the gates will open. Retrieve your ticket on the other side of the gate and hold on to it – you will need it to exit at your destination.

The much touted German-designed Maglev (magnetic levitation) train takes just eight minutes to travel the 20 miles (30 km) between Pudong Airport and the Longyang Lu subway station on the periphery of Shanghai, toward the eastern end of Line 2. En route it reaches speeds of 270 miles per hour (430 km/h). It runs every 20 minutes between 8:30am and 4:30pm, and costs ¥40 for those holding an inbound or outbound air ticket for the same day.

BUSES

City bus *(gonggong qiche)* networks are extensive and cheap. Most trips within Beijing and Shanghai city centers require a flat flare (no change given), which is clearly posted on the side of the bus; typically ¥1 or ¥2. Air-conditioned services are usually a little more expensive. However, traffic jams last all day in both cities, and no priority is shown to buses, which means journeys can be unnecessarily lengthy. The buses are almost always overcrowded – so much so that you are unlikely to be able to see out of the windows. These conditions are also perfect for thieves, so keep a careful eye on your belongings. Consider using buses only for short straight-forward journeys, or for suburban sightseeing.

Bus routes can also be tricky to navigate, particularly as most destinations and schedules are listed in Chinese only.

City buses – cheap but almost always overcrowded

TAXIS

The best way to get to places away from subway stations is by taxi *(chuzu qiche)*. Taxis are found in large numbers in both Beijing and Shanghai, and can be hailed easily in the street. When arriving at airports, avoid the touts who immediately surround you, and head instead to the taxi rank outside where you are less likely to be overcharged. Make sure the driver uses the meter, which drivers usually only start once the journey is actually under way – so wait a moment, then say, "Dabiao" (start the meter), if necessary. Taxis rarely have rear seat belts *(anquan dai)*, and those in the front may not work, although it is required by law that they be worn on expressways. Few taxi drivers speak English, so have your destination written down in Chinese by your hotel staff. Also get into the habit of picking up businesscards at places in areas that you might want to return to – such as your hotel.

Fares per kilometer (half mile) are clearly posted on the side of the car. These fares vary from ¥1.2 (very few, in Beijing only, and being phased out) to ¥3 (certain hotel-based more luxurious vehicles). The majority of taxis are ¥1.6 or ¥2 per kilometer. Flagfall of ¥10 includes the first three or four km. Rates automatically rise by 50 percent after 10 miles (15 km), and by 20–30 percent between 11pm and 5am. Most daytime city trips will come to no more than around ¥20. There is no need to tip (and the driver will be bewildered if you do).

Most taxi journeys are straightforward and trouble-free, and in general only on the run from the airport into town (and sometimes vice versa) will you occasionally

Bicycles – the traditional way to get around the city

run into problems, as less scrupulous drivers prey on new arrivals unfamiliar with the city or departing visitors in a hurry to catch their flight. Note that on the run to and from Beijing's Capital Airport you must pay the driver the road toll of ¥10 on top of the metered fare. But in addition to ignoring touts at airports and railway stations, avoid cabs waiting at popular tourist sites and those that call out to you. It is also generally wiser to walk away from your hotel and flag down a passing cab, as even at otherwise respectable hotels there can often be shenanigans involving kick-backs from taxi drivers to forecourt staff.

Taxis can also be hired for the day, and this is a convenient way to see sights just out of town. This is best arranged the previous day by flagging down vehicles in the street. Again, have hotel staff write down the details of what you want, including date, pick-up time and location, and the complete itinerary, and ask for a

Street sign in two scripts

东 长 安 街
DONGCHANGAN JIE 东

price ("Duoshao qian?"); have the driver write down his answer. You should also expect to pay any road, tunnel, or bridge tolls.

In smaller towns, motorcycle rickshaws *(sanlun motuoche)* and bicycle rickshaws *(sanlun che)* are a convenient and entertaining way to get around town. However, be careful if tempted to take these in Beijing or Shanghai – they frequently target tourists for substantial rip-offs.

CYCLING

Hiring a bicycle can be a great way to explore. Bike lanes are common (although usually not respected by drivers) and roadside repair stalls are everywhere. Both Beijing and Shanghai are flat and very cycle-able, but if you are not used to cycling in heavy traffic, it can be an intimidating experience. Make sure that any bike you rent has a lock provided. Handy bike stands are found all over and have an attendant to watch the bikes for a fee, usually ¥0.30.

ROAD NAMES

Main streets, avenues, and thoroughfares are often divided into different sections based on the four cardinal points. For example, Zhongshan Lu (Zhongshan Road) may be divided into Zhongshan Xi Lu (West Road) and Zhongshan Dong Lu (East Road). Similarly, you may also see Zhongshan *Bei* Lu (North Road) and Zhongshan *Nan* Lu (South Road). Road names in Beijing and Shanghai also display the Pinyin translation, but in smaller towns and remote destinations, only Chinese is used. Apart from *lu* (road), other key words to look out for are *jie* (street), *dajie* (avenue, literally "big street"), and the lanes or alleyways called *hutong* in Beijing and *long* in Shanghai.

A city taxi, a convenient way of getting around

General Index

Acknowledgments

Dorling Kindersley would like to thank the many people whose help and assistance contributed to the preparation of this book.

Design and Editorial
PUBLISHER: Douglas Amrine
PUBLISHING MANAGERS: Vivien Antwi, Jane Ewart

Proofreader
Ferdie McDonald

Photography Co-ordinator
Amanda Mengpo Li

Map Co-ordinators
Uma Bhattacharya, Casper Morris

Design and Editorial Assistance
Rachel Barber, Katie Bradley, Iris Chan, Caroline Jackson, Yang Jie
JACKET DESIGN: Tessa Bindloss, Sonal Bhatt

Additional Photography
Max Alexander, Simon Blackall, Demetrio Carrasco, Andy Crawford, Ian Cumming, Gadi Farfour, Eddie Gerald, Nigel Hicks, Dave King, Stephen Lam, Ian O'Leary, Colin Sinclair, Chris Stowers, Hugh Thompson, Linda Whitwam

Photography Permissions
The Publishers thank all the temples, museums, hotels, restaurants, shops, and other sights for their assistance and kind permission to photograph their establishments.

Picture Credits
Key: a-above; b-below/bottom; c-centre; l-left; r-right; t-top

AKG-IMAGES: Laurent Lacat 41tr; ALAMY IMAGES: Pat Behnke 30br; David Crausby 218c; Li Jiangshu/Panorama Stock 94br; Iain Masterton 221tl; Panorama Media (Beijing) Ltd. / Panorama Stock / 84br; Panorama Stock Photos/Zhang Zhenguang 146tr; Snap2000 Images / David Robinson 15c; Matthew Wellings 35cra; Ron Yue 34c. THE ART ARCHIVE: Bibliotheque Nationale, Paris 41cra, 143cr; Bibliotheque Nationale, Paris/Marc Charmet 20tr; British Library 18br, 20bl; British Museum/Eileen Tweedy 30tr; Freer Gallery of Art 26-27; Genius of China Exhibition 26tr, 39bc, 42bl; Musée Thomas Dobrée Nantes / Dagli Orti 49tl; National Palace Museum of Taiwan 22cl.

BIBLIOTHÈQUE NATIONALE DE FRANCE, PARIS: 18tr; BRIDGEMAN ART LIBRARY: 22cr, 23cl, 23cra; after Alexander, William (1767-1816) 48crb; Bibliotheque Nationale, Paris 6-7, 20cl, 23tr; *Portrait of T'ai T'sin Che-Tsou* (1638-61) 48bc; Giraudon 42br; Yu Zhiding (1647-1709) *The Depiction of the Poet Wang Yuang* (1634-1711) water colour 28tr.

©THE TRUSTEES OF THE BRITISH MUSEUM: 21tc, 26clb, 26bc, 26crb, 27bl, 27cb, 27br, 27cra, 27tr.

CHINA SPAN/KEREN SU: 29cl, 143cl; CHINAPIX: 122tr; Corbis: 49c, 52bl, 53tc; Asian Art & Archaeology, Inc. 39c, 40clb, 42ca, 44ca, 44bc; Tiziana and Gianni Baldizzone 21cr; Dave Bartruff 190cla; Bettmann 51tl, 51br, 52tl, 135br; Bohemian Nomad Picturemakers 189tl; Bohemian Nomad Picturemakers/ Kevin R Morris 143br; Burstein Collection 22br, *The First Emperor of the Han Dynasty Entering Kuan Tung* by Chao Po-chu 30, 41cb, 43t, 46bl; Christie's Images 40tr; ChromoSohmINC/Joseph Sohm 90br; Dean Conger 62cla, 153br, 195c; Ric Ergenbright 143bl; Macduff Everton 53cr, 53bl, 133tc; Free Agents Limited 24tr; Hulton-Deutsch Collection 81tl, 153bc; Robbie Jack 33bl; Kelly-Mooney Photography 75tc; Charles & Josette Lenars 45tr; Liu Liqun 93tr, 133cb; Carl & Ann Purcell 23crb; Roger Ressmeyer 72cr; Reuters 36bc, 223tr; Royal Ontario Museum 26bl, 27cr, 46t; Sean Sexton Collection 135; Stapleton Collection 31tr; Keren Su 34cr; Julia Waterlow 20br; Michael S. Yamashita 29br; CPA MEDIA: 48ca, 50tr, 135cl, 135tc; Bibliotheque Nationale Paris/ Oliver Harvgreave 46clb; Chinese Government (1961)/Meng Qingbiao 51crb.

DK IMAGES: ©The Trustees of the British Museum 26cl, Alan Hills 26tl.

FOTOE: 22tr; Zhang Weiqing 22clb.

GETTY IMAGES: Walter Bibikow 14; Hulton 65bc; Jeff Hunter 16t; The Image Bank 54-55; National Geographic 40cla; Photographer's Choice/John Warden 91tl; Stone /D E Cox 86; GRAND HYATT: 136t, 137bc, 165br; SALLY & RICHARD GREENHILL: 50tl, 51tr; S.A.C.U. 50br, 50cl.

IMAGINECHINA: 52crb, 93br; Jin Baoyuan 29tr; Adrian Bradshaw 133cla; Wu Changqing 88tr; Jiang Chao 95tl; CNS 31cr; Guo Guangyao 28cr; Jiang Guohong 32crb; Zhang Guosheng 69bl; Long Hai 30bc,

31crb, 125cra; Wu Hong 33br, 61br; Wei Hui 33cr; Li Jiangsong 21crb; Wang Jianxin 31clb; Huang Jinguo 29cr; Kan Kan 22cb; Zhou Kang 126tr; Zhou Kang Pzhk 75cr; Xu Ruikang 29tc; Chen Shuyi 73br; Lin Weijian 28bl, 122cl, 122cr; Shen Yu 28br, 123tl, 138br, 220br; Fang Zhonglin 130clb; Yi Zhou 123bl; Yin Zi 18-19c; INSTITUTE OF HISTORY & PHILOLOGY: Academia Sinica 18cl, 18cb.

THE KOBAL COLLECTION: Columbia 33tr; Tomson Films 33cla.

PANOS PICTURES: 19cra; PHOTO12.COM: OIPS 96cl; Panorama Stock 78bl, 89tl; Panoramic Stock 90cl; POPPERFOTO.COM: 50-51; 135cra, 135cb; Portman Ritz-Carlton: 176br.

RED GATE GALLERY, Beijing: 73; THE RED MANSION LTD.: Fang Lijun 32-33; Zhan Wang 32clb; Cang Xin 32cla; ROBERT HARDING PICTURE LIBRARY: 139tr; PanoramaStock 47tr.

SCIENCE & SOCIETY PICTURE LIBRARY: Science Museum 19bl; SHANGHAI MUSEUM: 126, 126cla, 126c, 126clb, 127, 127t, 127cr, 128tl, 128c, 128br, 129c, 129br; CHINA STOCK: 41bl, 45c, 45clb, 50clb, 51cra; SUPERSTOCK: age fotostock 118-119.

THAMES & HUDSON LTD: Eileen Tweedy 20-21c; TOPFOTO.CO.UK: British Museum 23bc, 49bl; The Museum of East Asian Art / HIP 47bc; THREE ON THE BUND: courtesy of Laris 188cl; TRANSRAPID: 137tr.

WERNER FORMAN ARCHIVE: 43crb; P'yongyang Gallery, North Korea 23cla; Peking Palace Museum 44crb; Private Collection 41br, 47c, 49br; Victoria & Albert Museum 43cb; Yang-Tzu-Shaw 42crb.

JACKET
Front - DK IMAGES: Chen Chao clb; Colin Sinclair main image. Back - DK Images: Chen Chao clb, cla; Colin Sinclair bl; PHOTO12.COM: Panoramic Stock tl. Spine: DK IMAGES: Chen Chao b; Colin Sinclair t.

Front Endpapers: GETTY IMAGES: The Image Bank / Andrea Pistolesi Ltr; SUPERSTOCK: age fotostock R br.

All other images © Dorling Kindersley
For further information see:
www.dkimages.com

SPECIAL EDITIONS OF DK TRAVEL GUIDES

DK Travel Guides can be purchased in bulk quantities at discounted prices for use in promotions or as premiums. We are also able to offer special editions and personalized jackets, corporate imprints, and excerpts from all of our books, tailored specifically to meet your own needs.

To find out more, please contact:
(in the United States) **SpecialSales@dk.com**
(in the UK) **Sarah.Burgess@dk.com**
(in Canada) DK Special Sales at **general@tourmaline.ca**
(in Australia) **business.development@pearson.com.au**

Phrase Book

The Chinese language belongs to the Sino-Tibetan family of languages and uses characters which are ideographic – a symbol is used to represent an idea or an object. Mandarin Chinese, known as Putonghua in mainland China, is fairly straightforward as each character is monosyllabic. Traditionally, Chinese is written in vertical columns from top right to bottom left, however the Western style is widely used. There are several romanization systems; the Pinyin system used here is the official system in mainland China. This phrase book gives the English word or phrase, followed by the Chinese script, then the Pinyin for pronunciation.

Guidelines for Pronunciation

Pronounce vowels as in these English words:

a	as in "father"
e	as in "lurch"
i	as in "see"
o	as in "solid"
u	as in "pooh"
ü	as the French u or German ü (place your lips to say oo and try to say ee)

Most of the consonants are pronounced as in English. As a rough guide, pronounce the following consonants as in these English words:

c	as ts in "hats"
q	as ch in "cheat"
x	as sh in "sheet"
z	as ds in "heads"
zh	as j in "Joe"

Mandarin Chinese is a tonal language with four tones, represented in Pinyin by one of the following marks ˉ ˊ ˇ ˋ above each vowel – the symbol shows whether the tone is flat, rising, falling and rising, or falling. The Chinese characters do not convey this information: tones are learnt when the character is learnt. Teaching tones is beyond the scope of this small phrase book, but a language course book with a cassette or CD will help those who wish to take the language further.

Dialects

There are many Chinese dialects in use. It is hard to guess exactly how many, but they can be roughly classified into one of seven large groups (Mandarin, Cantonese, Hakka, Hui etc.), each group containing a large number of more minor dialects. Although all these dialects are quite different – Cantonese uses six tones instead of four – Mandarin or Putonghua, which is mainly based on the Beijing dialect, is the official language. Despite these differences all Chinese people are more or less able to use the same formal written language so they can understand each other's writing, if not each other's speech.

In Emergency

Help!	请帮忙！	Qing bangmang
Stop!	停住！	Ting zhu
Call a doctor!	叫医生！	Jiao yisheng
Call an ambulance!	叫救护车！	Jiao jiuhuche
Call the police!	叫警察！	Jiao jiingcha
Fire!	火！	Huo
Where is the hospital/police station?	医院/警察分局在哪里？	Yiyuan/jingcha fenju zai nali ?

Communication Essentials

Hello	你好	Nihao
Goodbye	再见	Zaijian
Yes/no	是／不是	shi/bushi
… not …	不是	bushi
I'm from…	我是 … 人	Wo shi … ren
I understand	我明白	Wo mingbai
I don't know	我不知道	Wo bu zhidao
Thank you	谢谢你	Xiexie ni
Thank you very much	多谢	Duo xie
Thanks (casual)	谢谢	Xiexie
You're welcome	不用谢	Bu yong xie
No, thank you	不，谢谢你	Bu, xiexie ni
Please (offering)	请	Qing
Please (asking)	请问	Qing wen
I don't understand	我不明白	Wo Bu mingbai
Sorry/Excuse me!	抱歉／对不起	Baoqian/duibuqi
Could you help me please? (not emergency)	你能帮助我吗？	Ni neng bang zhu wo ma?

Useful Phrases

My name is ….	我叫 …	Wo jiao …
Goodbye	再见	Zaijian
What is (this)?	（这）是什么？	(zhe) shi shenme?
Could I possibly have …? (very polite)	能不能请给我 …?	Neng buneng qing ni gei wo …
Is there … here?	这儿有 … 吗？	Zhe'r you … ma?
Where can I get …?	我在哪里可以得到 …?	Wo zai na li keyi de dao …?
How much is it?	它要多少钱？	Ta yao duoshao qian?
What time is …?	… 什么时间？	… shenme shijian
Cheers! (toast)	干杯	Ganbei
Where is the restroom/toilet?	卫生间／洗手间在哪里？	Weishengjian/ Xishoujian zai nali?

Useful Words

I	我	wo
woman	女人	nüren
man	男人	nanren
wife	妻子	qizi
husband	丈夫	zhangfu
daughter	女儿	nü'er
son	儿子	er'zi
child	小孩	xiaohai
children	儿童	er'tong
student	学生	xuesheng
Mr./Mrs./Ms. …	先生／太太／女士	xiansheng/taitai/ nüshi

big/small	大／小	da/xiao
hot/cold	热／凉	re/liang
cold (to touch)	冷	leng
warm	暖	nuan
good/not good/ bad	好／不好／坏	hao/buhao/ huai
enough	够了	goule
free (no charge)	免费	mianfei
here	这里	zheli
there	那里	nali
this (nearby)	这个	zhege
that (nearby)	那	na
that (far away)	那个	nage
what?	什么？	Shenme?
when?	什么时候？	Shenme shihou?
why?	为什么？	Wei shenme?
where?	在哪里？	Zai nali?
who?	谁？	Shui?

Signs

open	开	kai
closed	关	guan
entrance	入口	rukou
exit	出口	chukou
danger	危险	weixian
emergency exit	安全门	anquanmen
information	信息	xinxi
restroom/toilet (men) (women)	卫生间／洗手间（男士）（女士）	Weishengjian/ Xishoujian (nanshi) (nüshi)
men	男士	nanshi
women	女士	nüshi

Money

bank	银行	yinhang
cash	现金	xianjin
credit card	信用卡	xinyongka
currency	外汇兑换处	waihui
exchange office		duihuanchu
dollars	美元	meiyuan
pounds	英镑	yinghang
yuan	元	yuan

Keeping in Touch

Where is a telephone?	电话在哪里？	Dianhua zai nali?
May I use your phone?	我可以用你的电话吗？	Wo keyi yong nide dianhua ma?
mobile phone	手机	shouji
sim card	卡	sim ka
Hello, this is ...	你好，我是 ...	Nihao, wo shi
airmail	航空	hangkong
e-mail	电子邮件	dianzi youjian
fax	传真	chuanzhen
internet	互联网	hulianwang
postcard	明信片	mingxinpian
post office	邮局	youju
stamp	邮票	youpiao
telephone booth	电话亭	dianhua ting
telephone card	电话卡	dianhua ka

Shopping

Where can I buy ...?	我可以在哪里买到 ...?	Wo keyi zai nali maidao ...?
How much does this cost?	这要多少钱？	Zhe yao duoshao qian?
Too much!	太贵了！	Tai gui le!
Do you have ...?	你有 ... 吗？	Ni you …… ma?
May I try this on?	我可以试穿吗？	Wo keyi shi chuan ma?
Please show me that.	请给我看看那个。	Qing gei wo kankan na ge.
bookstore	书店	shudian
clothes	衣服	yifu
department store	百货商店	baihuo shangdian
electrical store	电器商店	dianqi shangdian

ladies' wear	女式服装	nüshi fuzhuang
market	市场	shichang
men's wear	男式服装	nanshi fuzhuang
pharmacist	药剂师	yaojishi
picture postcard	图片明信片	tupian mingxinpian
souvenir shop	纪念品店	jinianpin dian
supermarket	超市	chaoshi
travel agent	旅行社	lüxing she

Sightseeing

Where is ...?	... 在哪里？	... zai nali?
How do I get to ...?	我怎么到 ...?	Wo zenme dao ...?
Is it far?	远不远？	Yuan bu yuan?
bridge	桥	qiao
city	城市	chengshi
city center	市中心	shi zhongxin
gardens	花园	huayuan
hot spring	温泉	wen quan
island	岛	dao
monastery	寺院	siyuan
mountain	山	shan
museum	博物馆	bowuguan
palace	宫殿	gongdian
park	公园	gongyuan
port	港口	gangkou
river	江，河	jiang, he
ruins	废墟	feixu
shopping area	购物区	gouwu qu
shrine	神殿	shendian
street	街	jie
temple	寺庙	si/miao
town	镇	zhen
village	村	cun
province/county	省／县	sheng/xian
zoo	动物园	dongwuyuan
north	北	bei
south	南	nan
east	东	dong
west	西	xi
left/right	左／右	zuo/you
straight ahead	一直向前	yizhi xiangqian
between	在 ... 之间	zai ... zhijian
near/far	近／远	jin/yuan
up/down	上／下	shang/xia
new	新	xin
old/former	旧	jiu
in	在 ... 里	zai ... li
in front of	在 ... 前面	zai ... qianmian

Getting Around

airport	机场	jichang
bicycle	自行车	zixingche
I want to rent a bicycle	我想租一辆自行车。	Wo xiang zu yiliang zixingche.
ordinary bus	公共汽车	gonggong qiche
express bus	特快公共汽车	tekuai gonggong qiche
minibus	面包车	mianbaoche
main bus station	公共汽车总站	gonggong qiche zong zhan
Which bus goes to ...?	哪一路公共汽车到 ... 去？	Nayilu gonggong qiche dao ... qu?
When is the next bus?	下一辆公共汽车是什么时候？	Xiayiliang gonggong qiche shi shenme shihou?
Please tell me where to get off?	请告诉我在哪里下车？	Qing gaosu wo zai nali xia che.
car	小汽车	xiaoqiche
ferry	渡船	duchuan
baggage room	行李室	xingli shi
one-way ticket	单程票	dancheng piao
return ticket	往返票	wangfan piao
taxi	出租车	chuzuche
ticket	票	piao
ticket office	售票处	shoupiao chu
timetable	时刻表	shikebiao

Accommodations

air-conditioning	空调	*kongtiao*
bath	洗澡	*xizao*
check-out	退房	*tui fang*
deposit	定金	*dingjin*
double bed	双人床	*shuangren chuang*
hair drier	吹风机	*chuifeng ji*
room	房间	*fangjian*
economy room	经济房	*jingji fang*
key	钥匙	*yaoshi*
front desk	前台	*qiantai*
single/twin room	单人／双人房	*danren/shuangren fang*
single beds	单人床	*danren chuang*
shower	淋浴	*linyu*
standard room	标准房间	*biaozhun fangjian*
deluxe suite	豪华套房	*haohua taofang*

Eating Out

May I see the menu?	请给我看看菜单。	*Qing gei wo kankan caidan*
Is there a set menu?	有没有套餐？	*You meiyou taocan?*
I'd like ….	我想要 …	*Wo xiang yao …*
May I have one of those?	请给我这个。	*Qing gei wo zhege*
I am a vegetarian	我是素食者。	*Wo shi sushizhe.*
Waiter/waitress!	服务员！	*Fuwuyuan!*
May I have a fork/knife/spoon	请给我一把叉／刀／汤匙。	*Qing gei wo yiba cha/dao/tangshi*
May we have the check please.	请把帐单开给我们。	*Qing ba zhangdan kaigei women*
breakfast	早餐	*zaocan*
buffet	自助餐	*zizhucan*
chopsticks	筷子	*kuaizi*
dinner	晚餐	*wancan*
to drink	喝	*he*
to eat	吃	*chi*
food	食品	*shipin*
full (stomach)	饱	*bao*
hot/cold	热／冷	*re/leng*
hungry	饿	*e*
lunch	午餐	*wucan*
set menu	套餐	*taocan*
spicy	酸辣	*suan la*
hot (spicy)	辣	*la*
sweet	甜	*tian*
mild	淡	*dan*
Western food	西餐	*xi can*
restaurant	餐馆	*canguan*
restaurant (upscale)	饭店	*fandian*

Food

apple	苹果	*pingguo*
bacon	咸肉	*xianrou*
bamboo shoots	笋	*sun*
beancurd	豆腐	*doufu*
bean sprouts	豆芽	*dou ya*
beans	豆	*dou*
beef	牛肉	*niurou*
beer	啤酒	*pijiu*
bread	面包	*mianbao*
butter	黄油	*huangyou*
chicken	鸡	*ji*
crab	蟹	*xie*
duck	鸭	*ya*
eel	鳗	*man*
egg	蛋	*dan*
eggplant	茄子	*qiezi*
fermented soybean paste	酱	*jiang*
fish	鱼	*yu*
fried egg	炒蛋	*chao dan*
fried tofu	油豆腐	*you doufu*
fruit	水果	*shuiguo*
fruit juice	果汁	*guo zhi*
ginger	姜	*jiang*
ice cream	冰淇淋	*bingqilin*

meat	肉	*rou*
melon	瓜	*gua*
noodles	面	*mian*
egg noodles	鸡蛋面	*jidan mian*
wheat flour noodles	面粉面	*mianfen mian*
rice flour noodles	米粉面	*mifen mian*
omelet	煎蛋饼	*jiandanbing*
onion	洋葱	*yangcong*
peach	桃子	*taozi*
pepper	胡椒粉，辣椒	*hujiaofen, lajiao*
pickles	泡菜	*paocai*
pork	猪肉	*zhurou*
potato	土豆	*tudou*
rice	米饭	*mifan*
rice crackers	爆米花饼干	*baomihua bing'gan*
rice wine	米酒	*mi jiu*
salad	色拉	*sela*
salmon	鲑鱼，大马哈鱼	*guiyu, damahayu*
salt	盐	*yan*
scallion	韭葱	*jiucong*
seaweed	海带	*haidai*
shrimp	虾	*xia*
soup	汤	*tang*
soy sauce	酱油	*jiangyou*
squid	鱿鱼	*youyu*
steak	牛排	*niupai*
sugar	糖	*tang*
vegetables	蔬菜	*shucai*
yoghurt	酸奶	*suannai*

Drinks

beer	啤酒	*pijiu*
black tea	红茶	*hong cha*
coffee (hot)	（热）咖啡	*(re) kafei*
green tea	绿茶	*lü cha*
iced coffee	冰咖啡	*bing kafei*
milk	牛奶	*niunai*
mineral water	矿泉水	*kuang quanshui*
orange juice	橙汁	*cheng zhi*
wine	葡萄酒	*putaojiu*

Numbers

0	零	*ling*
1	一	*yi*
2	二	*er*
3	三	*san*
4	四	*si*
5	五	*wu*
6	六	*liu*
7	七	*qi*
8	八	*ba*
9	九	*jiu*
10	十	*shi*
11	十一	*shiyi*
12	十二	*shier*
20	二十	*ershi*
21	二十一	*ershi yi*
22	二十二	*ershi er*
30	三十	*sanshi*
40	四十	*sishi*
100	一百	*yi bai*
101	一百零一	*yi bai ling yi*
200	二百	*er bai*

Time

Monday	星期一	*xingqiyi*
Tuesday	星期二	*xingqi'er*
Wednesday	星期三	*xingqisan*
Thursday	星期四	*xingqisi*
Friday	星期五	*xingqiwu*
Saturday	星期六	*xingqiliu*
Sunday	星期天	*xingqitian*
today	今天	*jintian*
yesterday	昨天	*zuotian*
tomorrow	明天	*mingtian*

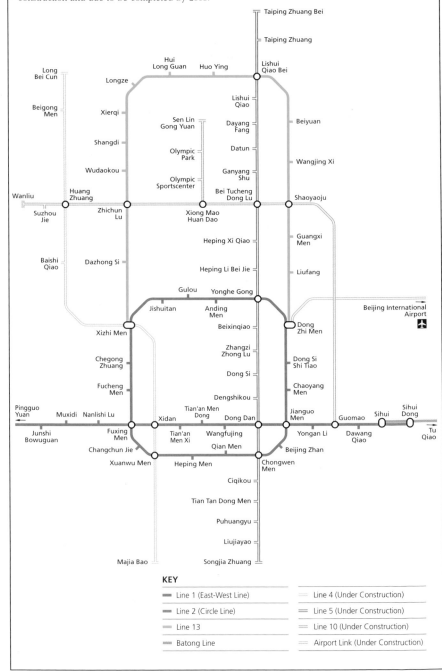

BEIJING SUBWAY

Line 1 crosses central Beijing and Line 2 runs around its perimeter, tracing the route once occupied by the walls of the Inner City. Semi-circular Line 13 is a light rail service that runs overground for much of its route. Lines 4, 5, 10, and the Airport Link shown here are currently under construction and due to be completed by 2008.

Taiping Zhuang Bei

Taiping Zhuang

Long Bei Cun

Hui Long Guan · Huo Ying · Lishui Qiao Bei

Beigong Men

Longze

Xierqi

Lishui Qiao

Sen Lin Gong Yuan · Dayang Fang · Beiyuan

Shangdi

Datun

Olympic Park

Wudaokou

Wangjing Xi

Olympic Sportscenter · Ganyang Shu

Wanliu · Huang Zhuang · Zhichun Lu · Bei Tucheng Dong Lu · Shaoyaoju

Suzhou Jie

Xiong Mao Huan Dao

Heping Xi Qiao · Guangxi Men

Baishi Qiao · Dazhong Si

Heping Li Bei Jie · Liufang

Gulou · Yonghe Gong

Jishuitan · Anding Men · Beijing International Airport

Xizhi Men · Beixinqiao · Dong Zhi Men

Chegong Zhuang · Zhangzi Zhong Lu

Dong Si Shi Tiao

Fucheng Men · Dong Si

Chaoyang Men

Dengshikou

Pingguo Yuan · Muxidi · Nanlishi Lu · Tian'an Men Dong · Dong Dan · Jianguo Men · Guomao · Sihui · Sihui Dong

Junshi Bowuguan · Fuxing Men · Xidan · Tian'an Men Xi · Wangfujing · Yongan Li · Dawang Qiao · Tu Qiao

Changchun Jie · Qian Men · Beijing Zhan

Xuanwu Men · Heping Men · Chongwen Men

Ciqikou

Tian Tan Dong Men

Puhuangyu

Liujiayao

Majia Bao · Songjia Zhuang

KEY

Line 1 (East-West Line)	Line 4 (Under Construction)
Line 2 (Circle Line)	Line 5 (Under Construction)
Line 13	Line 10 (Under Construction)
Batong Line	Airport Link (Under Construction)